ICETE Series

Serving Communities

Governance and the Potential of Theological Schools

Serving Communities is a radical contribution to the notion of governance. Dr Ferenczi does not give an upside-down approach, but explores its multifaceted reality. This book is a must read for leaders in theological education to impact and be relevant to the global challenges faced by churches and seminaries today.

Ashish Chrispal
Regional Director, Asia, Overseas Council

Few know the global theological education landscape better than Dr Ferenczi. Broadly grounded in historical perspective he brings together the three most critical pieces for analysis and progress in Bible schools and seminaries: leadership (governance), the local church and vision. Each chapter commands our attention with insights skillfully guiding us to a more promising future where the academy and the church synergize their energies for the equipping of people for ministry. Rarely does anyone weave such a globally coherent portrait showing where theological education and the church are and where they could be and, best of all, how to get there.

Duane H. Elmer
G. W. Aldeen Professor Emeritus of International Studies,
Distinguished Professor Emeritus of Educational Studies,
Trinity International University / Evangelical Divinity School

Sensible governance of theological seminaries and wise organizational leadership to advance Christian leaders in the multi-national, multi-religious and complicated socio-political contexts of Eurasia are the most crucial issues and challenges for educational leaders in the countries of the former Soviet Union. This book by Dr Jason Ferenczi is an invaluable contribution to the qualitative development of Eurasian theological schools after seventy years of the prohibition of spiritual education and after more than twenty-five years of a "theological educational ghetto" in terms of relationships with local governments. We are very much looking forward to having this book in the Russian language someday as well.

Taras Dyatlik
Regional Director for Eurasia Overseas Council,
Educational Development Director for Euro-Asian Accrediting Association

Serving Communities

Governance and the Potential of Theological Schools

Jason Ferenczi

Series Editor
Riad Kassis

© 2015 by Jason Ferenczi

Published 2015 by Langham Global Library
an imprint of Langham Publishing

Langham Partnership
PO Box 296, Carlisle, Cumbria CA3 9WZ, UK
www.langham.org

ISBNs:
978-1-78368-084-9 Print
978-1-78368-088-7 ePub
978-1-78368-101-3 PDF

Jason Ferenczi has asserted his right under the Copyright, Designs and Patents Act, 1988 to be identified as the Author of this work.

All rights reserved. No part of this publication may be reproduced, stored in a retrieval system or transmitted, in any form or by any means, electronic, mechanical, photocopying, recording or otherwise, without the prior written permission of the publisher or the Copyright Licensing Agency.

All Scripture quotations, unless otherwise indicated, are taken from the Holy Bible, New International Version®, NIV®. Copyright ©1973, 1978, 1984, 2011 by Biblica, Inc.™ Used by permission of Zondervan.

British Library Cataloguing in Publication Data
A catalogue record for this book is available from the British Library

ISBN: 978-1-78368-084-9

Cover & Book Design: projectluz.com

Langham Partnership actively supports theological dialogue and a scholar's right to publish but does not necessarily endorse the views and opinions set forth, and works referenced within this publication or guarantee its technical and grammatical correctness. Langham Partnership does not accept any responsibility or liability to persons or property as a consequence of the reading, use or interpretation of its published content.

Contents

Preface ix
Overview 1
1   Introduction 7
2   The Context of Theological Education 31
3   Building a Bridge to Governance 61
4   Listening to Theological Schools and Their Experiences 91
5   A Community of Trust 101
6   Alignment of the Parts 111
7   Strong, Enabling Leadership 127
8   Reflective Responsiveness 139
9   Education That Transforms 149
10 Planning for the Future 161
11 Four Institutions in Summary 175
12 Conclusions 181
Epilogue: A Library, a Farm, and a Train Station 203
Recommended Reading 207
Appendix A: Statement on Methodology 213
Appendix B: Protocol for Examination of Historical Documents . . 219
Appendix C: Protocol for Analysis of Board Meeting Minutes
    and Board Policy Manual 221
Appendix D: Protocol for Observation of Board Meeting 223
Appendix E: Protocol for Structured Interviews 227
Bibliography 231

Preface

I never would have anticipated that I would write a book about leading and governing theological schools. I have neither led nor governed a theological school; I am, in fact, a seminary dropout. Despite this, I have found much common cause with seminary leaders around the world and believe deeply and passionately in the transformative potential of theological schools. This belief was nourished during nearly fifteen years of labor at Overseas Council, when I had the opportunity to work with some of the world's finest theological educators. It was nourished by my study of history and later of education. But most of all, it was nourished by my fellowship with theological educators around the globe, hearing their own stories, their passion, and their struggles.

Despite this love for theological educators, I have at times been a loving critic of the *status quo* in theological education, always driven by a powerful sense of what *could* be. At times, my words, although offered with the best intentions, have been intemperate. I am deeply thankful for the grace shown to me in the global theological education community. Beyond that, I am deeply thankful for the way in which men and women around the world have taught, guided, and formed me in my journey. This book attempts to join together passion for what *can be* with a grace for what *is*. It is offered as an attempt to help theological schools achieve something even greater.

This study emerged in 2007 as I set aside a nearly completed PhD in Russian History and returned to Overseas Council in a leadership position. The combined advice of Bob Ferris, Manfred Kohl, and Duane Elmer led me, in different ways, to the study of education. In retrospect, the journey from history to education was far less abrupt than I had expected, as I found that many of the tools that I had learned in the study of history equipped me for insight in the educational world. It grew throughout my service as Vice President of International Partnership at Overseas Council (2007–2012) and into my role as Program Officer for Leadership at Cornerstone Trust (2012–present). It was nourished by my encounters with over 200 theological seminaries and the people who dwell in them in nearly 100 countries across the planet. Portions of it were indeed written in Brazil, Nigeria, Russia, Sri Lanka, Malaysia, and Indonesia.

While the weaknesses of this work are completely my own, it would not be possible without the input of many people around the world.

I am thankful to Overseas Council International (OCI), my employer during much of the process: while OCI contributed financially to my doctoral study, their greatest influence was the opportunities afforded to observe the work of theological schools around the world. I am thankful to my colleagues at Overseas Council: David Baer, Manfred Kohl, Scott Cunningham, Paul Theaker, and Cindy Pastrick, and especially to my international colleagues who became not only treasured colleagues, but dear friends: Ashish Chrispal, Bill Houston, Josué Fernández, Philippe Emedi, Taras Dyatlik, and Victor Nakah. These men and women have each contributed much to the success of this project and to me personally.

I am thankful to several colleagues and friends in other organizations who have repeatedly stretched me and encouraged me: Evan Hunter, Larry Smith, Riad Kassis, Jane Overstreet, and Paul Sanders.

I am thankful to my dissertation committee at Columbia International University. Ron Kroll ably chaired my committee and proved to be perhaps the finest copy editor I have known, a task far above the call of duty. Bob Ferris, and Duane Elmer never ceased to push me to deeper, broader, and better thinking and clearer expression, through this work and beyond. I am also thankful to Sam Barkat, who taught me much about leadership, humility, and navigating cultural difference, as well as Meri MacLeod, who always stretched my thinking on education.

I am also thankful for my colleagues at Cornerstone Trust, especially Aaron LeClaire, who have continued to stretch my thinking in ways I could scarcely have imagined when I joined the team in 2012. I am deeply thankful for the values that I have seen lived out day in and day out in the CT family and office.

And most of all, I am thankful to the women of my life: my daughters: Leah, Sophia, Amelia, and Clara and especially to my wife, Stefanii Morton Ferenczi: for uncounted hours of sacrifice during travel, writing, and "mental absence," and for your love and friendship.

Overview

The Challenge

There is no shortage of advice on the topic of leadership, and a significant body of literature exists addressing issues specific to leadership in theological education. Much less attention has been devoted to the question of the role of governing boards in theological schools. As continued changes cause theological schools to think ever more about how they relate to their dynamic context, the question of how governing boards contribute to this process and undergird executive leadership is more relevant than ever.

Such attention as has been paid to this topic had focused on the governance of theological schools in North America. Relatively little attention has been paid to governance of theological schools in other parts of the world, and in particular to the question of how governance process in theological schools is affected by cultural context.. This study thus examines governance in a number of theological schools in diverse Majority World contexts and seeks to understand how the governance process contributes to their ability to adapt to changing contexts. It focuses specifically on the interface between the executive leadership (the Chief Executive Officer and his/her team) and the governing board.

The Investigation

The methodology adopted in this study is rooted in structured grounded theory. In other words, it presents the lived experience of the various schools while seeking to discern trends from varied data including documents, observations, interviews, and other artifacts. That data is then used to formulate a tentative theory to stimulate further research.

This study is "structured" in that that author drew on the body of literature on theological education and governance in the formation of the research questions and interpretive categories. This literature is reviewed in chapters 2 and 3, with a special focus on how major trends impact discussions of governance in Majority World theological schools. The following key questions were formulated:

1. What characteristics contribute to effectiveness of theological school governance?

2. How does the cultural setting of theological schools relate to characteristics that contribute to governance effectiveness?

3. How do governing boards employ insights from internal and external relationships to enhance governance effectiveness?

The literature study also helped shape the interview and observation protocols that drove the interaction with four theological schools in the first half of 2011. These schools arose in differing historical circumstances in Asia, the Caribbean, Eurasia, and South America in the second half of the twentieth century.

Qualitative analysis was employed to discern emerging categories from the experience of these four schools. The research process is described in more detail in chapter 4.

Tentative answers to the research questions are presented in chapters 5 to 10, while in chapters 11 to 12 an attempt is made to draw conclusions from the data and suggest ways in which the governance process might be improved.

The Findings

The first research question concerned *the characteristics that contribute to effectiveness of theological school governance*. The qualitative analysis suggests that the following six categories are important:

1. **A Community of Trust** – that is, a fabric of relationship and trust within the institution and a sense of commonality in accomplishing the task of mission. This was usually expressed in terms of respect for and trust of leaders (especially CEOs) and the board. Equally important was expression of trust and support *by leaders* for their staff, faculty, and board members, *across the fabric of the community*.

2. **Alignment of the Parts** – that is, the relatively smooth interaction of various people and structures within the educational institution in a unified pursuit of its mission. This expressed itself in unity between the perceived needs of the context, the explicit academic curriculum, and the hidden and null curricula.

3. **Strong, Enabling Leadership** – The alignment of the various parts of the organization was in all cases dependent on a strong, enabling CEO figure. Strong, enabling leadership was not enough by itself. Rather, it was strong, enabling leadership in an aligned community of trust.

4. **A Shared Commitment to Education that Transforms** – This was expressed through at least three key concepts: a commitment to worldview change in students; a commitment to empowerment of students as agents of gospel change in lives, communities and societies; and a commitment to the unity of knowledge, belief, and actions in the educational process. Again, the relationship of this category to categories 1, 2, and 3 was mutually reinforcing.

5. **Reflective and Responsive Interaction with the Surrounding Community/Society** – This category was evidenced by awareness of and concern for broader social and cultural issues, interaction with a variety of both direct and indirect constituents of the theological school, and expression of the influence of this awareness and concern on the forms of education and administration practiced by the school.

6. **The Importance of Planning for the Future, Especially for Succession** – All the above categories remain deeply fragile and are subject to disruption in the event of an expected or unexpected leadership transition.

The second research questions concerned *the influence of cultural setting on governance in theological schools.* Here the results were somewhat unexpected. There was very little evidence of specific "cultural" forms of governance. It was very difficult to point to aspects of the governance process that were particularly "Asian" or "Latin American." Instead, the influence of culture on governance seemed to be institution-specific and localized, emerging from the particular historical context of the individual institutions.

The final research question concerned *how governing boards employ insights from internal and external relationships to enhance governance effectiveness*. This question was focused primarily on the exercise of governance by members of boards. The overall data, however, pointed to a broader concert of governance involving a spectrum of people associated with the educational institution. Board members rarely drew on insights from internal and external relationships. In all four institutions, such activity tended to take place more readily at the level of management, staff, and faculty. Board members were clearly aware of the concepts and engaged in internal and external relationships, yet at quite low levels with minimal influence on the direction of the institution. The potential for greater inputs from board members was clear, but it appears that their focus is on guarding values, assuring fiduciary responsibility, and acting as a protective buffer.

A Concert of Governance

The above findings point to the deep interdependence of the various parts of an organization – its governing board, executive leadership, management team, and faculty. In none of the observed schools was the governing board able in and of itself to achieve meaningful change. This leads to a theory of a "concert of governance." While this theory acknowledges the rightful final authority of the governing board, it suggests that meaningful, adaptive change within the institution, particularly in the strategic and generative frames of governance, requires insight and action from other groups within the institution as well. In such a model, the CEO plays a critical and central role. He or she must not be an autocrat but must understand his/her strengths and weaknesses and be able to bring people around herself/himself who complement and balance these strengths and weaknesses. The central calling of leadership in such a situation is drawing on and caring for others in the service of organizational mission.

Such an approach to governance is unquestionably messy, both in theory and in practice. One of the predominant models of governance, the Policy Governance Model of John Carver, is unquestionably simpler. A policy governance framework may assist a board to do better work, especially in the fiduciary sphere, yet truly effective governance requires determining that the institution is fulfilling its mission and meeting relevant needs effectively. True governance effectiveness must go broader and deeper than the Carver Model and must draw in more voices.

While the board itself is clearly the critical final authority in the governance process, the overall work of governance stretches beyond the boardroom and into the fabric of the institution as a whole, drawing on the insights, talents, and abilities of the CEO, the management, staff, and faculty, as well as that of the board.

The study concludes by suggesting that models and ideas presented by Chait, Ryan, and Taylor[1] – *generative governance* – and by Heifetz, Grashow, and Linsky[2] – *adaptive leadership* – may provide for a more complete understanding of governance.

---

1. R. P. Chait, W. P. Ryan, and B. E. Taylor, *Governance as Leadership: Reframing the Work of Nonprofit Boards* (Hoboken, NJ: John Wiley, 2005).
2. R. Heifetz, A. Grashow, and M. Linsky, *The Practice of Adaptive Leadership: Tools and Tactics for Changing Your Organization and the World* (Cambridge, MA: Harvard Business Press, 2009).

1

Introduction

Another trend . . . is the understanding of "community." With the ongoing urbanization, redefining the concept and reality of "community" is a practical need for China, and for the church. The positive part is that we are able to see new opportunities emerging. The negative part is that during this process, many "traditional" formulas may not work anymore. People are not yet used to such changes. I personally feel this might be the greatest challenge (and opportunity) for the church in this new era."

(CHINESE CHRISTIAN LEADER, 2014)

There is no "way out" in mission failures. There is no independent evaluation of strategy . . . so that the course can be set aright. It becomes personal, sentimental issue and silence is rule [rather] than speaking up for self-evaluation. Thus the manpower, the best minds and resources, property and equipment will be used for emotional (and spiritual so called) reasons and not for genuine church planting. Things get bigger and inertia so great that nothing can be changed until things rot and die. The whole mission philosophy needs evaluation, if it is proved ok than it must keep on going the way it is now moving, but if found wanting than bold steps must be taken. We have limited manpower, resources and of course time.

(SOUTH ASIAN LEADER, 2014)

We live in interesting times. As I have traveled throughout the world in recent years, interacting with various Christian ministries, I have been repeatedly struck by the sheer *complexity* of challenges and opportunities that we collectively face. Conflicts burn in a broad arc stretching from North Africa to Southeast Asia. Religious minorities face increasingly harsh social and/or governmental persecution in many parts of the world. Millions of pages and billions of words are spilled in universities, government ministries, and media concerning the importance of education, yet the outcomes of education seem to continue to stagnate globally. Social media and technology subtly (or not so subtly) disrupt and remake entire industries and sectors of society. Mass media becomes less a tool for conveying dispassionate information and more a tool for fanning flames of partisan discontent. Social polarization and conflict increase. Anger and indignation seem to be the emotions *du jour*. Leadership is perceived as ineffective. Hope fades.

Amidst this turbulent landscape, the church continues to wrestle with how to be salt and light. These are far from the most turbulent times the church has experienced. In many ways, this is a hopeful age. Even as many traditional churches shrink in Europe and, increasingly, North America, faith in Christ is increasing in nearly every corner of the globe.[1] Vibrant churches spring up around China's most prestigious universities. Middle Eastern Muslims displaced by conflict worship in traditional Christian churches, challenging everything Middle Eastern Christians thought they knew about being Christian in a predominantly Muslim world. African cities – from the slums of Nairobi and Luanda to the rich central business districts of Lagos and Abidjan – reverberate with praise on Sunday mornings. Nepali, Sudanese,

---

1. The "southward" shift of Christianity and the attendant rethinking of the task of mission and the nature of the church is a primary background for this study, which seeks to better understand how Christian institutions function in times of great change. This shift is covered in various ways by, among others, D. Robert, "Shifting Southward: Global Christianity since 1945," *International Bulletin of Missionary Research* 24, no. 2 (2000); A. Walls, "Christian Scholarship and the Demographic Transformation of the Church," in *Theological Literacy for the Twenty-First Century*, ed. R. L. Petersen and N. M. Rourke (Grand Rapids, MI: Eerdmans, 2002); S. Escobar, *The New Global Mission: The Gospel from Everywhere to Everyone* (Downers Grove, IL: IVP Academic, 2003); L. Sanneh and J. Carpenter, eds., *The Changing Face of Christianity: Africa, the West, and the World* (New York: Oxford University Press, 2005); P. Jenkins, *The New Faces of Christianity: Bible Believers in the Global South* (New York: Oxford University Press, 2006); M. Noll, *The New Shape of World Christianity* (Downers Grove, IL: IVP Academic, 2009); P. Borthwick, *Western Christians in Global Mission: What's the Role of the North American Church* (Downers Grove, IL: Intervarsity Press, 2012).

Chin, and dozens of other nationalities gather for church services in large and small cities across North America, Europe, and Australia. Communities of believers cluster in North American city centers, seeking to be truly in the city and for the city. No longer do all believers of evangelical conviction stand within the walls of their churches and mission compounds lamenting the fallenness of the outside world. Those walls have become porous as followers of Christ engage their societies more fully as agents of *shalom*.

As it has throughout its history, the church finds itself negotiating the dynamics of both the spiritual and the physical world – being in the world, but not of the world and dwelling in a kingdom that is at once already and not-yet. Perhaps more than in the recent past, believers of evangelical faith wrestle with what their faith has to say to the myriad challenges of this physical world. The church dwells in this dynamic world and is influenced by and poised to influence it. Approached from the Christian perspective of holistic mission or *misión integral*[2], the church has much to do in ministering to both spiritual and social aspects of these challenges. This is especially true as Christianity's center of gravity shifts to the south and east where many challenges are present in their starkest terms.[3] Such rapid change and pressing challenges,

---

2. This movement toward greater "holism" in mission is another primary background for this study. The church is indebted to C. René Padilla, Samuel Escobar, and others in Spanish-speaking Latin America for their groundbreaking work in this area. Padilla traces the history of evolution of this concept, in "Integral Mission and its Historical Development," in *Justice, Mercy and Humility*, ed. T. Chester (Carlisle: Paternoster, 2003). Wright (*The Mission of God: Unlocking the Bible's Grand Narrative* [Downers Grove, IL: Intervarsity Press, 2006]) develops a related idea of the mission of the people of God, a theological approach that deeply impacted the Cape Town Commitment (2011) emerging from the 2010 Lausanne Congress. I have personally been impacted in my thinking on this topic by informal inputs from Stephen Bauman and the team of World Relief and Matthew Frost and the team of TearFund-UK.

3. Although much of the groundwork of integral mission was formed in Latin America, African thinkers have more recently contributed markedly to this framework. Cf. E. Katongole and C. Rice, *Reconciling All Things: A Christian Vision for Justice, Peace, and Healing* (Downers Grove, IL: Intervarsity Press, 2008); R. Pohor and M. Kenmogne, *Théologie et vie chrétienne en Afrique* (Yaoundé, Cameroon: ADG Editions, 2012); R. Pohor and I. Coulibaly, *Christianisme authentique en Afrique contemporaine* (Abidjan, Côte d'Ivoire: Les Presses FATEAC, 2014), especially the essay by Ahoga in this volume. Some other inputs on this question from other regions include M. Maggay, "Towards Contextualization from Within: Some Tools and Culture Themes," in *Doing Theology in the Philippines*, ed. E. Acoba, John D. Suk, and the Asian Theological Seminary (Manila: OMF Publications, 2005); T. Gener, "Every Filipino Christian a Theologian: A Way of Advancing Local Theology in the 21st Century," in *Doing Theology in the Philippines*, ed. E. Acoba, John D. Suk, and Asian Theological Seminary (Manila: OMF Publications, 2005); L. Mapile, "Social Concern and Theological Education: A Philippines' Perspective," in *Tending the Seedbeds: Educational*

while daunting, also present opportunities. Reflecting on several decades of experience in educational administration, Nason suggests that such times of turmoil are "often the most productive for institutional change, since the pattern of the future can be definitely shaped."[4] This sentiment is echoed well by the Chinese Christian leader quoted at the beginning of this chapter.

What is the role of institutions in the future potential of the Christian church? We live, it seems, in an increasingly anti-institutional or post-institutional world.[5] Few established institutions – from politics to education to commerce – seem immune to disruption and deconstruction. The church is hardly immune, as multiple movements in North America and elsewhere call for less structured churches that are more responsive to their context.[6] Brooks, writing about the ineffective response to the 2014 Ebola outbreak in West Africa, sees this failure as rooted in a failure of governance and an unwillingness to take seriously the importance of institutions.

> A few generations ago, people grew up in and were comfortable with big organizations – the army, corporations and agencies. They organized huge construction projects in the 1930s, gigantic industrial mobilization during World War II, highway construction and corporate growth during the 1950s. Institutional stewardship, the care and reform of big organizations, was more

---

Perspectives on Theological Education in Asia, ed. A. Harkness (Quezon City, Philippines: Asia Theological Association, 2010); J. Searle and M. Cherenkov, *A Future and a Hope: Mission, Theological Education, and the Transformation of Post-Soviet Society* (Eugene, OR: Wipf & Stock, 2014).

4. J. W. Nason, *The Nature of Trusteeship: The Role and Responsibilities of College and University Boards.* Washington, DC: Association of Governing Boards of Universities and Colleges, 1982, 15–16.

5. H. Heclo, *On Thinking Institutionally* (Oxford: Oxford University Press, 2008).

6. I do not pretend to have any meaningful expertise in this area. I have in mind the emergence of non-denominational mega-churches in the 1990s–2000s such as Willow Creek in Chicago, Saddleback in southern California, and Mars Hill (two churches of same name in Seattle and Grand Rapids). Interestingly, most of these have become quite complex institutions in their own right. The "emerging church" (MacLarin, 2003) seems to have taken a different approach, one that is explored in the European context by Doornenbal (*Crossroads: An Exploration of the Emerging-Missional Conversation with a Special Focus on 'Missional Leadership' and Its Challenges for Theological Education* [Delft, the Netherlands: Eburon Delft, 2012]) and Soloviy (*Vynykaiucha tserkva* [Cherkassy, Ukraine: Colloquium, 2014]). Although less concerned about overcoming traditional structures, the Redeemer movement emerging from Tim Keller's work in New York City has certainly shared the theme of cultural engagement and raised questions of what "church" looks like. I cite these as just a few of the many non-traditional approaches to the structure of the Christian church.

prestigious. Now nobody wants to be an Organization Man. We like start-ups, disrupters and rebels. Creativity is honored more than the administrative execution. Post-Internet, many people assume that big problems can be solved by swarms of small, loosely networked nonprofits and social entrepreneurs. Big hierarchical organizations are dinosaurs . . . When the boring tasks of governance are not performed, infrastructures don't get built. Then, when epidemics strike, people die.[7]

At least in the West, we live in a world that is increasingly dominated by individual or localized action, often bonded through technology with other local initiatives. This obviously presents some wonderful new opportunities for collaboration around the many problems we face. Brooks, however, makes an important point that this need not be an either-or question. In addition to individuals who banded together to give to Ebola relief and single or small groups of medical professionals who traveled to West Africa, there is a desperate need for institutions that are capable of a broader yet nimble response. Institutions are still valid.

Similar trends are discernible in mission and the church. The 2000s saw an increasing call for churches to engage directly with partners "on the field."[8] Part of this emerged from a continuing sense that mission was "from everywhere to everywhere"[9] with a substantial part of the work of mission arising from the Majority World itself. Faith in traditional mission agencies shrank as the possibility of direct action was made possible by growing wealth, alongside ease of travel and communication. Major North American churches and their missions pastors in some cases became significant actors in the broader mission world. Similar questions about the role of institutions contributed to a critique of theological seminaries. From the 1980s, many began to ask if formal theological education is a sustainable or even desirable way to approach pastoral formation, a debate that continues today and will be discussed in chapter 2. Undoubtedly, many of these critiques have been positive and have led to positive change in mission organizations, theological

---

7. D. Brooks, "Goodbye, Organization Man," *The New York Times* (2014, September 15): A27.
8. B. Dyrness, *Let the Earth Rejoice!: A Biblical Theology of Holistic Mission* (Grand Rapids, MI: WIPF, 1998).
9. Escobar, *The New Global Mission*.

schools, and other church institutions. Some institutions have quietly slipped away, having fulfilled their purpose. Yet profound questions about the value of institutions continue to be a challenge for those who seek to lead organizations effectively.

A Double Precipice

While the church is a spiritual entity indwelled with the Holy Spirit, it also takes the human form of millions of all-too-human organizations and institutions. These range from small gatherings of believers in homes to multi-million-dollar parachurch organizations with infrastructure around the globe. These institutions are at once in this world and of the next. The tension between these realities is real. Leaders are forced to walk a sort of *double precipice*. On one side, there is the danger of too close an adherence to the latest business and management trends and an overweening sense of professionalism. At its worst, this precipice leads to hubristic pursuit of utopia in this world. On the other side is the equally dangerous precipice of over-spiritualization, of the sort referenced by the South Asian leader quoted at the beginning of this chapter. The church has used spiritual language to defend mediocrity and poor stewardship of resources far too long. Yet mediocrity is not the worst outcome. At its worst, this precipice can lead to toxic leadership, lack of accountability, and corruption.

In the best of times, the life of leadership on this double precipice is challenging, and we do not dwell in the best (or the simplest) of times. Perhaps as much as ever, we as humans look in all spheres of life for leaders who can address our common challenges and fears. In most cases, we expect too much from our all-too-human leaders. A recent study of innovation in theological schools in various parts of the world shined light on these unsustainable leadership expectations. MacLeod demonstrated that meaningful innovation in these theological schools was most often locally driven and inspired by an "uncommon ethos" that embodies at *once an openness to new ideas as well as a proactive approach to the local church.*[10] More often than not, this involved theological educators who were willing to take significant risk and sail into

---

10. M. MacLeod, "Unconventional Educational Practices in Majority World Theological Education: A Qualitative Research Study" (unpublished manuscript, 2013), Indianapolis, IN: Overseas Council.

largely uncharted waters in order to respond better to pressing needs. Life in these uncharted waters, however, is lonely and challenging.

> To a greater or lesser degree, schools are working under difficult conditions as they strive to understand and manage complex challenges related to long-term stability. Their endeavors occur within environments that are at times unpredictable and affected by external changes fraught with uncertainty, peer suspicion, resistance and conflict, and a sense of inadequate preparation.[11]

The decidedly locally based nature of innovation means that leaders often lack access to broader conversations and tools critical to the support of academic administrators in other contexts. The combination of this lack of tools, opposition, a frequent sense of being alone in innovative work, and the ever-present pressure of financial pressures places untold stress on innovators, raising significant question regarding the *human sustainability* of innovation and innovating institutions.

Ironically, the increased suspicion of institutions has not led to their withering away, but rather to ever-greater expectations placed on them and their leaders. The heyday of big institutions that Brooks describes, above, was one in which much was expected from government, big corporations, and other large bureaucratic institutions. Yet it was not usually expected quickly. The US Interstate Highway system, for example, took several decades to complete. Today, lightening-fast technology, rapid transportation, and globalization have all conspired to cause us to expect nimbleness, approachability, and rapid results. *We expect a lot – probably far too much – from those who lead. And these expectations take a toll.* If we accept that the institutions of the church throughout the world are valuable, then more focus needs to be placed on what allows these institutions to flourish. Central to this question is the flourishing of the leaders of these institutions. Those who are in some of the most critical positions are often those who are most challenged and least supported. How can institutions function in a better and healthier way in order to allow these institutions to achieve their full purpose? What role does board governance and governance more generally play in

---

11. Ibid., 25.

supporting these leaders and, ultimately, the missions of the organizations they lead? This is in many ways the central question of this study.

Leadership and Governance

There is no shortage of literature and discussion on leadership, including Christian leadership. Innumerable books, articles, videos, consulting services, academic institutes, and other activities are dedicated to thinking about how leaders can lead better. This has become a billion dollar industry in the United States, with thriving subsidiaries around the world.[12] Kellerman, one of the key players in leadership studies in the United States over the past several decades, issued a strong indictment of the field in her book *The End of Leadership*.

> . . . the leadership industry is much less than meets the eye. For whatever the industry's small, generally narrow successes, humankind writ large is suffering from a crisis of confidence in those who are charged with leading wisely and well, and from a surfeit of mostly well-intentioned but finally false promises made by those supposed to make things better.[13]

Kellerman calls for a renewed focus on leaders in relation to those who follow, and a more general focus on the context in which leadership is exercised. Kellerman concludes a long list of indictments of wrong assumptions made by the leadership industry as follows:

> We think leadership can be learned quickly and easily and that one form of leadership can be taught, simultaneously, to different people in different situations – a stretch at best. We think of context as being of secondary or even tertiary importance – which is wrongheaded. We think leader-centrically – that being

---

12. I do not use the term "subsidiaries" lightly. I do not suggest by this that all good leadership thinking comes from the United States. Rather, the majority of the commercial leadership industry (the types of things you see advertised in airline magazines) seems to derive from North America.
13. B. Kellerman, *The End of Leadership* (New York: Harper Collins, 2012), xiv.

a leader is better and more important than being a follower. Wrong again.[14]

Kellerman issues a helpful call to step back and see leaders and the institutions they lead in the broader and dynamic contexts in which they function. This call seems appropriate in light of the increasing challenges facing leaders in Christian organizations. The well-intentioned but limited focus on disembodied leadership training and the neglect of the broader context has, among other outcomes, led to an increasing amount of pressure placed on CEO (Chief Executive Officer) figures to climb continually to unreasonable heights.

While the leadership industry has much to say about team building and management of human resources, it often leaves the CEO figure remarkably alone with the biggest and most complex questions facing an organization. Chait, Ryan, and Taylor describe the increasing complexity of leadership in the nonprofit sector: "Trustees, employees, clients, and donors expect far more of nonprofit CEOs today than a genial personality, moral probity, managerial acumen, and a passionate commitment to the organization's social mission. Stakeholders, in a word, expect *leadership*."[15] This shift in expectations of the CEO have led, the authors argue, to the shift of many traditionally *governing activities* to the CEO's portfolio: "A substantial portion of the governance portfolio has moved to the executive suite."[16] Governing boards, however, have not kept pace, and continue to do many of the things they did in an earlier age. Chait, Ryan, and Taylor call for a new approach to governance that builds on traditional roles and focuses more on *generative* governance, thinking about not just what the organization is, but *what it can be*. Generative governance engages with exactly the kind of big-scale, paradigm-shifting questions that are often the biggest strain on the CEO and the overall sustainability of the organization. These are also the sorts of big-picture questions that most benefit from broader thinking.

---

14. Ibid., xx.
15. Chait, Ryan, and Taylor, *Governance as Leadership*, 3.
16. Ibid., 4–5.

Governance in Global Context

Nearly ten years ago, I attended a board meeting of a Christian nonprofit organization in Southeast Asia as a guest. The board was composed of a dozen or so members, including both elected members and representatives of the organization's founding North American institutions. A Christian leader in the nation chaired the meeting and the board included a number of highly successful local businessmen and women. Several members of the faculty and administration attended. The morning hours passed slowly as the board methodically worked its way through a quite lengthy agenda. Nearly every item on the agenda was a relatively small decision usually presented devoid of any larger context of the question. Should the organization remain part of a local network/fellowship, which involved paying a modest amount of dues? Should certain employees attend an upcoming conference? Should prices be raised in the organization's coffee shop? The most active participants in these discussions were members of the faculty and administration. Most of the board members sat with detached looks (this was in the days before iPhones and other such devices).

One particular issue around a staff matter, however, raised significant discussion among the entire board. It seemed to me as an outsider to be a minor issue, but it was clear from the discussion that there were some bigger picture issues involved. There seemed to be tension between some expatriate members of the board and local members. Some unnamed value was being debated indirectly. The secretary dutifully recorded everything that was said for the minutes. After twenty minutes of largely unsuccessful discussion, the chairperson adjourned the meeting for a tea break for fifteen minutes, the issue as yet unresolved. After forty-five minutes of fellowship over tea and cakes, the board reconvened. The chairperson began the session by stating that, since the issue being discussed prior to the break had been decided, they would move on to the next agenda item. I was rather stunned and fully expected some member of the board to intervene and declare that the issue was, indeed, not settled at all. But no one did. They moved on, rather seamlessly.

I do not know how the issue was resolved, but it became clear that something significant transpired during the tea break, something that addressed the obviously important and value-laden discussion. While there was probably some minute of the final decision, there was no meticulous minuting of the discussion that resolved it. The issue was clearly resolved quietly. No one was publically shamed for being on the wrong side. Governance had worked, even if not in the best possible way.

This raised at least two fundamental questions for me about the work of governance. First, was this board engaged in meaningful work? Although this board was struggling mightily to be a good governing body and clearly valued the work of the institution they governed, their process left much to be desired. They would almost certainly have been the first to declare that. Board members were clearly not engaged with the modest issues of policy brought before them. I suspect that many of the members would gladly have allowed management (who were probably better informed on the issues at hand) to make decisions on such issues. Were there other issues – significant issues, *generative issues* – that might have more effectively engaged this board?

My second question was about process. Although the board was attempting to use some modified form of Robert's Rules of Order, it was clear that when a real, conflicted decision had to be made, it was made in a less formal, more sensitive way. *I came away wondering how much governing was done over tea and cakes.* How did this board meeting in a Southeast Asian megacity differ from a board meeting in a similar organization in a megacity in Brazil? Or Nigeria? Or Los Angeles? To what degree is the practice of governance impacted by context and culture? These questions, along with an interest in the administration in theological schools in general, inspired this study.

Adaptive Governance?

Governance has been a growing theme in the literature around nonprofit organizations and educational institutions over the last twenty years. Although it has not reached anything approaching the size or scope of the "leadership industry" mentioned above, the "governance industry" in North America has churned out a number of books, articles, resources, consultants, and conferences on the subject of how to have a better board. A significant percentage of this work, as discussed in chapter 2, is based in the experience of board members themselves, with a smaller subset based in research. The quintessential work of this genre, John Carver's *Boards that*

Make a Difference[17] has been used by countless boards not only in North America, but globally. Undoubtedly, the outputs of this governance industry, including the Carver Model, have helped to strengthen board governance and institutions/organizations around the world. But what is lacking? What does this prodigious and ongoing output of resources have to say to the governing boards of Majority World Christian institutions? To what degree do the driving questions behind these works reflect the driving questions of these Majority World organizations? While it would be hubris to suggest that this study seeks an answer to this question, it does seek to better understand the actual governing process and environment of a few theological schools, in order to raise some more general questions about governance and leadership in a global context.

One of the leading questions in my mind as I entered into this project was to what degree are the understandings of board governance that operate in the nonprofit sphere (Christian and otherwise) conditioned by the historical and cultural context of North America, with its strong emphasis on voluntary associations, civil society and lay oversight? Historical literature does strongly suggest that the evolution of governing forms in the United States are closely tied to voluntary associations dating back to the colonial period of US history[18] (discussed further in chapter 2). This statement is not made to suggest that civil society or lay initiative was wholly unique to the United States. In fact, historical discussion of the nineteenth century in several other areas has raised contentious questions about the emergence of space for civil society in pre-Revolutionary Russia, late Imperial China, and a various European states.[19] Yet these movements almost always emerged in tension with the predominant models of society, rather than as one of the key threads of the fabric of society as in the United States. Authoritarian governments

---

17. J. Carver, *Boards That Make a Difference: A New Design for Leadership in Nonprofit and Public Organizations*. 3rd ed. (San Francisco, CA: Jossey-Bass, 2006).
18. P. D. Hall, "Cultures of Trusteeship," in *Inventing the Nonprofit Sector and Other Essays on Philanthropy, Voluntarism, and Nonprofit Organizations*, ed. P. D. Hall, (Baltimore, MD: Johns Hopkins University Press, 1992).
19. Cf. O. Crisp and L. Edmondson, eds., *Civil Rights in Imperial Russia* (Oxford: Clarendon Press, 1989); W. T. Rowe, "Symposium: 'Public Sphere'/'Civil Society' in China? Paradigmatic Issues in Chinese Studies, III," *Modern China* 19, no. 2 (1993): 139–157; N. Bermeo and P. Nord, eds., *Civil Society before Democracy: Lessons from Nineteenth-Century Europe* (Lanham, Md: Rowman & Littlefield, 2000); J. Bradley, *Voluntary Associations in Tsarist Russia: Science, Patriotism, and Civil Society* (Cambridge, MA: Harvard University Press, 2009).

in the twentieth century crushed most of these emerging movements. The legacy of these more recent government approaches in today's Russia, China, Brazil, and various other nations of Asia, Africa, and Latin America are far stronger than the flowerings of civil society more than a century ago. When we bring organizational governance models that emerged in the cultural soils of North America to other places, to what degree are we assuming that the North American situation is normative? To what degree are we ignoring other deeply ingrained modes of governance that have emerged within various cultures, including possible negative and positive elements of governance? To what degree does the unquestioned use of an outside model push the true work of governance into informal space (such as over tea and sweets!) in order to avoid conflict or avoid shame? The investigation of the four theological schools in this study does not seek to provide definitive answers to these questions. Rather, it seeks to provide a bit of descriptive framing of the actual governance process at work in these institutions to further clarify these questions.

Governance and Theological Education

As the Christian church seeks to fulfill the biblical mandate of ministering holistically, the question of well-trained leaders becomes central. Mature, equipped, and merciful servant leaders are essential.[20] Since the Middle Ages, Christian leaders have been trained within a system of theological education that arose in European universities and later broadened into a diverse system of seminaries, divinity schools, Bible colleges, and non-formal training programs functioning in some way in nearly every corner of the globe. In many ways, however, this system has run on "auto-pilot"; much of the fundamental architecture of curricula and organizational structures remained static and unexamined.[21] This model, developed largely in Europe and the United States, was exported in the second half of the twentieth century to other parts

---

20. R. K. Greenleaf, *Servant Leadership* (New York: Paulist Press, 1977).
21. I do not mean this as an all-encompassing statement; history rarely works this way. Undoubtedly, there has been significant discussion in many circles about what constitutes good theological education over the course of many decades. G. T. Miller (*Piety and Profession: American Protestant Theological Education, 1870-1970* [Grand Rapids, MI:

of the world, carrying with it much cultural baggage.[22] While some elements of this cultural baggage have been clear, others have been much less evident and examined. As the church addresses ongoing leadership needs, how can this system be examined in a way that is productive, affirming what works well while challenging to improve in some areas?

Over the past sixty years, and especially since 1980, the discourse on theological education has grown in both breadth and depth with a proliferation of works on the nature, content, history, and purposes of theological education. Although diverse in nature, nearly all works call for some form of renewal or change in theological education as it is practiced. For the purposes of this study, this diverse body of literature is referred to as "calls for renewal." This literature deals with many fundamental theological, philosophical, and educational questions regarding the purposes of theological education. Fewer studies give attention to institutional questions of how theological education is administered and governed. Despite differing approaches, a central theme emerges in the literature regarding the relationship of the theological school to its constituency and environment. Is the theological school able to understand and respond in a relevant way to the needs of its constituent churches and the society beyond? Is the theological school able to be "a constant source of intellectual rigor and prophetic vision, of spiritual energy, and as the support and inspiration for strong leadership and society-shaping influence in the churches"?[23] Despite thirty years of discussion, the tenor of recent works[24] suggests that these questions are far from settled.

Eerdmans, 2007]; and *Piety and Plurality: Theological Education since 1960* [Eugene, OR: Cascade Publications, 2014]) details these changes in the North American context from 1870 to the present. My point here is more directed to the majority-world situation since World War II.

22. M. L. Charter, "Theological Education for New Protestant Churches of Russia: Indigenous Judgments on the Appropriateness of Educational Methods and Styles," (Unpublished doctoral dissertation) Trinity Evangelical Divinity School. Deerfield, Illinois, 1997; O. Kalu, "Multicultural Theological Education in a Non-Western Context," in *Shaping Beloved Community*, ed. D. Esterline and O. Kalu (Louisville: Westminster John Knox Press, 2006).

23. R. K. Greenleaf, *Seminary as Servant: Essays on Trusteeship* (Peterborough, NH: Windy Row Press, 1983), 9.

24. E.g. L. M. Cannell, *Theological Education Matters: Forming Leaders for the Church* (Newburgh, IN: EDCOT Press, 2006); D. Aleshire, *Earthen Vessels: Hopeful Reflections on the Work and Future of Theological Schools* (Grand Rapids, MI: Eerdmans, 2008); L. G. Jones, "Something Old, Something New," *Christian Century* 131, no. 4 (2014).

This study approaches the question of renewal in theological education from a slightly different perspective, beginning with the governance-related questions that opened this chapter. This is based in the observation and assumption that renewal in theological education (or lack thereof) is influenced by the governance structures of the educational institutions where theological education takes place. Daniel Aleshire, who has served for twenty years as executive director of the Association of Theological Schools (ATS), observes that "almost all serious accrediting sanctions issued by ATS . . . have related to failures of governance, administration, or finances, and for many schools with sanctions related to finances, the underlying problem had as much to do with governance or administration as financial resources."[25] This observation parallels the experience of the Overseas Council International (OCI), a nonprofit organization serving more than one hundred theological schools outside of North America for nearly forty years. The focus on governance also arises from recent governance literature that suggests proper, visionary, and constituent-oriented governance is essential for all organizations and institutions during a period of dynamic change.[26] If the mission and structure of an institution is highly influenced by its environment, as most literature suggests,[27] governing boards must play a critical role in assuring responsiveness and relevance. Aleshire brings observation of theological schools and governance literature together in arguing that "board members are far more crucial to the integrity and capacity of theological schools in the present than they were in the past, and they will be even more important in the future. In fact, without thoughtful and creative board work, many schools may not have a future at all."[28] Effective, productive, and visionary boards of governance are a key – although understudied – element of renewal in theological education.

---

25. Aleshire, *Earthen Vessels*, 95.
26. D. H. Smith, *Entrusted: The Moral Responsibilities of Trusteeship* (Bloomington, IN: Indiana University Press, 1995); K. T. Scott, *Creating Caring and Capable Boards: Reclaiming the Passion for Active Trusteeship* (San Francisco, CA: Jossey-Bass, 2000); Chait, Ryan and Taylor, *Governance as Leadership*; D. Eadie, "Meeting the Governing Challenge: Applying the High-Impact Governing Model in your Organization" (Oldsmar, FL: Governing Edge Publications, 2007); Kellerman, *The End of Leadership*.
27. E.g. Hall, "Cultures of Trusteeship"; R. Abzug, and J. Galaskiewicz, "Nonprofit Boards: Crucibles of Expertise or Symbols of Local Identities," *Nonprofit and Voluntary Sector Quarterly* 30 (2001): 51–73.
28. Aleshire, *Earthen Vessels*, 165.

This study investigates how governing boards of theological schools in varying cultural contexts are contributing to renewal and responsiveness in the institutions they govern, in concert with the leaders, faculty, and staff of these institutions. Although the body of literature on boards in theological schools in North America is developing, very little is known about the practices, functions, and contributions of governing boards of theological schools outside of North America. This study seeks to contribute to deeper understanding of board function in Majority World theological schools, especially the governing board's role in relating to the institution's external environment. The study pursues the following qualitative research questions: What characteristics contribute to effectiveness of theological school governance? How does the cultural setting of theological schools relate to characteristics that contribute to governance effectiveness? How do governing boards employ insights from internal and external relationships to enhance governance effectiveness?

Definitions

This study seeks to gain a deeper understanding of governance as it is actually practiced in theological schools in a variety of contexts. As such, it utilizes an expansive definition of governance. Chait, Ryan, and Taylor argue that "governance is too complicated to reduce to simple aphorisms, however seductive, like 'boards set policies which administrators implement' or 'boards establish ends and management determines means.'"[29] Such a statement is, of course, a not-too-subtle critique of John Carver's *Policy Governance*. While the "simple" statements above contain truth and can prove useful within broader discussions of governance, this study understands governance as *assuring that an organization is reaching its full potential while remaining faithful to its values and ethos.* This definition presupposes the presence of what Chait, Ryan, and Taylor call "migratory governance,"[30] or the increasing assumption by senior organizational leaders of many of the traditional tasks of governance, such as strategic and financial planning. Chait, Ryan, and Taylor see this transition as a *fait accompli* and celebrate it as a positive step forward.

---

29. Chait, Ryan, and Taylor, *Governance as Leadership*, 5.
30. Ibid.

This "formulation of governance as leadership provides a more affirmative and constructive approach that *expands the pie* [emphasis added], provides more occasions and levers for leadership, and enhances the trustees' value to the organization. Just as significantly, governance as leadership enhances the organization's value to trustees."[31] This study was constructed around the expansive definition of governance articulated above with the goal of granting maximum space for observation of actual governance function in the observed institutions in a variety of cultures.

This study sees the governing board's role in assuring theological schools' responsiveness to their constituency and broader environment as a critical function of governance. Middleton's conception of "boundary spanning" is used as an organizing definition for this function in the context of governance.[32] Boundary spanning is based on the conception that governing boards are at once internal and external to an organization, and therefore able to see realities in ways that neither administrators (who are fully internal) or broader constituents (who are fully external) would be able to do. Boundary spanning is defined as "regulating exchanges of information and resources across boundaries between external and internal environments."[33] This study also relies heavily on Chait, Ryan, and Taylor's conception of generative thinking, or the idea that boards must think not only about what the institutions they govern are (fiduciary governance) or will be in the near term (strategic governance) but what institutions can and *should* be in light of external realities.[34]

The study employed the construct of "governance effectiveness" in its research methodology. This is a multi-faceted and potentially problematic concept that needs strict definition. The very use of the term "effectiveness" raises the question "effective in whose eyes?" an especially relevant question when complex constituencies are taken into account. For the purposes of this study, governance effectiveness is pursued in light of the board's ability to assist the institution it governs in responding to a changing environment through the employment of boundary spanning and generative thinking in

---

31. Ibid.
32. M. Middleton, "Nonprofit Boards of Directors: Beyond the Governance Function," in *The Nonprofit Sector*, ed. W.W. Powell (New Haven, CT: Yale University Press, 1987).
33. Ibid., 141.
34. Chait, Ryan and Taylor, *Governance as Leadership*.

relation to its context. Governance effectiveness in this sense is judged to be present when data reveal a substantial understanding of the board's role in assuring responsiveness of the institution to its environment as well as a willingness and ability to engage in generative thought that considers not just the present, but the future possibilities of the institution.

In addition to the concepts discussed above, several other terms used in the study require definition. The study seeks to understand governance in theological schools. For the purposes of this study, a theological school is defined as an institution providing training designed to equip leaders and/or members of Christian churches at the bachelor's degree level or higher with validation from a reputable outside agency (a national government or agency thereof, ATS, or an agency of ICETE – International Council for Evangelical Theological Education). When describing senior leadership of theological schools, the term CEO is used, denoting the chief administrative official of the school, referred to in various parts of the world as president, principal, rector, doyen, vice-chancellor, provost, and so forth. When describing board leadership, the term chairperson is used universally. The term board or board member is used to refer to governing bodies and their members, although quotes still make reference to council and other terms for such bodies used in other contexts. The term faculty is utilized to denote those engaged in the teaching functions of the institution, while staff is utilized in reference to non-teaching personnel. The term "management team" is utilized in reference to senior management of the institution overseeing strategic divisions or functions. These individuals are presumed to report directly to the CEO. At times, the term "leadership team" is used to denote this same group in direct quotations. The term "church" is generally used in a broad sense to describe a group of followers of Christ. The author acknowledges that not all followers of Christ, particularly those coming from other religious backgrounds, adopt the name "Christian" or use the term "church," due to negative contextual baggage of these terms. On occasion, the term "followers of Christ" is used synonymously with "church" to highlight this difference.

Another critical term is constituency. This study employs an expansive definition of this term, drawing on Andringa,[35] "those people who make a

---

35. R. C. Andringa and T. W. Engstrom, *Nonprofit Board Answer Book: Practical Guide for Board Members and Chief Executives* (Washington, DC: Board Source, 2002).

difference in achieving the mission" of the organization or institution. This wider definition stands in contrast to Carver's conception of constituency as those who have an *immediate* interest in the institution as a customer/student, donor, or provider of some other form of direct support or recognition.[36] Constituency in this study is defined as individuals, groups, or communities that draw real or potential benefit from the organization and who are able to contribute to the institution's success in direct or indirect ways. This study takes seriously Lynn and Wheeler's assertion that the theological school must value its relationship with the broader community, including non-ecclesial relationships.[37]

Another set of terms used in the study relates to context and culture. The context implies the broader environment of the theological school, including social structures both inside and outside the church. For the purposes of this work, context is defined broadly as the matrix of ecclesial, political, economic, cultural, and social surroundings that influence the theological school in direct and indirect ways on both a daily and long-term basis. The term culture composes a critical element of context. For the purposes of this work, culture is defined as the expression of basic values and understandings about the nature of reality, including epistemological, ontological, and axiological assumptions. It is assumed that these values and understandings are often embedded deeply and play an important, if discrete, role in the day-to-day life of a theological school. This definition of culture, applicable primarily to national, ethnic, or religious contexts, should not be confused with organizational culture, which is defined as "A pattern of shared basic assumptions that the group learned as it solved its problems that has worked well enough to be considered valid and is passed on to new members as the correct way to perceive, think, and feel in relation to those problems."[38] While broader definitions of culture and organizational culture share many similarities, especially in their embedded, often unarticulated nature, the relative scope and depth of broader culture must be acknowledged.

---

36. Carver, *Boards That Make a Difference*.
37. E. Lynn and B. L. Wheeler, *Missing Connections: Public Perceptions of Theological Education and Religious Leadership* (New York: Auburn Theological Seminary, 1999).
38. E. H. Schein, *Organizational Culture and Leadership* (San Francisco, CA: Jossey-Bass, 2004), 17.

Finally, the study employs educational terminology and spelling conventions used in the United States. This is most applicable when discussions of academic levels are used. "Graduate studies" in the context of this study adopts the American sense of the term, implying post-baccalaureate study. The researcher has taken the liberty of adjusting other terms used elsewhere (especially post-graduate) in transcripts of interviews. Transcripts and direct quotes also utilize spelling conventions of the United States.

What Comes Next

This study seeks to establish an understanding of governance practice in theological schools in a global perspective. While there has been considerable attention to governance of theological schools in North America, very little has been written about theological schools in the rest of the world. Such understanding serves multiple constituencies. Because the importance of governing boards continues to grow in a rapidly changing environment, the study provides case studies of how institutions in diverse contexts are engaging with their constituents as well as broader societal trends. It brings concrete examples and case studies that are more culturally relevant to governing boards in the types of institutions being studied. The study should also prove useful to those engaged in the growing field of board training and evaluation, such as OCI and ICETE member agencies. At present, such institutions draw largely on North American data and experiences. This study may reveal cultural dynamics that could be explored further to deepen understanding of institutional function in a given context. This further augments the researcher's interest in organizational dynamics in diverse cultural contexts, and specifically to cultural differences in the exercise of power and authority.

Chapter 2 sets a context for the study in the area of theological education. This focuses primarily on discussions of theological education since 1980 and with an eye primarily toward Protestant institutions. Literature dealing with or emerging from the Majority World is given special attention, although I have tried to see this discussion in the context of broader literature. Overall, I have focused on the evolution of this discussion from a conversation about fragmentation to a focus on theological education as mission and, more recently, the prophetic role of theological education.

Chapter 3 reviews literature on governance. This review focuses almost exclusively on the nonprofit and educational sectors. I have placed special focus on the literature on governance in theological education. Undoubtedly, a significant amount of wisdom could be gleaned from some of significant work on broader questions of governance in the public or corporate spheres, but that has proven beyond the limitations of this study. The review of governance literature also did not focus equally on all aspects of board governance. The study assumed that governing boards carry out the responsibilities of fiduciary oversight of the organization, which is well established in governance literature.[39] Although this is likely an overly optimistic assumption, more attention was given to aspects of governance related to assuring relevance of the organization within its context.

Chapter 4 presents the framework of the research study itself. After a short discussion of methodology (with additional data in the appendix) and limitations, I describe each of the four institutions involved, followed by a brief summary of the answers to the first research question, concerning *characteristics contributing to effectiveness of theological school governance*. These six characteristics are introduced and defined at the end of chapter 4.

Chapters 5–10 unpack each of these six characteristics as foundation stones of effective governance. As much as possible, these are elaborated in the voice of the data from the individual theological schools, in order to allow them to "speak with their own voice." At times, some historical background is given on each institution. Each chapter concludes with a brief conclusion on the potential impact and challenge for theological school leaders and board members. Chapter 11 summarizes outcomes and themes from each of the four institutions, which contributed significantly to the final discussion in chapter 12.

Chapter 12 takes up the final two research questions, namely how does the cultural setting of theological schools relate to characteristics that contribute to governance effectiveness? And how do governing boards employ insights from internal and external relationships to enhance governance effectiveness?

---

39. E.g. Nason, *The Nature of Trusteeship*; Chait, Ryan and Taylor, *Governance as Leadership*; B. R. Hopkins, *Legal Responsibilities of Nonprofit Boards. BoardSource Governance Series: Vol 2.*, 2nd ed. (Washington, DC: BoardSource, 2009); A. S. Lang, *Financial Responsibilities of Nonprofit Boards. BoardSource Governance Series: Vol 2.*, 2nd ed. (Washington, DC: BoardSource, 2009).

Finally, the grounded theory methodology is brought to conclusion by the development of a theory of a concert of governance. In short, this theory proposes that effective governance is centered in but also transcends the board, drawing in other key members of the community in an empowering way that aligns all of the parts of the organization to responsively fulfill its purpose. The implications of this theory for governance are then taken up, followed by implications for theological education. The chapter concludes with some additional areas for further study. An epilogue presents three brief vignettes of theological schools pursuing responsiveness.

Theological schools are complex institutions sitting functionally at the intersection of church, the academy, and broader society.[40] As such, they have multiple relationships and constituencies. Because of the historical development of dominant models of theological education in Europe, and later North America, and the global spread of those models via the missions movement,[41] theological schools function in extremely diverse contexts. As nationalization of boards, leadership, and faculty of theological schools has quickened in the past twenty years, such institutions have become laboratories for intense interaction of models of institutional governance, management, and structure. Changes specific to the sphere of theological education have been compounded by accelerating change in the broader sphere of global higher education.[42] Despite this change, little attention has been given to the lived experience of theological schools undergoing such changes in diverse cultural environments. Much remains to be learned regarding the influence of culturally distinct values on such matters as change, conflict, power, or leadership. It is my hope that this work sheds some helpful light on these processes within the context of theological schools. It is my hope as well that

---

40. Greenleaf, *Seminary as Servant*; W. L. Baumgaertner, "Accountability to Church and State," in *The Good Steward: A Guide to Theological School Trusteeship* (Washington, DC: AGB, 1983); M. Warford, "Stewards of Hope: The Work of Trustees," in *Building Effective Boards for Religious Organizations*, eds. T. P. Holland and D. C. Hester (San Francisco, CA: Jossey-Bass, 2000); C. R. Klein, "Boundary Spanning: Building Bridges between and Organization and Its Environment," in *Building Effective Boards for Religious Organizations*, ed. T. P. Holland and D. C. Hester (San Francisco, CA: Jossey-Bass, 2000).

41. R. Banks, *Reenvisioning Theological Education: Exploring a Missional Alternative to Current Models* (Grand Rapids, MI: Eerdmans, 1999); V. Steuernagel, "The Relevance and Effects of European Academic Theology on Theological Education in the Third World," *Evangelical Review of Theology* 27, no. 3 (2003): 203–212.

42. Cf. C. M. Christensen and H. J. Eyring, *The Innovative University: Changing the DNA of Higher Education from the Inside out* (San Francisco, CA: Jossey-Bass, 2011).

this work raises broader questions of leadership and organizational dynamics that can lead to ever more productive Christian organizations pursuing meaningful, holistic mission around the world.

2

The Context of Theological Education

The discussion of theological education and governance in the first chapter is neither unique nor novel. My goal in this work is to build a bridge between the two areas of inquiry, bring them together, and suggest how consideration of the two subjects together can be mutually beneficial to broader challenges. The following chapter seeks to build the foundation for this in considering recent literature on theological education. A key theme at the root of much of the diverse literature on renewal in theological education has been one of evaluation. Is theological education accomplishing what it sets out to do? Recent literature, especially a number of pieces written by Majority World theological educators, has increasingly posed this evaluative question in terms of the impact of theological education on the challenges of broader society. Often, these questions have been raised explicitly or implicitly in the framework of the *prophetic* role of theological education. Questions of how institutions/organizations respond to and influence their environments/contexts – increasingly dynamic in nature – is also an increasingly dominant theme in much recent literature on governance of educational and nonprofit organizations. A subtle shift has taken place, away from governance overseeing preservation of the *status quo* to governance as a means of generative thinking about the future. The relationship of institutions to their environment is a common theme that I will suggest has power to be an important bridging concept with shaping power for the future of theological education.

Renewal in Theological Education

Throughout its history, the church has always formed its people for service.[1] For many centuries, much of this formation was accomplished outside the bounds of formal education, through community-based formation and mentoring for ministry.[2] By the late eighteenth and nineteenth century, Protestant theological education, defined as professional ministerial

---

1. This chapter does not seek to delve into the fascinating questions of the history of the formation of leaders or, more specifically, of theological education in the pre-modern church. Cannell (*Theological Education Matters*) focuses effort in this area. Reed also explores this area in depth in *The Paradigm Papers: New Paradigms for the Post-Modern Church* (Ames, IA: BILD International, 1997). I look forward to the forthcoming work of a noted church historian, González (*The History of Theological Education* [Nashville, TN: Abingdon Press, 2015]) on these subjects. In terms of consideration of the foundational strata that have contributed to theological education, works by E. Farley, *Theologia: The Fragmentation of Unity of Theological Education* (Philadelphia, PA: Fortress, 1983); D. Kelsey, (*Between Athens and Berlin: The Theological Education debate* (Grand Rapids, MI: Eerdmans, 1993); D. Tracy, "On Theological Education: A Reflection," in *Theological Literacy for the Twenty-First Century*, eds. R. L. Petersen and N. M. Rourke (Grand Rapids, MI: Eerdmans, 2002); Walls, "Christian Scholarship and the Demographic; T. Groome, "Wisdom for Life: The Horizon of Theological Literacy," in *Theological Literacy for the Twenty-First Century*, eds. R. L. Petersen and N. M. Rourke (Grand Rapids, MI: Eerdmans, 2002; and S. M. Heim "Renewing Ways of Life: The Shape of Theological Education," in *Theological Literacy for the Twenty-First Century*, eds. by R. L. Petersen and N. M. Rourke (Grand Rapids, MI: Eerdmans, 2002) all make contributions.

2. Over the past thirty years, many have called in both theoretical and practical terms for a return to this "non-formal" model of formation. Cannell gives a helpful historical retrospective of this movement in "Nonformal Education: A Retrospective," *Common Ground Journal* 11, no. 2 (2014). Perhaps the most important figure in this movement in terms of non-formal theological education is Ted Ward, former professor at Michigan State University and Trinity Evangelical Divinity School. A collection of Ward's work, including many unpublished pieces, is found in the edition of *Common Ground Journal* published in Fall 2012 (Cannell, "Theme: The Social Philosophy of the Christian Educator, Gathering the Work of Ted Ward," *Common Ground Journal* 10, no. 2 [2013]). Perhaps Ward's greatest influence was through his mentoring of an entire generation of Christian educators, including many who have played a vital role in theological education in the Majority World (cf. D. H. Elmer and L. McKinney, *With an Eye to the Future: Development and Mission in the 21st Century: Essays in Honor of Ted Ward* [Monrovia, CA: MARC Publications, 1996]). Another aligned but distinct field of thinking revolves around Theological Education by Extension (TEE), which shares both values and practice with both formal and non-formal theological education (cf. R. Winter, *Theological Education by Extension* [Pasadena, CA: William Carey Library, 1969]; S. G. Snook, *Developing Leaders Through Theological Education by Extension: Case Studies from Africa* [Wheaton, IL: Billy Graham Center ,1992]; R. Kinsler, *Diversified Theological Education: Equipping all God's people* [Pasadena, CA: William Carey International University Press, 2011]). At present (2015), much creative work in TEE is being done through Increase (http://www.increasenetwork.org/), based in Malaysia. While this work does not address this important field of labor, whose boundaries increasingly overlap with a lot of "formal" theological education, this body of literature and practice is critical to consider when thinking about the future of theological education.

preparation, was increasingly accomplished through formal means. An entire ecosystem of seminaries, Bible colleges, divinity schools, and other modes of formal theological education have emerged. These systems arose first in Europe and North America, deeply embedded in the cultural and academic structures of those areas.[3] Such systems of theological education were transplanted to Africa, Asia, and Latin America beginning in the nineteenth century, usually through the work of European or North American missionaries. The first wave of such institutions arose in the late nineteenth and early twentieth centuries through the work of Presbyterian, Baptist, Methodist, and Anglican/Episcopal missions. Another, larger group grew from the 1950s onward, based in evangelical mission work.[4] Recent shifts in global Christianity toward the east and south have resulted in an increasingly globalized theological education, with African, Asian, and Latin Americans playing a larger role.[5] This in turn has led to the development of a dialogue around the role of theological education in various regions.[6] The increasingly multicultural and diverse nature of theological education in the West has also broadened the overall nature of the conversation.[7]

---

3. V. L. Brereton, *Training God's Army: The American Bible School, 1880-1940* (Bloomington and Indianapolis, IN: Indiana University Press, 1990); Kelsey, *Between Athens and Berlin*; Banks, *Reenvisioning Theological Education*; Steuernagel, "The Relevance and Effects"; Cannell, *Theological Education Matters*; Kalu, "Multicultural Theological Education"; G. Cheesman, *The Bible College Movement in the UK* (Frankfurt, Germany: Vdm Verlag, 2009).

4. Y. Allen, *A Seminary Survey: A Listing and Review of the Activities of Theological Schools in Africa, Asia, and Latin America* (New York: Harper, 1960).

5. Jenkins, *The New Faces of Christianity*; C. Ott and H. A. Netland, *Globalizing Theology: Belief and Practice in an Era of World Christianity* (Ada, MI: Baker Academic, 2006); T. C. Tennent, *Theology in the Context of the World Christianity: How the Global Church is the Way We Think about and Discuss Theology* (Grand Rapids, MI: Zondervan, 2007); C. J. H. Wright, "The Challenge of the Brain Drain within Theological Education," 2012 Global Consultation on Theological Education, South Hamilton, MA, 2012.

6. D. V. Esterline and O. U. Kalu, eds., *Shaping Beloved Community* (Louisville, KY: Westminster John Knox Press, 2006); D. Werner, D. Esterline, N. Kang, and J. Raja, eds., *Handbook of Theological Education in World Christianity: Theological Perspectives, Ecumenical Trends, Regional Surveys* (Oxford, UK: Regnum, 2010); I. Phiri and D. Werner, *Handbook of Theological Education in Africa* (Oxford: Regnum, 2013); H. Antone, W. Longchar, H. Bae, H. P. Ho, and D. Werner, eds., *Asian Handbook for Theological Education and Ecumenism* (Oxford: Regnum, 2013).

7. A. F. Evans, R. A. Evans, and D. A. Roozen, *The Globalization of Theological Education* (Maryknoll, NY: Orbis, 1993); Walls, "Christian Scholarship"; A. Mathews, "The Theological is Also Personal: The 'Place' of Evangelical Protestant Women in the Church," in *Theological Literacy for the Twenty-First Century*, eds. R. L. Petersen and N. M. Rourke (Grand Rapids, MI: Eerdmans, 2002); A. Padilla, "Living in the Hyphen: Theological Literacy from an

Questions about the nature and effectiveness of theological education have existed for generations.[8] From the 1980s, a number of substantive works raised significant philosophical, educational, and theological questions about theological education, with most works calling for some type of reform. Although these works were diverse, most spoke in some form to the question of the "fragmentation" of theological education and the tensions between various aspects of the general theological curriculum.[9] Banks[10] and Ott[11] provide a much deeper review of these debates than is possible here. In recent years, the debate has more meaningfully engaged voices from around the world. Indeed, Majority World voices continue to grow in discussions of theological education and attempts at reform. This is a trend that is likely to and must continue. As Wright suggests, there is a need for Western institutions to move out of their "host" positions and allow greater agency to non-Western theological schools. "We need a reversal of roles, so that the relationship can deepen and be enriched."[12]

The literature on theological education can be approached in a variety of ways. I will present below seven frameworks of literature relating to theological education. In each case, I will mention a few key works, and provide some additional suggestions, focusing particularly on Majority World voices. I will then discuss several major themes that I believe are central to these debates, with an eye toward framing praxis and action moving forward. Although I will draw from a global source base in tracing these themes, I

Hispanic American Perspective," in *Theological Literacy for the Twenty-First Century*, eds. R. L. Petersen and N. M. Rourke (Grand Rapids, MI: Eerdmans, 2002); T. Brelsford and J. Senior, "Theological Thinking as Contextual Practice," in *Contextualizing Theological Education*, eds T. Brelsford and P. A. Rogers (Cleveland, OH: Pilgrim Press, 2008).

8. This study focuses predominantly on the theological education debates that arose in the late 1970s in North America and continue today. However, these discussions were heavily influenced by earlier works, including Niebuhr, Williams, and Gustafson (*The Advancement of Theological Education* [New York: Harper Brothers, 1957]) and discussions connected to the Theological Education Fund and its various mandates. Pearson (*Supporting Asian Christianity's Transition from Mission to Church: A History of the Foundation for Theological Education in South East Asia*. The Historical Series of the Reformed Church in America, No. 68. [Grand Rapids: Eerdmans, 2010]) details some of this history in the context of Asia.

9. Farley, *Theologia*; Kelsey, *Between Athens and Berlin*.

10. Banks, *Reenvisioning Theological Education*.

11. B. Ott, *Beyond Fragmentation: Integrating Mission and Theological Education* (Oxford, UK: Regnum Books, 2001).

12. Wright, "The Challenge of the Brain Drain."

will approach these themes primarily for their relevance to Majority World theological education.

Much of the literature concerning theological education could be classified as emerging from a *theological/philosophical* framework. This is hardly surprising, given that most of those writing in this area have been theologians, biblical scholars, or others actively engaged in theological teaching. Farley and Kelsey are two of the emblematic works in this genre, with Farley's concept of "fragmentation" and Kelsey's "Athens-Berlin" tension/dichotomy influencing much other writing.[13] These works have tended to be descriptive, analyzing theological education as a phenomenon, with the focus at the conceptual level, rather than practical outworkings. Banks is another paradigm-shifting work in this genre, shifting the conversation fundamentally in the direction of seeing theological education as mission and an integral part of the *missio Dei*.[14] Ott also contributed significantly to an understanding of theological education as holistic mission.[15]

---

13. Farley, *Theologia*; Kelsey, *Between Athens and Berlin*.
14. Banks, *Reenvisioning Theological Education*.
15. B. Ott, *Understanding and Developing Theological Education*, trans. Tom Keefer, (Carlisle: Langham Global Library, 2015). The literature in this philosophical/theological framework is vast. Some significant works include: J. Hopewell, "A Congregational Paradigm for Theological Education," *Theological Education* 21 (1984); O. Costas, "Educación teológica y mission," in *Nuevas alternativas de educación teológica*, ed. C. R. Padilla (Buenos Aires: Nueva Creación, 1986); I. Zokoué, "Educating for Servant Leadership in Africa," *Evangelical Review of Theology* 9, no. 1 (1990); F. Herzog, "Athens, Berlin, and Lima," *Theology Today* 51, no. 2 (1994); W. Chow, "An Integrated Approach to Theological Education," *Evangelical Review of Theology* 19, no. 2 (1995); M. Stackhouse, *Apologia: Contextualization, Globalization, and Mission in Theological Education* (Grand Rapids, MI: Eerdmans, 1998); B. Edgar, "The Theology of Theological Education," *Evangelical Review of Theology* 29, no. 3 (2005); A. Kirk, "Re-envisioning the Theological Curriculum as if the *Missio Dei* Mattered," in *Theological education as mission*, ed. P. Penner (Schwarzenfeld, Germany: Neufeld Verlag, 2005); T. Pilli, "Toward a Holistic View of Theological Education," in *Theological Education as Mission*, ed. P. F. Penner (Schwarzenfeld, Germany: Neufeld Verlag, 2005); L. Stelio Rega, "Revendo paradigmas para a formaçao teológica e ministerial," in *Educação teológica transformadora*, ed. A. C. Barro and M. W. Kohl (Londrina, Brazil: Descoberta, 2006); W. H. Houston, "Theological Models of Biblical Holism with Reference to Theological Colleges in Africa." (Unpublished D.Min. dissertation), Gordon-Conwell Theological Seminary, South Hamilton, MA, 2008; Aleshire, *Earthen Vessels*; J. K. Asamoah-Gyadu, "Called to Make a Difference: Theological Education and Mission in Twenty-First Century Africa," *Ogbomosho Journal of Theology*, XV, no. 2 (2010); Mapile, "Social Concern and Theological Education"; J. Thomas, "Practical Theology: A Transformative Praxis in Theological Education toward Holistic Formation," *Journal of Theological Education and Mission* 1, no. 1 (2010); J. N. Amanze, "Contextuality: African Spirituality as a Catalyst for Spiritual Formation in Theological Education in Africa," *Ogbomosho Journal of Theology*, XVI, no. 2 (2011); M. Throup, "Towards Integration: Reenvisioning Theological Education as Worship,"

Another important framework of literature comes from the *educational* perspective. Just as many of the works from a theological/philosophical framework were written by theologians, this genre has emerged primarily from those trained in education. A few of the works that could be ascribed to this framework are Cole,[16] Ferris,[17] Groome,[18] Senanayake,[19] Enns,[20] Elmer,[21] Cannell,[22] Harkness,[23] Chong,[24] and Estefanos.[25] Shaw, while also a clear example of the "how to" genre, discussed below, is framed in educational thought and practice and contributes significantly to this framework of approaching theological education.[26] Many of these writers have been either taught or influenced by Ted Ward, who from the earliest stages of the theological education debates, raised probing questions about the nature and structure of theological education.[27] Though writers in this area generally shared with

---

The Theological Educator 1 (2011). Retrieved 14 Aug 2011. www.eeaa.org/TTE.htm.; G. T. Smith, "Theological Education as Formation in Wisdom," Presented at ATA Consultation on Models of Theological Education: Manila, Philippines, 2011; Doornenbal, *Crossroads*; D. Suazo Jiménez, *La función profética de la educación teológica evangélica en América Latina* (Barcelona, Spain: Editorial Clie, 2012), and M. Theocharous, "Not Living on Bread Alone: Theological Education as Prophetism," *Evangelical Review of Theology* 38, no. 3 (2012).

16. V. B. Cole, "Toward Integration in the Theological School Curriculum," *Evangelical Review of Theology* 23, no. 2 (1990).

17. R. W. Ferris, *Renewal in Theological Education: Strategies for Change* (Wheaton, IL: Billy Graham Center, Wheaton College, 1990).

18. Groome, "Wisdom for Life."

19. A. N. L. Senanayake, "Developing Culturally Relevant curriculum for Theological Education in Asia," in *Educating for Tomorrow: Theological Leadership for the Asian Context*, ed. M. W. Kohl and A. N. L. Senanayake (Bangalore, India: SAIACS Press, 2007).

20. M. Enns "Theological Education in Light of Cultural Variations of Reasoning: Some Educational Issues," in *Theological Education as Mission*, ed. P. Penner (Schwarzenfeld, Germany: Neufeld Verlag, 2005).

21. D. H. Elmer, "Theology Informs Mission and Education," in *Theological Education as Mission*, ed. P. Penner (Schwarzenfeld, Germany: Neufeld Verlag, 2005).

22. Cannell, *Theological Education Matters*.

23. A. Harkness, "De-schooling the Theological Seminary: An Appropriate Paradigm for Effective Pastoral Formation," in *Tending the Seedbeds: Educational Perspectives on Theological Education in Asia*, ed. A. Harkness (Quezon City, Philippines: Asia Theological Association, 2010).

24. C. Chong, "Christian Education Encounters 21st Century Globalization: The Singapore Experience," *Christian Education Journal* 3, no.10, Supplement (2013).

25. S. Estafanos, "Defying the Pharaohs: Contemporary Educational Challenges for the Evangelical Church in Egypt," *Christian Education Journal* 3, no. 10, Supplement (2013).

26. P. Shaw, *Transforming Theological Education: A Handbook for Integrative Learning* (Carlisle, UK: Langham Global Library, 2014).

27. Cannell, "Theme."

the theological/philosophical school a concern about fragmentation, many were quicker to suggest means to overcome fragmentation, usually through refinements or radical changes to the curriculum. A subtle tension between these first two approaches to thinking about theological education has long been present.

A third framework of literature is distinguished by its concern for the *product* of theological education. This framework has generally been concerned about what kinds of *leadership* theological schools produce.[28] This concern has often been expressed in terms of what kind of leadership is being formed for a particular geographic region.[29] A volume edited by Petersen and Rourke[30] approaches this question from the perspective of "theological literacy." The work of Greenleaf[31] is emblematic in this field, written by a businessman who was a decided outsider to theological education, yet was deeply concerned about the necessity of theological education for its broader social potential. A number of other writers from within theological education have also approached debates from this perspective, concerned for the kinds of church and societal leaders flowing from theological schools. These authors share the broader concern for theological education's ability to produce leaders who are able to influence both the church and society. This genre has been fueled by an increasing concern in the global church for holistic mission.

---

28. Greenleaf, *Servant Leadership*; Greenleaf, *Seminary as Servant*; M. W. Kohl, "Theological Education: What Needs to Be Changed?," in *Educating for Tomorrow: Theological Leadership for the Asian Context*, ed. M. W. Kohl and A. N. L. Senanayake (Bangalore, India; SAIACS Press, 2007); Jones, "Something Old, Something New."

29. Cf. C. R. Padilla, *New alternatives in Theological Education* (Oxford, UK: Regnum, 1985); N. Saracco, "La búsqueada de nuevos modelos de educación teológica," *Encuentro y diálogo* 4 (1988); D. Noelliste, "Theological Education in the Context of Socio-Economic Deprivation," *Evangelical Review of Theology* 3 (2005); A. C. Barro, "A educação teológica e os seus desafios para uma sociedade em transformação," in *Educação teológica transformadora*, ed. A. C. Barro and M. W. Kohl (Londrina, Brazil: Descoberta, 2006); A. Akrong, "The Challenges of Theological Education in Ghana," *Journal of African Christian Thought* 10, no. 2 (2007); Mapile, "Social Concern and Theological Education"; Searle and Cherenkov, *A Future and a Hope*.

30. R. L. Petersen, and N. M. Rourke, *Theological Literacy for the Twenty-First Century* (Grand Rapids, MI: Eerdmans, 2002).

31. Greenleaf, *Servant Leadership*; Greenleaf, *Seminary as Servant*.

A fourth framework of literature is *historical* approaches to theological education. This genre includes, among others, Marsden,[32] Sunquist,[33] Miller,[34] and Searle and Cherenkov.[35] The works of Aleshire,[36] while venturing far beyond the historical framework, are deeply informed by the author's understanding of the history of North American theological education. This framework is relatively empty in much of the Majority World.[37]

A fifth framework of literature consists of *research studies* concerning theological education. These studies employ forms of social science research methodology, either qualitative or quantitative, to contribute to understandings of theological education. A large amount of this work consists of dissertations completed in the last decade or so by theological educators.[38] Many of these, unfortunately, have not yet seen publication. Another

---

32. G. Marsden, *Reforming Fundamentalism: Fuller Seminary and the New Evangelicalism* (Grand Rapids, MI: Eerdmans, 1987).

33. S. Sunquist, "Asian Theological Education: The Long View," in *A Cultured Faith: Essays in Honour of Prof. G.P.V. Somaratna on His Seventieth Birthday*, ed. P. Mihindiskulasariya, I. Poobalan, and R. Caldera (Colombo, Sri Lanka: CTS Publishing, 2011).

34. Miller, *Piety and Profession*; Miller, *Piety and Plurality*.

35. Searle and Cherenkov, *A Future and a Hope*.

36. Aleshire, *Earthen Vessels*; and "Governance and the Future of Theological Education," *Theological Education* 44, no. 2 (2009).

37. This seems a field of inquiry that is particularly ripe for further research, especially the history of evangelical theological schools in Africa, Asia, and Latin America. I have been particularly encouraged by the good work done in Russia, Ukraine, and other parts of the former Soviet Union to document the history of theological education through the development and publication of archival materials, oral history, and other resources, much of it under the care of the Euro-Asian Accrediting Association (www.e-aaa.org). In one case, this has led to a small museum that explores theological education and leadership development among Ukrainian-speaking churches in the rich broader context of the history of the evangelical movement. Taras Dyatlik's forthcoming doctoral dissertation will also contribute considerably to this field.

38. A few examples include I. Shamgunov, "Listening to the Voice of the Graduate: An Analysis of Professional Practice and Training for Ministry in Central Asia" (Unpublished doctoral dissertation), University of Oxford, UK, 2009; J. Feliciano-Soberano, "Patterns of Epistemological Beliefs among Filipino Students at a Graduate Seminary in Manila: Cultural Perspectives and Pedagogical Implications" (Unpublished doctoral dissertation), Trinity Evangelical Divinity School, Deerfield, Illinois, 2011; J. A. M. Neto, "Un análisis bíblico-histórico de la formación con base en la iglesia local y sus implicaciones para las iglesias evangélicas tradicionales del nordeste brasileño" (Unpublished Doctoral Dissertation), Seminario Teológico Centroamericano, Guatemala City, Guatemala, 2012; M. Tankler, "Harmonizing Individual and Ecclesiastical Expectations with the Institution of Theological Education" (Unpublished Doctoral Dissertation), Asbury Theological Seminary, Wilmore, KY, 2013; P. P. Cornelius, "Bridging the Expectation-Reality Gap: Exploring a Transformational Model for Theological Education in India," (Unpublished Doctoral

significant body of literature has arisen from research conducted by the Auburn Center for the Study of Theological Education at New York's Auburn Theological Seminary.[39] These studies focus exclusively on North American theological education, but contribute significantly to better understanding of leadership, governance, and many financial and management issues relating to theological education.[40] A number of articles in *Theological Education* also report on research studies conducted by ATS and other entities,[41] often with the support of the Lilly Endowment. MacLeod,[42] a study of nine theological schools globally, each of which had pursued some sort of meaningful innovation, is rich in insight – and challenges – for theological educators. An in-depth qualitative study of theological education in Central and Eastern Europe[43] is unique in that it bridges between formal and non-formal theological education and interviews a host of people across theological schools, the church, and emerging leaders. The study presents a number of helpful and challenging questions for theological educators. Finally, a 2011–2013 survey of theological institutions on a global level revealed much about the state of a wide-ranging group of theological schools.[44]

A sixth framework of literature consists of works designed to provide immediate, practical advice to theological educators. I have chosen to call this genre *"how to" literature*. This area has grown in recent years. In the North American arena, Lewis and Weems[45] provides guidance to seminary

---

Dissertation), Fuller Theological Seminary, School of Intercultural Studies. Pasadena, California, 2014; and E. R. Hunter, "Stakeholder Perspectives of Contextual Engagement of PhD Programs at Select Evangelical Seminary in the Majority World" (Unpublished doctoral dissertation), Trinity Evangelical Divinity School, Deerfield, IL, 2014.

39. www.auburnseminary.org/religion-and-research

40. Cf. B. G. Wheeler, et al., *Leadership That Works: A Study of Theological School Presidents* (New York: Auburn Center for the Study of Theological Education, 2010); H. M. Blier and B. G. Wheeler, *Report on a Study of Doctoral Programs That Prepare Faculty for Teaching in Theological Schools* (New York: Auburn Center for Theological Education, 2010).

41. Cf. T. D. Lincoln, "How Master of Divinity Changes Students: A Research-Based Model," *Teaching Theology and Religion* 13, no. 3 (2010).

42. MacLeod, "Unconventional Educational Practices.

43. S. Patty, "A View of Theological Education in Central and Eastern Europe: A Joint Project of Mission Eurasia and Josiah Venture in Partnership with Dialogues in Action" (unpublished manuscript), 2015.

44. D. V. Esterline, D. Werner, and T. Johnson, *Global Survey on Theological Education: 2011-2013*. Presented at WCC Consultation in Busan, Korea, November 2013.

45. G. D. Lewis and L. H. Weems, *A Handbook for Seminary Presidents* (Grand Rapids, MI: Eerdmans, 2006).

presidents, while Billman and Birch[46] provides a resource to academic deans. In the last decade, a number of resources have emerged specifically focused on Majority World theological institutions and the issues they face. Hardy,[47] Ott,[48] Deininger and Eguizabal,[49] and Shaw[50] all contain significant practical advice on nearly all aspects of theological education. Kafang provides a description of the broad operation of six theological seminaries in Nigeria.[51] The website theologicaleducation.org, administered jointly by the European Evangelical Accrediting Association and Overseas Council, provides additional practical literature.

A final, seventh, framework of literature revolves around some *international documents and publications* whose goal was to spur renewal in theological education. Among evangelical schools, the *ICAA Manifesto* of 1983[52] served as a call for reform in all aspects, including contextualization, church-ward orientation, continuous assessment, community life, servant molding, and cooperation (it should be noted that ICAA was the predecessor of ICETE). The Nairobi Manifesto (1998) built upon the ICAA Manifesto in the African context, affirming the need for relevance to the African context, servant molding, integrated programs, and a church-ward orientation. Ferris explored ways in which institutions around the world were implementing the ideas of the *Manifesto*. Ferris' work provides both reflections on commonalities observed among selected schools, and broad-ranging suggestions for curriculum and institutional reform implementing the spirit of the *Manifesto*.[53] The *Cape Town Commitment*,[54] although much

---

46. K. D. Billman and B. C. Birch, eds., *C(H)AOS Theory: Reflections of Chief Academic Officers in Theological Educations* (Grand Rapids: Eerdmans, 2011).
47. S. Hardy, *Excellence in Theological Education* (Green Point, South Africa: Modern Printers, 2006).
48. Ott, *Understanding and Developing Theological Education*.
49. F. Deininger and O. Eguizabal, *Foundations for Academic Leadership* (Nürnberg, Germany: VTR Publications, 2013).
50. Shaw, *Transforming Theological Education*.
51. Z. B. Kafang, *Higher Theological Education: An Overview of Six Protestant Theological Institutions in Nigeria* (Jos, Nigeria: Pyla-Mak Services Ltd, 2009).
52. Ferris, *Renewal in Theological Education*, 139–146.
53. Ibid., 127–136.
54. *The Cape Town Commitment*, The Lausanne Movement. Retrieved November 29, 2011. www.lausanne.org/en/documents/ctcommitment.html.

broader in its approach to global mission, included a number of challenges for theological educators.

Themes in the Literature

Miller, explaining the title of his history of North American theological education from 1970 onwards, *Piety and Plurality*, asserts that one of the chief themes of the past forty years has been "irreducible diversity."[55] This holds true as well in global theological education and the literature surrounding it. A review of the literature, however, does reveal a number of important themes which have evolved over the years, with new currents emerging. I will trace below several of these themes, including the challenge of integration, the rise of the missional model of theological education, cultural literacy, experience and reflection, orality, the broadening of the curriculum, and youth/globalization and technology. I will close this section by discussing what I see as three summative themes that prove especially helpful in understanding the role of governance in theological education. These three themes are thinking about theological schools as ecosystems, the human aspect of theological schools, and the idea of the prophetic role of theological education.

One of the most consistent themes in the theological education debates has been the call *for greater integration*. Farley pioneered this call for integration across both academic disciplines and the domains of knowledge, skills, and character.[56] This idea of integration stands in opposition to what Farley argues has been the fragmentation that has emerged since Schleiermacher's elaboration of the four-fold curriculum of biblical studies, theological studies, historical studies, and practical theology in the early nineteenth-century Berlin. Kelsey[57] contributed to this argument by describing the tension/dichotomy between elements of theological education that take their inspiration from the Greek concept of *paideia* (Athens) and those that draw their inspiration from the nineteenth-century German research university

---

55. Miller, *Piety and Plurality*, x.
56. Farley, *Theologia*. While Farley's diagnosis continues to influence theological education, a number, including Ferris (*Renewal in Theological Education*), Banks (*Reenvisioning Theological Education*), and Ott (*Beyond Fragmentation*) have critiqued his prescription for change as incomplete.
57. Kelsey, *Between Athens and Berlin*.

concept of *Wissenschaft* (Berlin). Few participants in the debate have denied the need for or importance of greater levels of integration, although practical solutions have been diverse and contradictory. A number of integrative centers have been proposed as a way to orient the broader theological curriculum. Again, these have emerged from various disciplinary perspectives and with differing methods of implementation. These integrative centers have included holistic mission,[58] worship,[59] the *missio Dei*,[60] the congregation,[61] reflective practice,[62] pastoral formation,[63] and wisdom.[64]

While the idea of fragmentation continues to inform literature on theological education, Robert Banks' *Reenvisioning Theological Education* shifted the contours of the conversation. The second major theme, **the idea of mission as an organizing principle for theological education** has gradually taken root on Banks' foundation, drawing strongly on the missiological thinking of Bosch.[65] This approach seems to be increasingly taken for granted in contemporary literature. Banks faults many previous thinkers, including Farley and Kelsey, for their willingness to raise a problem and a possibility, yet in the end return to the situation as it is, assuming that many elements are unchangeable. Banks also steps back from the classical-vocational debate to interrogate basic educational assumptions latent in the prevailing systems and to call for a more explicitly biblical understanding, based on the teaching methods of Christ. Banks' missional model focuses on training that is highly interactive, with mentoring and community playing key roles. The goal is to see "intellectual, spiritual, and practical concerns form a seamless whole."[66] Overall, it draws heavily on Jesus' discipleship model and Paul's collegial models of teaching. Banks' missional model provides a hopeful basis for

---

58. Barro, "A educação teológica"; and "Holistic Mission as a Vision for the Seminary," presented at Asia Theological Association (ATA) Consultation on Models of Theological Education: Manila, Philippines, 11 May 2011.
59. Throup, "Towards Integration."
60. Banks, *Reenvisioning Theological Education*.
61. Hopewell, "A Congregational Paradigm."
62. A. Thoman, "Leadership Development, Part 1: Churches Don't Have to Go It Alone," *Christian Education Journal* 6, no. 2 (2009).
63. Kelsey, *Between Athens and Berlin*.
64. Smith, "Theological Education."
65. D. J. Bosch, *Transforming Mission: Paradigm Shifts in the Theology of Mission* (Maryknoll, NY: Orbis, 2011).
66. Banks, *Reenvisioning Theological Education*, 126.

theological training that functions as a unifying whole, embracing both cognitive and affective domains, while stressing application of all learning. Peter Penner's *Theological Education as Mission*,[67] comprising a series of papers delivered at a 2005 conference in Prague, contributes significantly to this missional model of theological education.

A third theme in the literature is the need for theological education to become more **contextual and to include increased cultural understanding and literacy as an outcome.** This theme is often grounded in missiological thinking on contextualization, especially the work of Walls.[68] Walls sees the Christian faith as embodying both an indigenizing principle (where the faith comes to dwell within the culture of believers) and a pilgrim principle (where Christian faith remains countercultural). This theme is also frequently linked with a call for the greater involvement of the church in theological education, or in the words of Cannell, "theological education is valid only if the community is broadened to include the church."[69] This theme is increasingly present in writers on the subject of theological education in the Majority World, including Yung,[70] Enns,[71] Lee,[72] Barro,[73] Akrong,[74] Kalu,[75] Caldwell,[76] Asamoah-Gyadu,[77] Amanze,[78] Theocharous,[79] Estafanos,[80] and Searle and Cherenkov,[81] although the individual writers' approaches to the question

---

67. P. Penner, *Theological Education as Mission* (Schwarzenfeld, Germany: Neufeld Verlag, 2005).
68. A. Walls, *The Cross-Cultural Process in Christian History* (Maryknoll, NY: Orbis, 2002).
69. Cannell, *Theological Education Matters*, 261.
70. H. Yung, *Mangoes or Bananas? The Quest for Authentic Asian Christian Theology* (Eugene, OR: Wipf and Stock, 1997).
71. Enns, "Theological Education."
72. M. Lee, "The Asianization of Theological Education," *Journal of African Christian Thought* 9, no. 2 (2006).
73. Barro, "A educação teológica."
74. Akrong, "The Challenges of Theological Education."
75. Kalu, "Multicultural Theological Education."
76. L. W. Caldwell, "How Asian is Asian Theological Education?" in *Tending the Seedbeds: Educational Perspectives on Theological Education in Asia*, ed. A. Harkness (Manila: Asia Theological Association, 2010).
77. Asamoah-Gyadu, "Called to Make a Difference."
78. Amanze, "Contextuality."
79. Theocharous, "Not Living on Bread Alone."
80. Estafanos, "Defying the Pharaohs."
81. Searle and Cherenkov, *A Future and a Hope*.

differ. Hiebert's idea of "critical contextualization"[82] seems to be a common framework for this question.

While the question of contextualization is frequently raised in philosophical/theological literature, it also figures heavily in literature arising from the educational and leadership frameworks; indeed, few works since 2010 do not touch on this subject in some form. This is evident in increasing calls for theological education to have as an outcome a heightened sense of cultural literacy. MacLeod unpacks this concept in a description of "unusual sensitivity to context" that undergirds much of the innovation in the theological schools explored in that study.[83] A persistent theme is the need for theological education to encourage and instill in students higher capacities for cultural literacy, rather than merely transferring to them established content. Perhaps the most summative statement to this end comes from Ted Ward, in his introduction to a volume of his works collected in the *Common Ground Journal*:

> The Christian educator views mission in terms of its responsibilities for teaching and learning. We are preparing and equipping the leaders of leaders.
>
> Our most pressing responsibility is to critically separate two images of that task. The first image is unfortunately common, that preparing people who will be grounded in formal theology, able to preach and to officiate in the modes and ceremonies of religious activity he or she believes to be most common, based on his own experience and fitting as he or she has experienced most common in the nation or region in which their own religious experiences occurred. The second image is much closer to the biblical mandate, that of developing leaders who are grounded in biblical truth and skilled in cultural and linguistic adaptation, so that their lifestyles, language patterns, and interactional skills are flexible, sensitive, and responsive. Toward this end, the missioner's experience will need to grow larger and more diverse in order to accommodate and embrace religious

---

82. P. G. Hiebert, *Transforming Worldviews: An Anthropological Understanding of How People Change* (Grand Rapids, MI: Baker, 2008).
83. MacLeod "Unconventional Educational Practices."

practices common to Christians of the less familiar culture. This sort of expansion and transformation of cultural perspective will require human interactions, including hours, days, and weeks of comprehensive dialogues with a wide variety of new friends.[84]

Brelsford and Rogers also explore this theme in a volume of essays reflecting on their experience in the context of their institution, Candler School of Theology.[85] Bounds,[86] writing in that volume, raises the helpful example of "helping students figure out their theological bookshelves" – helping them to determine what theological questions they have and how classic works like Augustine speak to those. Rather than simply filling students with content *about* Augustine, the goal of teaching becomes helping students find in a church father a wise counselor regarding their own questions. Brelsford and Senior carry this further,[87] speaking of helping students to uncover and understand the *functional theologies* that are at work in their thinking, and to gain *both* a right understanding of what God is doing, as well as how we as humans are interpreting it.

Calls for improved skills of culture reading, especially from Majority World writers, frequently point to the essential nature of this skill for understanding the functional theological frameworks that undergird cultures.[88] Much of this literature is grounded in the work of Bediako and his exploration of the intersection of theology and culture.[89] In the Asian context, Yung has also contributed substantially to this conversation.[90] Amanze[91] and

---

84. T. Ward, "Preparing and Equipping the Leaders of Leaders," *Common Ground* 10, no. 2 (2013): 11.

85. T. Brelsford and P. A. Rogers, eds., *Contextualizing Theological Education* (Cleveland, OH: Pilgrim Press, 2008).

86. E. M. Bounds, "Theological Reflection in Contextual Education," in *Contextualizing Theological Education*, ed. T. Brelsford and P. A. Rogers (Cleveland, OH: Pilgrim Press, 2008).

87. Brelsford and Senior, "Theological Thinking as Contextual Practice."

88. While in this case, I raise this as a working question in African and Asian realities, I do not mean to suggest that the West is immune to functional cultural understandings that are inimical to the gospel. It seems to me that the West has often been quick to point to majority-world syncretism without adequate reflection on our own syncretistic "baptism" of elements of Western culture.

89. K. Bediako, *Theology and Identity: The Impact of Culture upon Christian Thought in the Second Century and in Modern Africa* (Carlisle, UK: Regnum Books International, 1999).

90. Yung, *Mangoes or Bananas?*

91. Amanze, "Contextuality."

Asamoah-Gyadu[92] both raise this issue in the African context, asking how theological education relates to, informs, builds on, and, when necessary, corrects underlying elements of African spirituality. Motty speaks of the need to "evaluate our audience's culture competently and also understand how people learn in the local culture."[93]

A distinct yet related theme is the call for theological education to move away from knowledge transfer to one that causes students to mine their own experience and *engage in active reflection on how the Bible and theology inform their situation.* This theme often draws explicitly or implicitly on conceptions of adult education/andragogy,[94] transformative education,[95] and the educational thinking of Paulo Freire.[96] Estafanos, in exploring the role of Christian education and theological education in the Egyptian church, points to what he sees as an unnecessary dichotomy between experience and Scripture, philosophy and theology.

> A wrong idea in the Presbyterian Church in Egypt is that talking about personal experience either leads to spiritual pride if the experience is positive, or is simply an exercise in begging for sympathy if the experience is negative. While this rejection of real life experience results in divorce of theory and practice, it also results in absence of a contextual theology that is born from and rooted in Egyptian culture.[97]

Coppedge speaks of the potential impact on both the individual and the broader community of a more experience-rich approach to theological education: "let us teach how to engage the Word of God so that . . . significant

---

92. Asamoah-Gyadu, "Called to Make a Difference."
93. B. Motty, "Forward," in *Beyond Literate Western Practices: Continuing Conversations in Orality and Theological Education*, ed. S. E. Chiang and G. Lovejoy (Hong Kong: Condeo Press/International Orality Network, 2014), 13–14.
94. M. S. Knowles, F. H. Elwood, and R. A. Swanson, *The Adult Learner: The Definitive Classic in Adult Education and Human Resources* (New York: Butterworth-Heinemann, 2005).
95. J. Mezirow, *Transformative Dimensions of Adult Learning* (San Francisco, CA: Jossey-Bass, 1991); P. Cranton, *Understanding and Promoting Transformative Learning: A Guide for Educators of Adults* (San Francisco, CA: John Wiley, 2006).
96. P. Freire, *Pedagogy of the Oppressed* (New York: Continuum, 2000).
97. S. Estafanos, "Defying the Pharaohs: Contemporary Educational Challenges for the Evangelical Church in Egypt," *Christian Education Journal* 3, no. 10, Supplement, (2013): S-169.

questions can be addressed as they arise personally, communally, and even nationally."[98] Watson sees special relevance of this approach to experience-based learning in the Indian context, where he suggests that a greater focus on the church's *Sitz im Leben* can counter a "culture of lethargy" that he sees in many Indian theological schools.[99] Kalu sums up this approach by calling for greater "formation-by-engagement."[100]

Another theme emerging in some recent writers is the importance of *acknowledging diverse readings of the Scripture*. While this element has long been present among more ecumenical participants in the conversation, a number of evangelical writers have raised issues of how the theological conversation continues to be shaped by the missionary legacy and the contours of Western theology, as well as subtle or not-so-subtle suppression of minority voices. Kalu, writing about African theological education from 1970 to 2000, suggests that African education and theological education are areas where the "tensile strength of the missionary heritage" remains particularly strong.[101] Theocharous stresses this point explicitly, pointing to the importance of theological educators being especially able to navigate differing perspectives.[102] Shaw also makes this point.[103] Wright hints at some of the potential fruits of this richer, more global conversation in an address to global theological educators, pointing to the possibility of enjoying "the exciting and perhaps very unfamiliar tastes and smells of a different theological and cultural cuisine – the rich and nourishing theological food with which God wants to bless the whole of his church, north and south, east and west."[104]

---

98. W. Coppedge, "Training in the Ugandan Context," in *Beyond Literate Western Practices: Continuing Conversations in Orality and Theological Education*, ed. S. E. Chiang and G. Lovejoy (Hong Kong: Condeo Press/International Orality Network, 2014), 36.

99. H. M. Watson, "The Theological Educator: An Indian Perspective," *Currents in Theology and Mission* 40, no. 2 (2013).

100. Kalu, "Multicultural Theological Education," 227.

101. Ibid., 226.

102. Theocharous, "Not Living on Bread Alone."

103. P. W. H. Shaw, "New Treasures with the Old: Addressing Culture and Gender Imperialism in High Level Theological Education," in *Tending the Seedbeds: Educational Perspectives on Theological Education in Asia*, ed. A. Harkness (Quezon City, Philippines: Asia Theological Association, 2010).

104. Wright, "The Challenge of the Brain Drain."

An emerging theme centers on the subject of *orality*. Orality concerns approaches that take seriously the learning preferences and frameworks of those who cannot read and the much larger number of people in the world who are oral-preference learners. While orality has been a significant theme in evangelistic work for many years, leading to significant breakthroughs in places like Bihar,[105] it has only come to influence theological education more recently. Two recent volumes have compiled the learning of conferences on the subject of orality in theological education, with the goal of "moving beyond Western, literate models."[106] Motty, the CEO of a leading Nigerian seminary, believes that "theological educators must help the literate learners and/or societies to understand the value that oral learners have."[107] Sessoms details his own journey in orality as well as providing much practical advice on oral leadership training, primarily in the non-formal context in Asia.[108] Orality may indeed be a key to breakthroughs in impact of theological education in a way similar to the approach's impact on evangelistic activities in many parts of the world. Thornton, reflecting on his experience in Latin America, asserts that "answers will come only as we understand Latin culture in all its diversity and then shape and deliver the message in a culturally appropriate way. This is orality at work in its broadest sense."[109]

A significant theme in theological education in the past decade, especially in Africa, has been *the broadening of the curriculum* of theological schools. This has resulted not only in new programs outside the traditional theological disciplines, but also in the transformation of many African (and a few other)

---

105. Cf. A. Abraham, "Contextualized Theological Education for Oral Learners with Particular Reference to the Unreached, Unengaged People Groups in North India: Lessons Learnt and the Challenges," in *Beyond Literate Western Practices: Continuing Conversations in Orality and Theological Education*, ed. S. Chiang and G. Lovejoy (Hong Kong: Condeo Press/International Orality Network, 2014).

106. S. Chiang and G. Lovejoy, eds., *Beyond Literate Western Practices: Orality and Theological Education* (Hong Kong: Condeo Press/International Orality Network, 2013); Chiang and Lovejoy, eds., *Beyond Literate Western Practices: Continuing Conversations in Orality and Theological Education* (Hong Kong: Condeo Press/International Orality Network, 2014).

107. Motty, "Forward," 14.

108. R. Sessoms, "On Tablets of Human Hearts" (forthcoming, 2015).

109. W. P. Thornton, "Orality and Theological Education in Latin American Culture," in *Beyond Literate Western Practices: Continuing Conversations in Orality and Theological Education*, ed. S. Chiang and G. Lovejoy (Hong Kong: Condeo Press/International Orality Network, 2014), 60–61.

theological schools into Christian universities.[110] Several flagship evangelical schools in both Anglophone and Francophone Africa have taken this path or are in the process of transformation. While these transformations have taken place for a number of reasons, most African leaders narrate the reason for this as deeply rooted in a sense of mission. This most often takes the form of a desire for broader level thought leadership in society that is based in theological thinking *writ large* yet also engages other disciplines and modes of thought. Asamoah-Gyadu suggests that the increasingly complex nature of African urban reality and the dynamic nature of churches are making the "professional pastoral" approach to theological education insufficient.[111] Reflecting on the state of the discussion in Eurasia, Searle and Cherenkov state that "the debate has moved on and the main focus has shifted away from contextualization of theological education and toward the contextual integration of theological studies with both ministerial practice and other non-theological academic disciplines."[112] Thomas explores practical theology as a broadening paradigm for theological education.[113]

A final general theme in the literature relates to subjects of *youth, technology,*[114] *and globalization.* Chong has explored these issues in the context of contemporary Southeast Asia, emphasizing the importance of focusing on the next generation, stressing multiple models of education, and setting development of cross-cultural skills as a central learning objective.[115]

---

110. This is a complex movement that has drawn much attention. The emergence of Christian universities in the Majority World has been well documented by Carpenter, Glanzer, and Lantinga (*Christian Higher Education: A Global Reconnaissance* [Grand Rapids: Eerdmans, 2014]). Both the Nagel Center at Calvin College under the leadership of Dr Joel Carpenter (http://www.calvin.edu/nagel/) and the International Association for the Promotion of Christian Higher Education (IAPCHE) under the direction of Dr Mwenda Ntarangwi are deeply engaged in this movement.

111. Asamoah-Gyadu, "Called to Make a Difference."

112. Searle and Cherenkov, *A Future and a Hope*, 86.

113. Thomas, "Practical Theology."

114. I have intentionally not taken up any of the voluminous literature on online theological education. My own thinking on this subject has been deeply enriched by the work of Dr Meri MacLeod (www.digitalseminarian.com), an authority on the subject.

115. C. Chong, "The Rise of the Net-Generation: Implications for Educational Renewal in the Seminary Classroom," in *Building Lives for Ministry: Collected Essays of Alliance Bible Seminary 110th Anniversary Consultation on Theological Education*, ed. Wai-Luen Kwok (Hong Kong: Alliance Bible Seminary, 2009); Chong, "Christian Education."

Undoubtedly, one could find any number of additional themes in the vast and varied literature on theological education. The above list is, admittedly, highly subjective and neglects the richness of the parts in order to present the whole. It is also formed and framed very much by the dual nature of this work, exploring both governance and theological education in the broader framework of challenges facing the church. In light of building a bridge toward the next major topic, the literature on governance, I want to suggest below three summative themes emerging from the literature on theological education that are particularly valuable as we begin to think about governance and, ultimately, the way that Christian institutions respond to the myriad challenges of our day.

First, there is an increasing understanding of *theological schools as ecosystems* in and of themselves,[116] as well as a part of complex ecclesial, social and academic ecosystems. I first encountered this concept in Benefiel,[117] who uses the term to discuss theological schools' relationship with the church and other stakeholders. Brelsford, although not using the ecological metaphor, builds on this idea in a discussion of interlocking constituencies:

> Graduate professional theological education . . . has three primary contexts and three primary constituencies to whom it must be responsible: academy, church, and society. To contextualize theological education . . . is to engage in theological education with a conscious intent *to integrate* these three contexts; to locate learning in all three contexts; and to hold teaching, learning, and knowledge in each of these contexts accountable to the others.[118]

Aleshire further strengthens the idea of ecology. "If change [in theological education] is to come, it will occur because a system of influences has interacted in such a way that the change occurs both in the broader ecology and in individual schools."[119] Beyond this fragile external matrix of

---

116. I am indebted to my friend and colleague, Scott Cunningham. Our conversations on this topic, as well as his later elaboration of a "four-circles model" of sustainability of a theological school, were deeply enriching to me.

117. R. Benefiel, "The Ecology of Evangelical Seminaries," *Theological Education* 44, no. 1 (2008): 21–27.

118. Brelsford, *Contextualizing Theological Education*, 1 (emphasis added).

119. D. Aleshire, "Response to 'Stewards of the Gospel,'" in *Stewards of the Gospel*, ed. R. Vallett (Grand Rapids: Eerdmans, 2011), 227.

relationships, theological schools are also complicated, human ecosystems on the inside, a theme that will emerge strongly in the remainder of this book. The hidden curriculum of theological schools – how leaders, faculty, staff and students act and interact *outside* the classroom – often has greater impact on learning than what happens *inside* the classroom.[120] Shaw dwells the most on the issue of the hidden curriculum, as well as providing many helpful resources,[121] while Dharamraj unpacks this issue in the context of her and her colleagues' teaching in a theological school in India.[122]

The ecological metaphor focuses our attention on the human relationships that constitute the theological school. While issues such as financial management, curriculum review, and human resource policies are important, the importance of the hidden curriculum and the human relations that form it deserve far more attention. Theological schools, simply put, are not machines; their management is more art than science. Colwill[123] dissects various metaphors used to describe organizations. The machine metaphor or framework, dominant in leadership theory in the early twentieth century and still latent in many organizations today, stresses the function of the various human parts of an organization in service of an efficient whole, much as a particular gear or screw contributes to the function of a motorbike or clock. "The individual role was shaped to fit the organization's needs",[124] leading to compartmentalization, and in the worst cases, dehumanization. In this framework, management was highly bureaucratic and compartmentalized.

---

120. Charter, "Theological Education"; D. V. Esterline, "Multicultural Theological Education and Leadership for a Church without Walls," in *Shaping Beloved Community*, ed. D. V. Esterline and O. U. Kalu (Louisville, KY: Westminster John Knox Press, 2006).

121. Shaw, *Transforming Theological Education*.

122. H. Dharamraj, "We Reap What We Sow: Engaging Curriculum and Context in Theological Education," *Evangelical Review of Theology* 38, no. 3 (2014).

123. D. Colwill, "The Use of Metaphor in Consulting for Educational Change," in *Consulting for Organizational Change*, ed. A. F. Buono and D. W. Jamieson (Charlotte, NC: Information Age Publishing, 2010). I am deeply indebted to Dr Colwill for sharing with me this article which would likely not have crossed my path otherwise. Besides her discussion of metaphor in describing organizations in general, she also traces three other dominant metaphors: the organism, the human brain, and the energy wave. This is worthy reading and could be quite useful for staff or board retreats to raise unfamiliar ways of thinking about how an organization works together. The greatest value of these metaphors lies, in my opinion, in their ability to "excavate" working assumptions that are not articulated within a community. I believe that the machine metaphor is much more active in many Christian organizational subconsciences than we realize.

124. Ibid., 119.

"The compartmentalization of a large, bureaucratic organization often caused *fragmentation*, competition, and conflict between departments, functions, groups, and individuals."[125] To what degree have theological schools been managed through a machine framework? In what ways could this machine framework of leadership and management have contributed to the fragmentation that Farley rightly diagnosed? While the literature on theological education has put forth many suggestions and solutions for curricular change, refocusing of mission, and new financial strategies, perhaps the very conception of the management structure of the seminary needs greater consideration? How can these structures be more profoundly redemptive and human in their nature? This question is taken up further in the subsequent chapters on alignment and transformational education.

A second, related summative theme, *the human aspect of life in theological schools,* has emerged significantly in literature in the past decade. Groome develops this theme broadly and deeply.[126] Shaw's discussion of the hidden curriculum is foundational, and his presentation and unpacking of this idea at many conferences of theological educators over the past decade has certainly impacted my thinking.[127] Dharamraj fleshes out this idea in practice, pointing that the hidden curriculum is two-fold, including both what we do *not* teach, as well as *what we don't realize we are teaching.*[128] Greenleaf raised this issue more than thirty years ago in his essays on the potential role of seminaries, calling for a "theology of persons" and a "theology of institutions,"[129] which can in turn work itself out in a result of "transforming leadership"[130] and theological schools that reach their true potential. Cannell raised this issue concretely as well, citing the institutionalization of theological schools as a great point of danger.[131] Suazo Jiménez picks up this theme, drawing on both Greenleaf and Cannell, subjecting the dominant, hierarchical approach to theological school management and governance to theological critique:

---

125. Ibid., emphasis added.
126. Groome, "Wisdom for Life."
127. Shaw, *Transforming Theological Education.*
128. Dharamraj, "We Reap What We Sow."
129. Greenleaf, *Seminary as Servant*, 15.
130. Ibid., 13.
131. Cannell, *Theological Education Matters.*

On the other hand, the incarnation also challenges issues which transcend the work of professors or the content of the curriculum in order to influence as well institutional questions. For example, what implications does the incarnation of Jesus have for the exercise of power and authority in institutions of theological education? If the birth of Christ denounces great power (*poder regio e imperial*) it is necessary also to question institutional power. Christian institutions (including seminaries) all too often reflect structures, actions, and attitudes of power common in society. . . . Institutions have come to be an end in and of themselves and exist for their own benefit, many times at the expense of people.[132]

Searle and Cherenkov, reflecting on the particularly worn-out nature of the Soviet machine-like framework for society, argue that, in contemporary Ukraine, "the time is coming for communities united by ideas and values, communities that trust each other and are coming together to develop their vision of the future . . . The time has come for bold, yet responsible, evangelical entrepreneurs who are willing to take risks for the sake of the gospel."[133] Asamoah-Gyadu also approaches this question from a theological perspective, although he turns the conversation more to the impact of theological education than the structures that comprise it. "As Christian salvation is affirmed in the context of theological education, it is imperative to understand that true salvation is not only experiential but also brings peaceful co-existence among all people"[134] These critiques seem to present a fundamental challenge for theological schools. This question is taken up in the subsequent chapter on responsive reflectiveness.

If there is a key summative theme emerging in recent literature, particularly literature arising from Majority World theological educators, it is the idea of *the prophetic role of theological education*. By suggesting this overarching theme, drawing on the title of David Suazo Jiménez' work,[135] I am consciously imposing a category to unite what are, inherently,

---

132. Suazo Jiménez, D. *La función profética*, 98.
133. Searle and Cherenkov, *A Future and a Hope*, 139.
134. Asamoah-Gyadu, "Called to Make a Difference," 14.
135. Suazo Jiménez, *La función profética*.

disparate voices, including Lara Proença,[136] Stelio Rega,[137] Suazo Jiménez,[138] Theocharous,[139] Dharamraj,[140] Tiénou,[141] Ahoga,[142] and Searle and Cherenkov,[143] among others. This also has some commonality with a series of articles on the "public character" of theological education relating to an ATS project in 2000.[144] Yet this category speaks in fresh ways to the long-running challenge of fragmentation in theological education,[145] as well as the now solidly established framework of theological education *as mission*.[146] The theme of the prophetic role of theological education brings together calls for deeper engagement with the many cultures where the Christian church exists, the necessity of tools for understanding these cultures, a profoundly critical stance to culture – including dominant evangelical culture – and a profound voice of hope to the church and broader society.

A number of these authors approach the subject of the prophetic role of theological education from a specialization or a strong grounding in biblical studies. Suazo Jiménez traces the prophetic function through both the Old and New Testaments, drawing this into dialogue with the practice of theological education in Latin America.[147] Dharamraj,[148] an Old Testament scholar, draws on her own and her colleagues' teaching of the Old Testament to demonstrate the insufficiencies as well as the possibilities of the theological

---

136. W. Lara Proença, "De 'casa de profetas' a seminaries teológicos: A preparação vocacional em perspectiva histórica," in *Educação teológica transformadora*, ed. A. C. Barro and M. W. Kohl (Londrina, Brazil: Descoberta, 2006).

137. Stelio Rega, "Revendo paradigmas."

138. Suazo Jiménez, *La función profética*.

139. Theocharous, "Not Living on Bread Alone."

140. Dharamraj, "We Reap What We Sow."

141. T. Tiénou, "Epanouissement du christianisme en Afrique," in *Christianisme authentique en Afrique contemporaine*, ed. R. Pohor and I. Coulibaly (Abidjan, Côte d'Ivoire: Les Presses FATEAC, 2014).

142. A. Ahoga, "Christianisme et context de vie," in *Christianisme authentique en Afrique contemporaine*, ed. R. Pohor and I. Coulibaly (Abidjan, Côte d'Ivoire: Les Presses FATEAC, 2014).

143. Searle and Cherenkov, *A Future and a Hope*.

144. E.g. D. Jones, J. Greenman, and C. Pohl, "The Public Character of Theological Seminaries: An Evangelical Perspective," *Theological Education* 37, no. 1 (2000).

145. Farley, *Theologia*; Kelsey, *Between Athens and Berlin*.

146. Banks, *Reenvisioning Theological Education*; P. Penner, "Introduction," in *Theological Education as Mission*, ed. P. Penner (Schwarzenfeld, Germany: Neufeld Verlag, 2005).

147. Suazo Jiménez, *La función profética*.

148. Dharamraj, "We Reap What We Sow."

curriculum for transformation. Lara Proença draws on the "house of the prophets," or the formation of prophets in the Old Testament as a paradigm for countering aspects of contemporary Brazilian theological education that are insufficient.[149] Theocharous sets an Old Testament framework:

> Throughout Israel's history the voice of the prophets accompanied God's people in the best of times and the worst of times. It critiqued, challenged, condemned but also empowered, comforted, and healed. Prophets took God's revelation seriously; they took God's people seriously; *but they took their ever-changing context and how God worked in the unfamiliar, hostile surrounding world just as seriously.*"[150]

Suazo Jiménez approaches the life of Christ as the life of a prophet, pointing to how a traditional Latin American evangelical understanding of Christ's life is severely limiting:

> Traditionally, evangelical believers have been taught to see the Jesus of the Gospels as the Son of God who came basically to die. Therefore, his earthly ministry, his teachings, his confrontations with the religious and political leaders of Israel are understood only as preparation for his death, without considering either soteriological or prophetic elements. If one speaks of following Jesus, this limits to individual aspects of spiritual and devotional character (prayer, intimacy with God, model as a teacher, and others) which is of course good. However, very little is said about Jesus as a prophet who confronts the powers of his time, who denounces the evils of Jewish society of the first century and announces both judgment and the Kingdom of God.[151]

These prophetic elements from both testaments have much to contribute to our understanding of the role of theological education.

Various authors detail a number of things that have stood and stand in the way of a truly prophetic role for theological education. One of the key barriers has been the lack of full-throated, confident engagement

---

149. Lara Proença, "De 'casa de profetas' a seminaries teológicos."
150. Theocharous, "Not Living on Bread Alone," 1 (emphasis added).
151. Suazo Jiménez, *La función profética*, 73–74.

with culture, often based in tacit assumption of the lack of worth of non-Western cultures. Tiénou, speaking of the "blossoming of Christianity in Africa," points to the necessity of precision in using the term Africa, in order to avoid the semantic baggage that sees Africa as somehow immutable or unchanging. "The vocabulary 'contemporary Africa' expresses a rejection of the idea of traditional, primitive Africa, always outside of history. This Africa has ceased to exist. Contemporary Africa is a continent like all the others."[152] Others[153] raise similar concerns about the failure of theological education to engage deeply with the cultural and religious contexts of other regions of the world, leading to a significant tension between what is taught and thought in seminaries and the surrounding milieu. Ahoga, writing from the context of Francophone Africa, speaks of the "tension between the theology of the theologian and his living environment (*milieu de vie*) or the context of application of his theology."[154] In many ways, these comments echo and embody the work of Andrew Walls, who has long called for more confident Christian engagement with non-Western cultures, following earlier examples of Christian intellectual engagement and contextualization in the era of the early church as well as in medieval Europe and elsewhere.[155]

The area of language and use of language represents a particular limitation to full engagement of theological thinking in theological schools with issues of context. Walls, writing of the role of Christian scholarship in the global church, speaks of the importance of vernacular languages in this process of engagement, arguing that it is necessary to "go beyond language, the outer skin of culture, into the processes of thinking and choosing and all the networks of relationship that lie beneath language, turning them all toward Christ."[156] Abraham[157] brings this to a very practical level, pointing to the importance of the use of the vernacular languages of North India in fruitful evangelistic and leadership development efforts in North India, a point related to those

---

152. Tiénou, "Epanouissement du christianisme," 18.
153. Dharamraj, "We Reap What We Sow"; Searle and Cherenkov, *A Future and a Hope*; and Caldwell, "How Asian is Asian theological education?"
154. Ahoga, "Christianisme et context de vie," 21.
155. Walls, "Christian Scholarship."
156. Ibid., 171.
157. Abraham, "Contextualized Theological Education."

of Howell[158] and Sule-Saa[159] in the West African context. Ahoga points to the fact that structures of education, with their heavy reliance on writing and reading, have been imported from the West, but the interface of these approaches in a largely oral context has not been adequately considered.[160] This lack of connection between the work of theologians and their contexts – including the languages and modes of thought and writing – is inhibiting the prophetic role of theological education.[161]

Another significant limitation to the prophetic role of theological education circles back to a much earlier phase of the theological education debates – fragmentation. While Farley[162] raised this issue in relation to the integration of the various threads of the theological curriculum, more recent writing has focused on the inherent lack of interdisciplinary thinking in theological education, and the necessity of tools from the disciplines of anthropology, sociology, history, and others for understanding culture. It is important to say that this call for a broader "tool kit" does not aim to make out of seminarians sociologists or economists, or to assume uncritically some of the internal values and structures of these disciplines that may be contrary to a biblical approach to life. Rather, these tools should be framed in a theological perspective to help to amplify sensitivity to context, a trait that emerges in my research as very important in the leadership and culture of a theological school. Stelio Rega, explores the tensions of this approach in the Brazilian context, where he argues that evangelical theological vocabulary has been impoverished.

---

158. A. M. Howell, "Beyond Translating Western Commentaries: Bible Commentary Writing in African Languages," *Journal of African Christian Thought* 13, no. 2 (2010).

159. S. S. Sule-Saa, "Owning the Christian Faith Through Mother-Tongue Scriptures: A Case Study of the Dagomba and Konkomba of Northern Ghana," *Journal of African Christian Thought* 13, no. 2 (2010).

160. Ahoga, "Christianisme et context de vie," 32.

161. This seems to be an area of increased activity and study. The Akrofi-Christaller Institute in Akropong, Ghana (http://www.acighana.org/) remains at the forefront of considering the uses and values of vernacular languages in African theological education, while the New India Evangelistic Association in Kerala, South India (http://www.nieamission.org/) has taken a lead in this area in South Asia. The International Orality Network (http://www.orality.net/) has concentrated significant attention on these issues and their relation to theological education, as has The Seed Company (https://theseedcompany.org/).

162. Farley, *Theologia*.

> In the field of evangelical literature, the drawing *(o seqüestro)* of vocabulary from other fields of human knowledge, such as economics, psychology, and law is evident, whereas the theological vocabulary cannot be updated, in semantic terms, for dealing with the dilemmas of contemporary man . . . the ministerial vision, sometimes even within seminaries, is more pragmatic, functional than theological and biblical.[163]

This pragmatic approach to ministry, a concern echoed by Suazo Jiménez,[164] Searle and Cherenkov[165] and others, leaves the church unprepared to truly respond to the questions of its context. The avoidance of cross-disciplinary engagement, rather than protecting theology from external pollution, has quite the opposite effect in leading to the church's uncritical appropriation of ideas and concepts from other disciplines without adequate theological thought. Instead, theology and theologians must engage in the work of synthesis on these issues in collaboration with the church.

Another significant impediment to the prophetic role of theological education is the failure of the church and theological school to speak meaningfully, biblically, and theologically into issues and injustices. A closely related impediment is the temptation of pride and self-serving or autocratic leadership. Lara Proença, writing from the Brazilian context, speaks of the "fragility" of the Brazilian church. This fragility, he argues, "is due, in large part, to the failure to prepare leaders who can lead God's people."[166] Yet Lara Proença's critique is not a typical lament over untrained pastors, for he points first and foremost not to lack of knowledge, but to character issues, particularly temptations to character issues that are prolific in the Brazilian church: the temptation of numbers, the view of religious work as a path to gain person growth and success, the cult of personality and autocratic leadership. This, he argues, has contributed to the "trivialization" *(banalização)* of the office of pastor.[167] Lara Proença calls for theological educators to take seriously the Old Testament paradigm of formation of prophets, as well as the New Testament

---

163. Stelio Rega, "Revendo paradigmas," 144.
164. Suazo Jiménez, *La función profética*.
165. Searle and Cherenkov, *A Future and a Hope*.
166. Lara Proença, "De 'casa de profetas' a seminaries teológicos," 34.
167. Ibid., 39.

models of Jesus' teaching as a means of forming leaders of character and humility that more fully express the wholeness of the gospel in contemporary Brazilian context.[168] Theocharous, writing from the Greek context, stresses the important role of the theological educator as interpreter and prophetic critic, able to see beyond the "pious talk" that is common in the church to see and proclaim the degree to which "our narrative has been compromised" by unbiblical narratives in surrounding culture.[169]

> This is the burden of the prophets. They carry the weight of the people of God on their shoulders. They cannot settle, become comfortable, feel at home. The role of evangelical theological education is to encourage, support and equip prophets who will be able to identify our fertility cults which claim our allegiance. They will be able to expose our pious talk that deceives us and reveal hidden allegiances we are unaware of. They will be able to show us life beyond "bread," by rescuing our texts from oblivion, re-reading them for us and opening our ears to what the Spirit says through the other, show us truths from unexpected places.

This presents a vision of the prophetic theological educator as a kind of an itinerant, always aware of God's leading amidst the changing realities of context.

What does this summative theme of the prophetic role of theological education add to our current understanding of the role of an increasingly global theological education? In many ways, it builds on major themes of the past, suggesting ways beyond the fragmentation through a very intentional orientation of theological formation to the responsive work of holistic mission. This orientation of theological education as mission actualizes the integral missiological thinking of Andrew Walls, David Bosch, René Padilla, and Christopher Wright, among many others, in the work of theological education. Walls' conceptions of the gospel as "liberator of culture"[170] and of the need for "deep translation" of the gospel into the world's cultures[171] are

---

168. Ibid., 44.
169. Theocharous, "Not Living on Bread Alone."
170. A. F. Walls, *The Missionary Movement in Christian History: Studies in Transmission of Faith* (Maryknoll, NY: Orbis, 2004).
171. Walls, "Christian Scholarship," 171.

especially applicable to the work of theological education. These frameworks provide a secure biblical/theological/philosophical starting point for thinking about theological education, an adequate response to the question of *why?* The robust literature on educational praxis in theological education, particularly work inspired by Ted Ward, provides adequate framework for a response to *how?* Suazo Jiménez' work,[172] however, takes this one step further, linking a theological education rooted in holistic mission to the pedagogical principles and ideals of Paulo Freire,[173] calling for evangelical theological education to be consciousness-raising and humanizing. This linkage seems to be a particularly fruitful potential stream of thinking. Finally, the prophetic vision articulated by many of the authors discussed above, builds on the *how* and the *why* foundations above to provide a teleological foundation – *to what end?* Indeed, this seems to be a particularly flourishing phase in thinking about evangelical theological education and theological education more broadly, with a significant foundation for even more creative work in the future.

---

172. Suazo Jiménez, *La función profética*.
173. Freire, *Pedagogy of the Oppressed*.

3

Building a Bridge to Governance

How does the extended conversation about the purposes, methods, and ends of theological education relate to governance? What role might a conversation about governance have in providing institutional foundation stones for responsive evangelical theological education around the world? The three summative themes in the literature on theological education all point to elements of a bridge between the two topics. First, the idea of the ecology of theological education begins to deconstruct the prevailing, implicit understanding of theological schools as machines, or, in other words, as hierarchical institution whose structures are inconsequential to the overall impact of theological education. This theme of ecology, together with the strong focus on the human element of theological schools, points us to a much more complex understanding of the leadership and governance of theological schools, one that focuses less attention on structures and processes and more on relationships and influence. Structures and processes – management – remain critically important, but must increasingly be looked upon through a framework of human relationships, all rooted in the ultimate mission of the institution. The summative theme of the prophetic role of theological education is critical to understanding this ultimate mission, and turns the understanding of the institution of a theological school further away from internal structures to external impact. How are relationships best structured to achieve these prophetic, transformative ends? The results of research, as reported in the following chapters, strongly affirm the importance of leadership and governance in meaningful renewal and ultimate impact in the theological schools studied. I will return to this theme in chapter 12. Below, however, I will take up a review of recent literature on governance. First, I will outline the main themes of some paradigm-shaping works in the field, such as Carver's *Boards that Make a Difference* and *Governance as Leadership* of Chait, Ryan, and Taylor. Second, I will draw special focus on works dealing with governance of theological schools. I will conclude the chapter with some thoughts on how these two bodies of literature intersect in concrete ways.[1]

As Hall[2] and Scott[3] argue, the nonprofit or "third" sector has played a critical role in American history. James,[4] Salamon et al.,[5] and Anheier and Salamon[6] demonstrate that the role of the nonprofit sector continues to grow in almost every nation. Hall demonstrates that the voluntary association, or lay governance, has been critical to the success of the nonprofit sector in the United States and has contributed markedly to the economic and political success of the nation in the past 150 years.[7] In the past two decades, events such as corporate scandals and the failure of board oversight in the recent financial crisis have led to increased attention to an oversight of corporate governance.[8] Legislation designed to improve corporate governance function, such as the Sarbanes-Oxley Act of 2002, have required higher levels of diligence on the part of corporate boards. This has, in turn, affected the nonprofit environment

---

1. In the original dissertation (2012), this literature review essay was written prior to my field research and analysis. The main purpose of this review was its contribution to the sample selection and interview and observation protocols that guided my field research (see Appendix A). In re-working this chapter for publication, I have drawn on my experience in field research, as well as my thinking and reading since the completion of my dissertation. The final result is, therefore, more broadly descriptive than the original dissertation chapter.
2. Hall, "Cultures of Trusteeship."
3. Scott, *Creating Caring and Capable Boards*.
4. E. James, *The Nonprofit Sector in International Perspective: Studies in Comparative Culture and Policy* (New York: Oxford University Press, 1989).
5. L. M. Salamon, et al., *Global civil society: Dimensions of the nonprofit sector* (Baltimore, MD: Johns Hopkins Comparative Nonprofit Sector Project, 1999).
6. H. K. Anheier and L. M. Salamon, "The Nonprofit Sector in Comparative Perspective," in *The Nonprofit Sector, a Research Handbook,* ed. W.W. Powell and R. Steinberg (New Haven, CT: Yale University Press, 2006).
7. Hall, "Cultures of Trusteeship."
8. K. Eichenwald, "In String of Corporate Troubles, Critics Focus on Boards," *New York Times* (2003, September 21). Retrieved April 8, 2009, from http://www.nytimes.com; R. Abzug and J. S. Simonoff. *Nonprofit Trustees in Different Contexts* (Aldershot, England: Ashgate, 2004); H. Landy, "Executives Took, but Directors Gave," *New York Times* (2009, April 4). Retrieved 8 April 2009, from http://www.nytimes.com.

in the United States, leading to greater oversight of governance activity.[9] Alongside these legal changes, management professionalism has risen in the nonprofit sector,[10] creating greater expectations for board performance on the part of many nonprofit managers. Yet despite its import, governance models remain relatively understudied.[11]

Considerable work on the history of governance in the corporate, nonprofit, and educational spheres has helped to inform the structures of governance. Much of this underscores the importance of environment in the formation of governance structures. In the corporate world, Morck and Steier trace the development of corporate governance models in the Americas, Europe, and Asia, demonstrating how these have been influenced both by contextual differences as well as the forces of globalization.[12] Hall, an American historian, contributes to the understanding of the development of governance structures in eighteenth- to twentieth-century America, again citing the importance of context in forming "cultures of trusteeship," where "cultures of philanthropy and voluntarism . . . parallel cultures of economic and political life."[13] This is demonstrated by historical exploration of trusteeship in the contexts of Cleveland, Boston, and New York in the nineteenth and twentieth centuries. The contextual nature of trusteeship is seen in the history of academic governance as well. Cowley traces the origins of American academic governance to medieval Bologna, Paris, Oxford, and Cambridge.[14] In each case, Cowley cites the influence of the environment on governance structures, from statist government influence in early modern France to the influence of academic associations, donors, and the federal government in late twentieth-century American higher education. Duryea,[15]

---

9. M. Moore, "Nonprofits to Face Sarbanes-Like Scrutiny from IRS," *Boston Business Journal*. (2009, January 9). Retrieved 26 January 2009, from http://boston.bizjournals.com; Carver, *Boards That Make a Difference*.
10. Chait, Ryan, and Taylor, *Governance as Leadership*, 2–3; Hall, "Cultures of Trusteeship," 139.
11. Abzug and Simonoff. *Nonprofit Trustees*.
12. R. K. Morck and L. Steier, *The Global History of Corporate Governance* (Chicago, IL: University of Chicago Press, 2005).
13. Hall, "Cultures of Trusteeship," 140.
14. W. H. Cowley, *Presidents, Professors, and Trustees: The Evolution of American Academic Government* (San Francisco, CA: Jossey-Bass, 1980).
15. E. D. Duryea, "Evolution of University Organization," in *The University as an Organization*, ed. J. A. Perkins (New York: McGraw-Hill, 1973).

writing in the context of the effects of 1960s-era student movements on American higher education, resulting in a transfer of power from boards to strong CEOs to faculty and finally to students over the course of the twentieth century. Nason traces this shift of power to the "unraveling of consensus" in educational institutions, and a move from "governance by consensus to governance by conflict."[16] Nason's sense of unraveling is echoed in some of the most influential literature on academic administration, which suggests that higher education is now engaged in multiple and divergent conversations or "cultures".[17]

Beyond this background material, the literature on boards divides into two main groups: prescriptive literature and social scientific literature. The first is a vast corpus of prescriptive literature written to give board chairpersons, board members, and nonprofit managers practical, immediately applicable advice on how to improve board function. The work of Carver[18] is among the most widely cited and studied, but Houle,[19] Scott,[20] Andringa and Engstrom,[21] Stahlke,[22] Chait, Ryan, and Taylor,[23] Brown,[24] Eadie,[25] and McKenna[26] have also played a critical role. The second major category is the theoretical/empirical literature on board function based on social scientific theory. These works, including Abzug and Galaskiewicz,[27] Abzug and Simonoff,[28] and Ostrower

---

16. J. W. Nason, *The Nature of Trusteeship*, 6.
17. M. D. Cohen and J. G. March, *Leadership and Ambiguity: The American College Presidency* (Boston, MA: Harvard Business School Press, 1986); W. H. Bergquist and K. Pawlak, *Engaging the Six Cultures of the Academy* (San Francisco, CA: Jossey-Bass, 2008).
18. Carver, *Boards That Make a Difference*.
19. C. O. Houle, *Governing Boards* (San Francisco, CA: Jossey-Bass, 1989).
20. Scott, *Creating Caring and Capable Boards*.
21. Andringa and Engstrom, *Nonprofit Board Answer Book*.
22. L. Stahlke, *Governance Matters: Relationship Model of Governance, Leadership, and Management* (Toronto, ON: GovernanceMatters, 2003).
23. Chait, Ryan, and Taylor, *Governance as Leadership*.
24. J. Brown, *The Imperfect Board Member: Discovering the Seven Disciplines of Governance Excellence* (New York: Wiley, 2006).
25. Eadie, "Meeting the Governing Challenge."
26. D. L. McKenna, *Stewards of a Sacred Trust* (Winchester, VA: ECFA Press, 2010).
27. Abzug and Galaskiewicz, "Nonprofit Boards."
28. Abzug and Simonoff, *Nonprofit Trustees in Different Contexts*.

and Stone,[29] are generally mildly critical of the prescriptive literature for its lack of theoretical and analytical basis. The predominant focus of much of this research work has been board composition. If there is a recurring theme in the literature over the past thirty years, it is that governance continues to fail in too many circumstances.

Amidst the professionalization of the nonprofit sector, stricter legal requirements, and a desire to see board service become more fulfilling and functional, a host of prescriptive works have appeared to give immediate, practical guidance to board members and nonprofit managers. Many of these are paired with a consulting function, such as Carver's International Center for Policy Governance (www.policygovernance.org) and the broader BoardSource (www.boardsource.org). This governance industry continues to grow, helping corporations and institutions to adapt, thereby avoiding extinction, in a rapidly changing environment.[30] Carver, the most prolific, has conducted thousands of seminars in as many organizations, trained 250 consultants, and conducted training in nineteen countries.[31]

The most widely cited prescriptive work on governance is Carver's *Boards That Make a Difference: A New Design for Leadership in Nonprofit and Public Organizations*, first published in 1995. Carver works from the concept of policy governance,[32] based on the assumption that "the purpose of governance is to ensure, usually on behalf others, that an organization achieves what it should achieve while avoiding those behaviors and situations that should be avoided."[33] This is accomplished by the setting of board policies that define ends, rather than means, toward which the organization can and must work. In Carver's model, policy equals expression of explicit values.[34] Policies fall into four main categories. First are *ends*, which state and keep the institution focused on its core mission on behalf of stakeholders. Second are *executive limitations*, which establish that which management cannot do to achieve

---

29. F. Ostrower and M. Stone, "Governance: Research Trends, Gaps, and Future Prospects," in *The Nonprofit Sector: A Research Handbook*, ed. W. W. Powell and R. Steinberg (New Haven, CT: Yale University Press, 2006).
30. T. Paligorova, *Industry 2020*. Prague: Penta Investments, 2001. Retrieved January 26, 2009 from http://www.pentainvestments.com/files/vizia2020/3-001-PaligorovaTeodora-ENG.doc.
31. Carver, *Boards That Make a Difference*, vii.
32. Ibid., xxvii.
33. Ibid.
34. Ibid., 37.

the mission, thereby creating a space in which they can operate without board action. Third are policies governing *board-management relations*, determining how power passes through the organization. Finally, Carver cites *board process* policies, which determine how the board itself works in setting policy. Carver's Policy Governance Model is depicted as "a platform technology for governance," that can be applied to any kind of organization in any situation.[35] Carver stresses that policy governance is not something that can be implemented partially, but must be fully utilized in an organization.[36]

Carver's Policy Governance Model is tested by Nobbie and Brudney,[37] which served as the first systematic study of the policy governance model. This research examined, among other things, degrees of implementation of policy governance, perceptions of improved performance in various terms on part of board chairpersons and CEOs, and comparisons to other organizations that either had no board training or had training from another organization (BoardSource). This study built upon Brudney and Murray's study[38] that suggested that no one model or combination of models of governance proved to be strongly associated with perceived success of a board change effort. Overall, Nobbie and Brudney's study suggested that most organizations using policy governance did implement it fully. They also found heightened perceptions of effectiveness among those surveyed. However, their study found no meaningful difference in perception of effectiveness between those organizations employing policy governance and those receiving training and support from BoardSource.[39] This suggests that a board's willingness to take its task seriously and to seek help in considering the best ways to carry out its tasks is more important than the implementation of any one platform or model. While the Carver Model underscores many key elements of governance, research like Nobbie and Brudney suggest that the solution to

---

35. C. Oliver, "Policy Governance and Other Governance Models Compared," *Board Leadership* 64 (2002): 6.
36. Carver, *Boards That Make a Difference*.
37. P. D. Nobbie and J. L. Brudney, "Testing the Implementation, Board Performance, and Organizational Effectiveness of the Policy Governance Model in Nonprofit Boards of Directors," *Nonprofit and Voluntary Sector Quarterly* 32, no. 4 (2003).
38. J. L. Brudney and V. Murray, "Do Intentional Efforts to Improve Boards Really Work?," *Nonprofit Management and Leadership* 8, no. 4 (1998).
39. Nobbie and Brudney, "Testing the Implementation," 592.

the challenge of good governance may be more complex and may be more related to human relations than to specific forms.

Brown represents a genre of governance literature that follows closely on the trends of broader management and leadership.[40] Brown frames his work theoretically on Carver,[41] yet focuses on the collective or relational nature of a board. Brown argues that many boards are made up of people with many skills, yet in the boardroom, "individual competence can lead to collective incompetence."[42] Brown's focus is on building a board with healthy relationships and uplifting leadership that can together tackle the key issues of policy governance. Brown's work provides a practical and useful approach and his stress on the relational nature of governance is welcome.

Chait, Ryan, and Taylor's work[43] also fits into the broad category of prescriptive literature, although their practically oriented book is based deeply on the authors' own more theoretical and empirical work.[44] The work is based on the premise that the growing literature on governance has ignored many of the lessons learned by those investigating broader questions of leadership. They argue that governance must be considered a form of leadership, and be informed by research in that field. Like leadership, governance must be seen as a "dynamic, multidimensional concept".[45] The authors outline three key modes of governance as leadership. The first is the traditional fiduciary mode, focusing on stewarding the assets and mission of the organization. The second mode is strategic, focusing on the organization's medium-term life cycle. The final mode of governance is that of generative work, or the board's engagement with the broader environment and the problems and opportunities these present. Generative governance is thinking deeply about the organization's reason for being.[46] Chait, Ryan, and Taylor break from the rigidity of the Carver model,[47] arguing that generative work leads to some

---

40. Brown, *The Imperfect Board Member*.
41. Carver, *Boards That Make a Difference*.
42. Brown, *The Imperfect Board Member*, xviii.
43. Chait, Ryan and Taylor, *Governance as Leadership*.
44. E.g. B. E. Taylor, R. P. Chait, and T. P. Holland, "The New Work of the Nonprofit Board," *Harvard Business Review* (Sep-Oct 1996).
45. Chait, Ryan and Taylor, *Governance as Leadership*, xvii.
46. Ibid., 79–80.
47. Carver, *Boards That Make a Difference*.

ambiguity in terms of sharing of tasks between board and management,[48] yet they argue that only through this can real governance occur. Overall, while these authors stress the similarity, if not universal, nature of trusteeship in the nonprofit sector,[49] their framework of governance allows for considerable maneuverability to meet the unique needs of each organization within its context.

The second major category of literature addressing governance is based in more empirical and social scientific approaches to questions. As stated above, some work, such as that of Chait, Ryan, and Taylor[50] advances prescriptive ideas based on previous empirical work. The social science literature argues that there is need for deeper exploration of the construct of governance, so as not to lead to a dissonance between the theoretical and the actual.[51] Reaction to prescriptive approaches is present even within the prescriptive literature itself. Scott argues that the majority of board literature and consulting activities focus on administrative processes and management skills, not "the capacity for perceiving and responding to complexity."[52] This critique is at the heart of the reaction to prescriptive governance forms. In their review of recent literature, Ostrower and Stone affirm Middleton's contention[53] that the literature supports the idea that there is no "one size fits all" model for governance.[54]

This reaction to the "one size fits all" model rebels against the idea of organizations as rational entities, adhering instead to an epistemological approach encompassed in neo-institutional theory.[55] This approach sees institutional realities emerging from a complex conversation of internal

---

48. Chait, Ryan and Taylor, *Governance as Leadership*, 99.
49. Ibid., xxii.
50. Chait, Ryan and Taylor, *Governance as Leadership*.
51. E. L. Patterson, "Theological Boardsmanship: A Descriptive and Comparative Study of Some Identified Elements of Board Effectiveness" (Unpublished doctoral dissertation), Claremont Graduate School, Claremont, CA, 1992, 17.
52. Scott, *Creating Caring and Capable Boards*, 10.
53. M. Middleton, "Nonprofit Boards of Directors: Beyond the Governance Function," in *The Nonprofit Sector*, ed. W.W. Powell (New Haven, CT: Yale University Press, 1987).
54. Ostrower and Stone, "Governance," 612.
55. P. J. DiMaggio and W. W. Powell, "The Iron Cage Revisited: Institutional Isomorphism and Collective Rationality in Organizational Fields," *American Sociological Review* 48, no. 2 (1983); Abzug and Simonoff, *Nonprofit Trustees*.

and external forces through "differentiating and homogenizing processes."[56] This leads to a focus on the institution's interaction with its environment. Bradshaw et al. is a fierce critique of prescriptive forms,[57] especially those of Carver.[58] Much like Chait, Ryan, and Taylor,[59] Bradshaw argues for attention to broader literature on organizational dynamics and leadership that calls for greater flexibility within organizations.[60] In reviewing the literature on governance, Bradshaw contends that there is "no ideal governance model but there are certain governance functions which must be fulfilled."[61] Bradshaw believes that these can be approached in a number of functional, pragmatic ways, involving members of the constituency and staff members, as well as more traditional governing figures in the functions of governance. Diniz cites an example of such a governance structure in a rural health care organization in India, although Diniz stresses that the rural community context and nature of the work make such a governance structure possible.[62] Savage asserts that "there is no single right way today to organize a board or develop council, congregational, or organizational leadership."[63] Taken together with the work of Hall,[64] discussed above, this reaction to the prescriptive literature opens up important lines of inquiry for a study of governance in the specific context of theological schools in a variety of environments and may serve as the basis for a useful corrective to prescriptive forms.

This neo-institutional focus, together with broader cultural concerns arising from the civil rights and women's movements, have caused a significant amount of research literature on governance to focus on board composition,

---

56. Abzug and Simonoff, *Nonprofit Trustees*, vii.
57. P. Bradshaw, et al., "Nonprofit Governance Models: Problems and Perspectives." Paper presented at the ARNOVA Conference, Seattle, WA, 1998.
58. Carver, *Boards That Make a Difference*.
59. Chait, Ryan and Taylor, *Governance as Leadership*.
60. Bradshaw, et al., "Nonprofit Governance Models," 5.
61. Ibid., 9.
62. L. Diniz, "The Changing Face of Non-Traditional NGO Governance: The Case of the Chinmaya Rural Primary Health Care and Training Centre (CRTC), India," *FES Outstanding Graduate Student Paper Series* 10, no. 1 (2005). Retrieved April 17, 2009, from http://www.yorku.ca/fes/research/docs/2004/Diniz_2004_OGSPS.pdf.
63. T. J. Savage, "Beyond Hierarchies: Transforming Power and Leadership," in *Building Effective Boards for Religious Organizations*, ed. T. P. Holland and D. C. Hester (San Francisco, CA: Jossey-Bass, 2000), 121.
64. Hall, "Cultures of Trusteeship."

including factors of gender, educational background, and class. Ostrower and Stone cite this as one of the two largest categories of recent literature, along with board-management relations.[65] They conclude that while empirical studies demonstrate that board composition influences how boards function, it is not clear exactly how this process works, and even less clear how composition may impact effectiveness.[66] This provides a worthy caution that while diversity of voice and representation is a worthy goal, the presence of a diverse board in and of itself does not guarantee greater function.

Several tools and concepts developed in the field of anthropology prove useful in exploring governance in diverse cultures. Hall's conception of high contexts and low contexts can help to understand differences in board function in different cultures.[67] In Hall's conception, high context cultures employ communication that presumes the presence of an existing in-group, or a group that has a high degree of understanding of nuance and non-verbal communication. In such circumstances, less is said explicitly, but more may be communicated implicitly. At times, significant communication may be invisible to outsiders. Such high context cultures include Africa, Asia, Latin America, and the Romance-language-speaking nations of southern Europe. In contrast, Germany, Scandinavia, the United States, and the United Kingdom would constitute low context cultures, where more communication would take place in an explicit, verbal way. The concept of power distance[68] is equally useful in examining cross-cultural board function. Hofestadt's concept of low power distance cultures includes places where decision making is generally perceived as democratic and participatory in nature, as opposed to more hierarchical and closed decision making that occurs in cultures with high power distance. While these concepts have been developed in much broader perspective, their utility in understanding governance function is high.

---

65. Ostrower and Stone, "Governance."
66. Ibid., 614.
67. E. Hall, *Beyond Culture* (New York: Anchor, 1976).
68. G. Hofestadt, *Culture's Consequences: Comparing Values, Behaviors, Institutions, and Organizations across Cultures* (Thousand Oaks, CA: SAGE, 2001).

The Board's Interpretive Role – Boundary Spanning and Generative Thought

The literature on governance identifies several interrelated functions of a governing board, including guarding the organizational mission,[69] fiduciary oversight[70] and other organizational functions.[71] The focus of this study is the governance function that calls on the board to serve in boundary spanning and generative thought roles, acting as liaison and interlocutor between the organization and its environment, and considering how the organization can best achieve this at present and in the future. The literature on governance, both prescriptive and empirical, gives attention to this important dialogical process by which an organization is enabled to function well in relation to a changing external environment. This study approaches this concept through Middleton's concept of "boundary spanning."[72] Yet this understanding is enriched by other authors' approaches to governance functions relating to the institution's environment, including Chait, Ryan, and Taylor's concept of generative thinking,[73] Smith's concept of interpretation,[74] and Scott's concept of relational bonds.[75] It draws on concepts present in the literature, such as legitimacy, ownership, power, and community.

This conception of governance as boundary spanning follows on broader trends in business, leadership, and education. Senge's concept of the learning institution[76] has a similar focus on interaction with the environment. The greatest challenge, according to Senge, is an inability of an organization's leadership to see changes in the environment when "the organization as a whole cannot recognize the impending threats, understand the implications of those threats, or come up with alternatives."[77] Heifetz, Grashow, and Linsky

---

69. E.g. R. Cooley and D. Tiede, "What Is the Character of Administration and Governance in the Good Theological School?" *Theological Education* 30, no. 2 (1994).
70. E.g. Smith, *Entrusted*; Chait, Ryan and Taylor, *Governance as Leadership*.
71. E.g. Nason, *The Nature of Trusteeship*.
72. Middleton, "Nonprofit Boards of Directors."
73. Chait, Ryan and Taylor, *Governance as Leadership*.
74. Smith, *Entrusted*.
75. Scott, *Creating Caring and Capable Boards*.
76. P. M. Senge, *The Fifth Discipline: The Art and Practice of the Learning Organization* (New York: Doubleday, 2006).
77. Ibid., 18.

stress the need to move beyond leadership that focuses on technical, everyday problems and to focus more on leadership that addresses truly adaptive challenges, those that call for more fundamental thinking about the future of the organization in its environment.[78] In the field of education, Kaufman calls for a focus on external needs assessment, stressing that "we are not in a vacuum, and our results [as educators] are seen and judged by those outside of the schools – those external to it."[79] Lynn affirms this call for external needs assessment, but argues for seeing institutions holistically, understanding not only the external environment, but also the historical trends that have shaped the internal environment.[80] All of these works stress that organizations, including theological schools, do not exist in a vacuum, but are products of historical forces and are influenced by a constantly changing environment. Scott terms a governing board's awareness of all of these environmental factors *deep knowledge* of the organization.[81]

Middleton's concept of boundary spanning[82] provides a frame for thinking about boards in interaction with both the organizations they govern and the broader context. Middleton holds that:

> Boards are part of *both* the organization and its environment. *Environment* means all external elements that are salient to the organization as a whole, its subunits, or its members in their performance of activities that are organization related but that fall outside its authority. . . . Boards of directors are part of the organization because they are responsible in the broadest sense for its wellbeing and for ensuring that it fulfills its stated purpose. They are part of the external environment in the sense that their members are drawn from and often have primary affiliations to other groups in the community. Thus, boards, as boundary-

---

78. Heifetz, Grashow, and Linsky, *Practice of Adaptive Leadership*.
79. R. A. Kaufman, *Needs Assessment: Concepts and Applications* (Miami, FL: Education Technology Publications, 1979), 66.
80. R. L. Lynn, "Coming over the Horizon," in *Good Stewardship: A Handbook for Seminary Trustees*, ed. B. E. Taylor and M. L. Warford (Washington, DC: Association of Governing Boards, 1991).
81. Scott, *Creating Caring and Capable Boards*.
82. Middleton, "Nonprofit Boards of Directors," 141.

spanning and control units, have an important role in regulating exchanges of information and resources across boundaries.[83]

This concept allows the board to see both inside and outside the organization, and to draw strength from both. Middleton's concept adheres to Greenleaf's definition of trusteeship, namely that "institutions need two kinds of leaders: those who are inside and carry out the active day-to-day roles, and those who stand outside but are intimately concerned, and who, with the benefit of some detachment, oversee the active leaders. These are the trustees."[84]

In a concrete way, Middleton's concept of boundary spanning envisions boards that carry out four key functions:

1. Developing exchange relationships with external parties to ensure the flow of resources into and out of organization.

2. Interpreting information gained from exchange relationships to make the internal organizational adjustments necessary to meet environmental demands.

3. Buffering the organization from the environment and thus protecting it from external interference.

4. Reducing environmental constraints by influencing external conditions to the organization's advantage.[85]

The effectiveness of this concept is grounded empirically in the studies of governance in the health care sector by Pfeffer,[86] who demonstrates that the boards with the highest perceived effectiveness are those who are able to interact best with the needs of the environment. Although the board as intermediary with the institution's environment has not played the central role in research on governance that it did twenty years ago,[87] the concept has

---

83. Ibid.
84. Greenleaf, *Servant Leadership*, 40.
85. Middleton, "Nonprofit Boards of Directors," 143.
86. J. Pfeffer, "Size, Composition, and Functions of Hospital Boards of Directors: A Study of Organization-Environment Linkage," *Administrative Science Quarterly* 18 (1973).
87. Ostrower and Stone, "Governance."

more recently been adopted by Abzug and Simonoff[88] and has been brought into dialogue with the concept of legitimacy, as discussed below.

The concept of governing boards as boundary spanners resonates with some other recent conceptions of board governance. Chait, Ryan, and Taylor's conception of generative work also stresses and builds upon the board's boundary spanning role.[89] Drawing on the language of external needs assessment in Kaufman,[90] the authors lament that all too often, a board's opportunity to shape an organization for impact on society is self-limited to internal processes and procedures. Chait, Ryan, and Taylor argue that generative thinking must look outward and not be bound to internal processes, but rather *shape* these processes.[91] Generative work is the task of posing "great questions".[92] Bringing this concept into dialogue with Middleton, it is clear that generative work occurs on the boundaries of the organization, based on both knowledge of internal organizational reality and external problems and opportunities. While Middleton's concept locates the task in relationship to the organization and the environment, Chait, Ryan, and Taylor's concept outlines a cognitive process by which boundary spanning can occur.[93] Chait, Ryan, and Taylor suggest the utility of Bolman and Deal's concept of "frames,"[94] including the structural, human resource, political, and symbolic frames, in the work of generative governance.

Smith's work on the moral aspects of governance critiques both the prescriptive literature and the social science orientation of empirical literature on governance.[95] Such literature focuses on discrete aspects of governance, "rather than attempting to define desirable ends or goals or purposes for trusteeship."[96] Smith argues "that the *moral* duties of trustees of nonprofit institutions derive from the unique structure of their relationships

---

88. Abzug and Simonoff, *Nonprofit Trustees in Different Contexts*.
89. Chait, Ryan, and Taylor, *Governance as Leadership*.
90. Kaufman, *Needs Assessment*.
91. Chait, Ryan, and Taylor, *Governance as Leadership*, 80–81.
92. Ibid., 82.
93. Ibid.
94. L. G. Bolman and T. E. Deal, *Reframing Organizations: Artistry, Choice, and Leadership* (San Francisco, CA: Jossey-Bass, 2003).
95. Smith, *Entrusted*.
96. Ibid., 3.

with beneficiaries and donors."[97] Smith defines these duties both in terms of fiduciary responsibility and interpretation of how the institution can best serve in the environment. "Trustees should be reflective, that the board should be a community of inquiry, more precisely, a community of interpretation."[98] Patterson also develops a similar idea relating specifically to the field of theological institutions, citing the importance of the board to be a buffer and interpreter between the institution and its constituency.[99]

In a similar way, Scott frames the function of a board in terms of its ability to mediate between self-interests and the common good through "relational bonds" and a deep knowledge of the potential of the organization.[100] Scott holds that,

> Effective [trustee] leadership integrates altruism and authority. It is an integration that evokes the moral and ethical use of power and authority through position, knowledge, and skills to bring about changes in the well-being of individuals, institutions, and communities . . . the leader lives in and operates out of a world of multilayered complexity, sharing a particular view and interpreting the experience in compelling ways that enables others to develop trust and to risk being and doing.[101]

Smith's, Patterson's, and Scott's conceptions further strengthen Middleton's concept by infusing the concept of boundary spanning with moral values of leadership.

Like Carver,[102] Eadie focuses more on structures than relationships.[103] Yet Eadie goes beyond Carver, stressing that governance must go "well beyond the old-fashioned notion of governing as merely 'policy making'".[104] Effective governance, Eadie argues, is not merely a matter of policy, but of a "never-ending stream of decisions and judgments about very concrete products and

---

97. Ibid., 4 (emphasis in original).
98. Ibid., ix.
99. Patterson, "Theological Boardsmanship," 63.
100. Scott, *Creating Caring and Capable Boards*, 11, 38.
101. Ibid., 39.
102. Carver, *Boards That Make a Difference*.
103. Eadie, "Meeting the Governing Challenge."
104. Ibid., 7.

documents."[105] Perhaps the most provocative element of Eadie's work is the suggestion that governance is a team effort, practiced best by a "strategic governing team,"[106] composed of board, CEO, and senior executives. Although stressing the need for proper structures, Eadie affirms the importance of developing both the professional and relational architecture in a way that is resonant with some of the works discussed above. The "board-savvy CEO" is especially important to the process, coordinating and aiding the process. The CEO's ability to employ the "soft side" of his or her competencies in the relational sphere is especially important to governance process. This desire for broader participation in governance is echoed by other authors. It is embraced by Freiwirth and Letona.[107] Writing from a more radical perspective, they call for and posit examples of the "democratization" of governance, where "governance responsibility is shared across the organizational system among the key sectors of an organization – that is, its constituents, or members, staff, and board."[108] In the nonprofit sphere, they argue especially for the participation of those being served. "If the voices of those who are directly impacted by our actions are not included in key decision-making processes, we too often arrive at wrong conclusions or delusions that are incongruent with our constituencies' needs, let alone with our mission."[109] Burch Basinger raises a related issue by pointing out that the Carver Model "locates the work of the board in the realm of ends, and hands the means of getting there over to the president and the president's team."[110] This can be a very helpful distinction, avoiding micromanagement by the board. This approach, however, fails to fully take into account shared governance as practiced in most North American theological schools. "This doesn't mean that policy governance is necessarily and always at odds with shared governance, but Carver's emphasis on the exclusivity of the board-president relationship and his use of the word 'staff' to describe all other persons within the organization

---

105. Ibid., 19.

106. Ibid., 16.

107. J. Freiwirth and M. E. Letona, System-wide Governance for Community Empowerment," *The Nonprofit Quarterly* 13, no. 4 (2006).

108. Ibid., 25.

109. Ibid., 24.

110. R. Burch Basinger, "Where policy is good governance," *InTrust Magazine* (Summer 2008). Retrieved 7 Dec 2011. http://www.intrust.org/magazine/pastarticle.cfm?column=33&id=567, 25.

may be a problem."¹¹¹ Eadie,¹¹² Freiwirth and Letona,¹¹³ and Burch Basinger¹¹⁴ all raise issues surrounding the line that exists between the board and the staff, suggesting in subtle and not-so-subtle ways the need for broader participation in the governing process.

An understanding of the board's interpretive role within its environment raises questions about a number of key variables at work in the conversation, including the concept of legitimacy, the role of power, understandings of ownership and constituency in organizations, and the role of community in governance. Each of these concepts contribute significantly to an understanding of effective governance in diverse contexts.

Abzug and Galaskiewicz develop the concept of "legitimacy"[115] in relation to governing boards, suggesting that board members, especially elite board members, have the ability to confer upon an organization a sense of gravitas, import, and trustworthiness simply by their association with institutional governance. Such legitimacy is based in the background, expertise, and character of those who serve. Based on DiMaggio and Powell's theory of construction of organizational legitimacy,[116] Abzug and Galaskiewicz develop this idea further to suggest that preserving legitimacy is an interpretive function in which the board seeks to perceive the best interest of the organization.[117] They define two kinds of legitimacy, the first being downward, or elite, legitimacy in the eyes of government and higher authorities. The second is upward, or grassroots, legitimacy, meaning respect in the eyes of stakeholders. These two types of legitimacy can, and often do, create a tension between possible paths forward. As Abzug and Galaskiewicz argue, there is often not merely one community interest, there are at times many.[118] This idea of derived legitimacy through mediating this tension is closely related to Smith's conception of interpretation, or "ability to reconcile

---

111. Ibid., 26.
112. Eadie, "Meeting the Governing Challenge."
113. Freiwirth and Letona, "System-wide Governance."
114. Burch Basinger, "Where policy is good governance."
115. Abzug and Galaskiewicz, "Nonprofit Boards."
116. DiMaggio and Powell, "The Iron Cage Revisited."
117. Abzug and Galaskiewicz, "Nonprofit Boards," 54.
118. Ibid.

an organization's distinctive vision with the overall good of society."[119] It also resembles Scott's conception of the board's role in negotiating between the individual interest, the organizational interest, and broader societal good.[120]

This conception of legitimacy lies at the heart of many conflicts over the strategic direction of an organization. The tension between downward and upward legitimacy can create significant tensions within an organization. This is especially true in the realm of education, where the growth of multiple influences, including those from governments, faculty, and students, all vie to determine the ultimate vision of the institution.[121] Many times, a host of potentially good, legitimate choices may be available. Yet it is the role of the board to determine which of the choices represent the most effective, integrity-filled way forward for the organization. It is in such difficult scenarios that a board's ability to be a community of interpretation is critical. In describing the ideal community of interpretation, Smith states, "the optimal trustee is someone willing and able to discuss and assess the identity of the organization, someone with moral insight, sensitivity, savvy, and the ability to consider options reasonably."[122] As the environment of higher education around the globe grows more complex, the ability to maintain organizational legitimacy in the eyes of multiple influences will be even more important.

A subtle tension arises in the literature concerning the issue of ownership and constituency. Carver defines this in stark terms, differentiating between "moral owners," those to whom a board feels accountable, and "primary beneficiaries," or those whom a board serves.[123] In an educational institution, this would see the moral owners as donors and, in many cases, government, while the primary beneficiaries would be students. Within this model, the role of the faculty is unclear, as is the role of the broader community of the educational institution. While Carver's distinctions are helpful, they must serve as points of dialogue for the board in interpreting their response to various groups of stakeholders who feel a claim to the organization's mission.

---

119. Smith, *Entrusted*, 16.
120. Scott, *Creating Caring and Capable Boards*.
121. C. Kerr and M. L. Gade, *The Guardians: Boards of Trustees of American Colleges and Universities* (Washington, DC: Association of Governing Boards, 1989), 9–10.
122. Smith, *Entrusted*, 109.
123. Carver, *Boards That Make a Difference*, 185–186.

In this way, Smith's interpretive model may be useful.[124] Smith takes the most radical approach of any of the literature, arguing that at times, a board must decide to take an institution in the direction that serves the good of society, while perhaps failing to honor the desires of closer-at-hand constituencies.[125] Smith cites examples of organizations whose original purposes become irrelevant (e.g. the March of Dimes) or those whose activities are challenged by the spirit of a later time, such as charitable foundations whose mission can grow beyond that of the founders. "The boardroom should be the place where the past and future, particularity and common good, are reconciled."[126] While a useful caution against doctrinaire immutability within an organization, Smith's understanding of responsibility to constituency may be too broad. In their review of broader literature, Ostrower and Stone point out that this "ability to reinterpret purpose in light of current notions of common good" may go too far.[127] Carver's strict interpretation of constituency and Smith's broader interpretation may prove a useful and productive paradox in the boardroom, as boards seek to negotiate between multiple competing constituencies. Scott's call for boards to have a "capacity for perceiving and responding to complexity"[128] seems especially apt.

The concept of power is also central to proper understanding of governance. Board membership not only brings to the organization an individual's legitimacy; it also grants part of the authority and prestige of an institution to the individual board member. This can prove to be a challenge in some cases, where a board member's personal or social desires for power can corrupt organizational function. Ultimately, a board must create an environment that balances board members' personal aspirations[129] to form a single, focused community of trustee leaders, able to acknowledge their individual self-interest, while balancing it with regard for the common good.[130] The concept of power also plays a key role in a major area of inquiry regarding governance, namely the relationship between board and professional staff.

---

124. Smith, *Entrusted*.
125. Ibid., 16.
126. Ibid., 18.
127. Ostrower and Stone, "Governance," 613.
128. Scott, *Creating Caring and Capable Boards*, 10.
129. Middleton, "Nonprofit Boards of Directors," 143.
130. Scott, *Creating Caring and Capable Boards*, 40, 46.

This can create a tension between academically or professionally oriented management, who would see the greater good in standards or, in the case of education, accreditation, whereas board members may refer instead to what is best for the community.[131] Prescriptive governance literature[132] would argue that the board must have the final say as the final authority. While this is true, good governance (and the very demands of the real world) would lead to a more complex interplay of power between the board and the management.[133] Even some recent prescriptive literature acknowledges that the line between board and management can become fuzzy at times.[134] Middleton characterizes the best approach as "an interdependent relationship between people who see the organization from different perspectives."[135] Again, consideration of the concept of power in relation to governance points to the importance of dialogue and ability to wisely discern the best interests of the organization within its context.

The focus of recent literature on dialogue, interpretation, and discernment leads to another concept that arises frequently, namely the importance of community and relationships among board members. Simply put, the best boards are those that are able to respectfully but passionately discern the best ways forward. Middleton points to the import that boards have strong ties among members, despite diverse backgrounds. Without such ties, an "unclear identity" may come to exist among a board.[136] Such assumptions closely parallel the concept of the learning community[137] and the idea of "relational trust" as a foundation for productive work and institutions.[138] In the prescriptive literature, Brown calls for a greater focus on "healthy" boards, not just "smart" boards,[139] while Andringa and Engstrom stress the importance of board meetings including time for board fellowship.[140] Within

---

131. Hall, "Cultures of Trusteeship," 139.
132. E.g. Carver, *Boards That Make a Difference*; Houle, *Governing Boards*.
133. Ostrower and Stone, "Governance," 617–618.
134. E.g. Chait, Ryan, and Taylor, 2005; Andringa and Engstrom, 2002
135. Middleton, "Nonprofit Boards of Directors," 151.
136. Ibid., 149.
137. Senge, *The Fifth Discipline*.
138. P. J. Palmer, *The Courage to Teach: Exploring the Inner Landscape of a Teacher's Life* (San Francisco, CA: John Wiley, 2007).
139. Brown, *The Imperfect Board Member*, xviii.
140. Andringa and Engstrom, *Nonprofit Board Answer Book*, 6, 155–156.

Christian organizations, such approaches call for the gathering of the board around the common work of the gospel. Ostrower and Stone empirically conclude that such positive relationships do contribute to increased board effectiveness.[141] Overall, the literature stresses the need for a community able to think wisely about the future of an organization.

Theological Schools and Their Environment

Theological schools exist within a rapidly changing external environment. External threats and complex inner challenges have raised the question "can theological schools govern themselves into the future?"[142] Some research suggests that theological schools continue to prepare pastors for a church that existed thirty years ago, giving students skills to study the Bible and interpret theology, but not to lead today's church.[143] Reflecting on the system of theological training, Cannell makes the assertion that "the church has not consistently been well served by the schools and school-like institutions to which it has delegated the responsibility to prepare its leaders."[144] Akrong makes a similar point in the African context. "If theological education is to be relevant at all, it must be capable of giving answers to the faithful by relating their questions to the transforming power of the gospel that gives new life to individuals and communities."[145] If the situation is as dire as these reports and investigations suggest, theological schools risk irrelevancy in the face of an increasingly complex environment.

While the challenges are great, theological schools retain great potential, and meaningful innovation is happening. Greenleaf stresses theological schools' ability to be "powerful leaven in the culture,"[146] yet he admits that this is rarely reached. Greenleaf points out that seminaries, as they stand, are largely "marginal" institutions.[147] Klein paints a rather negative picture

---

141. Ostrower and Stone, "Governance."
142. Aleshire, *Earthen Vessels.*
143. J. Woodyard, *The M. J. Murdock Trust Review of Graduate Theological Education Programs in the Pacific Northwest* (Vancouver, WA: M. J. Murdock Trust, 1994).
144. Cannell, *Theological Education Matters*, 11.
145. Akrong, "Challenges of Theological Education," 27.
146. Greenleaf, *Seminary as Servant*, 1.
147. Ibid., 10.

of the situation of governance in theological education institutions in North America, arguing that many board members have an "expansive loyalty" to an institution without sufficient understanding or knowledge of the work of the institution itself.[148] Klein echoes Greenleaf[149] regarding the potential of seminaries for impact, stressing their unique position at the "intersection" of various influences.

> The governing boards of theological schools, standing as they do at the intersection of school and church, and church and society, are poised to ask the guiding questions and to press for the deeper insights. Theirs is a role that has not yet lived up to its potential. Boards may benefit from conceiving of their schools as 'learning organizations' that seek to avoid the double danger of blind drift and mindless adaptation. They must become inveterate askers of hard questions that expose reality, while at the same time they are no less supporter of seminary leaders who articulate a vision for the school. Study – of themselves as boards and of the institution – must be their motto. The stewardship of the vocation of their schools demands no less.[150]

Taylor and Warford also point to the import of the governing board of a theological school in assuring relevance, lamenting that most boards are "custodians of the status quo."[151] Despite the challenges, Aleshire remains deeply hopeful about the future of theological schools, though he argues that boards will need to "understand their work as more than just fiduciary care of the school and its mission."[152]

While theological schools share much commonality with other organizations, especially in other educational spheres, they are characterized by a unique theological trust relationship with the church, where preservation of theological integrity is crucial. Cooley and Tiede call on boards to identify,

---

148. C. R. Klein, *Perspectives on the Current Status of an Emerging Policy Issues for Theological Schools and Seminaries.* AGB White Paper No. 1. (Washington: AGB, 1991), 2–3.
149. Greenleaf, *Seminary as Servant.*
150. Klein, *Perspectives*, 33–34.
151. B. E. Taylor and M. L. Warford, *Good Stewardship: A Handbook for Seminary Trustees* (Washington, DC: Association of Governing Boards of Universities and Colleges, 1991), 3.
152. Aleshire, "Governance and the Future," 19.

support, and fulfill the organization's mission above all.[153] Unlike the for-profit world or most nonprofit or educational organizations, governance of theological schools involves theological stewardship as well. Boards must ascertain that institutions continue to adhere to the theological and biblical beliefs that informed their founding. This task has grown more complex. The influences on theological schools are many, ranging from faculty members, diverse constituent denominations and churches, independent or governmental accreditation bodies, students, and diverse communities of which the institutions are part.[154] Within many evangelical institutions, boards face the question of how institutions that once trained young men for church-based ministry should confront needs for broader training of women, lay people, and non-traditional students for wider ministry. As the many evangelical churches, especially in the Majority World, seek a more balanced focus on evangelism and works of social justice,[155] the call for discernment regarding institutional mission will continue to grow.

The literature on governance in theological education tends to follow many approaches of the broader literature, including prescriptive literature, some descriptive literature, and a small corpus of evaluative work, mainly in the form of dissertations. An even smaller body of work addresses the biblical/theological foundations of governance in theological education. Smith[156] and Scott[157] examine the moral dimensions of governance based in ethics and Scott's conception of "holding in trust." Both work within a theistic framework. McKenna expands this understanding in terms of biblical reflection. McKenna argues that "an appointment to a seminary board is an invitation to a sacred trust . . . the roots [of which] are biblical."[158] McKenna unpacks governance as stewardship in light of the creation account of Genesis 2:15, ensuring that institutional resources are invested in a way

---

153. Cooley and Tiede, "What Is the Character," 63.
154. Aleshire, *Earthen Vessels*.
155. Cf. T. Yamamori and C. R. Padilla, eds., *The Local Church: Agent of Transformation* (Buenos Aires, Argentina: Ediciones Kairos, 2004).
156. Smith, *Entrusted*.
157. Scott, *Creating Caring and Capable Boards*.
158. D. L. McKenna, "Mission and Ministry," in *Good Stewardship: A Handbook for Seminary Trustees*, ed. B. E. Taylor and M. L. Warford (Washington, DC: Association of Governing Boards, 1991), 9.

that will multiply and guard "the quality of present and future programs."[159] Secondarily, he grounds stewardship in the Pauline concept of vocation in Ephesians 4:1. While this call is admirable, it can quickly become introverted and focus only on the preservation of the internal environment of a seminary. Later in his work, McKenna addresses the board members' role in stewarding human resources of a seminary, grounding in the idea of *koinonia* (intimate participation in a community or communion). Again, this is deployed only in terms of shepherding the staff of the seminary.[160] McKenna returns to these themes in a longer treatment of the board's role specifically in relationship to CEO selection and orientation.

A volume edited by Holland and Hester[161] further explores governance within the context of religious organizations and adds to many of the themes developed in the literature discussed above. Warford argues that too much thinking on governance has been backward looking and overly concerned with oversight, when the ultimate role of board members should be "stewards of hope."[162] While stressing the import of fiduciary work, Warford focuses more on the need for lively arguments and discussions about the future of the organization. In this, a differentiation is made between a "formal model" of governance and a "functioning model" of governance,[163] with the functioning model focusing more on the web of relationships among all parties in the organization. Klein contributes the perspective of theological seminaries,[164] building on Middleton's conception of boundary spanning.[165] Too many board members, Klein argues, do not have an expansive enough understanding of their role.

> Unless this bridge building function is fully recognized and actively engaged, boards miss opportunities to strengthen their organizations by sustaining communications and deepening

---

159. Ibid., 11.
160. Ibid., 14–15.
161. T. P. Holland and D. C. Hester, eds., *Building effective boards for religious organizations: A handbook for trustees, presidents, and church leaders* (San Francisco, CA: Jossey-Bass, 2000).
162. Warford, "Stewards of Hope."
163. Ibid., 11.
164. Klein, "Boundary Spanning."
165. Middleton, "Nonprofit Boards of Directors."

connections. Organizations become impoverished, shortsighted, and insular, without well-developed ties to the outside world.[166]

Hester argues further that governance is fundamentally a practice of faith or a theological task, placing governance within a "larger, sacred, vocational context."[167]

Approaching the work of governance from an explicitly biblical perspective, Stahlke argues that governance should be seen as part of the structure of biblical relationships, invoking authority (and its limitations), responsibilities (and attendant expectations), and accountability.[168] The central idea of Stahlke's work is the "inversion" of the traditional organizational chart to look more like a tree. The board forms the trunk, funneling resources and providing ultimate support. The roots in turn tap deep into the resources, while management constitutes the main branches and the ultimate fruit is born by these branches. The relationships between these parts, Stahlke argues, must be managed with clear understandings of authority, expectations, and accountability based on godly relationships. A spirit of the board as an enabling entity and a broader spirit of empowerment of all parties within the organization infuses Stahlke's work. Although it relies heavily on the Carver Model for its structure, Stahlke's work also affirms the strong need for relational strength affirmed by other authors. The work's weakness is in its relative lack of dialogue with other literature and its lack of citations. Stahlke is unique in its attempt to expound a full-scale practical theory of governance based on biblical understandings of leadership and authority.[169]

The prescriptive literature on governance in theological education tends to take a form similar to many broader works. Lewis and Weems provide advice to CEOs of seminaries on a wide variety of topics, including a chapter on the CEOs' relationship with the board of directors.[170] Like several other works, this stresses the initiative of the CEO in managing the work of the board, rather than the roles and responsibilities of board members themselves.

---

166. Klein, "Boundary Spanning," 122.
167. D. C. Hester, "Practicing Governance in the Light of Faith," in *Building Effective Boards for Religious Organizations*, ed. T. P. Holland and D. C. Hester (San Francisco, CA: Jossey-Bass, 2000), 63.
168. Stahlke, *Governance Matters*.
169. Ibid.
170. Lewis and Weems, *A Handbook for Seminary Presidents*.

A significant number of works reflect an individual's experience in seminary governance.[171] Taylor and Warford provide the broadest overview of the tasks of board members in theological schools, providing both theoretical and practical advice.[172] An increasing number of organizations have devoted attention to the area of governance in theological schools in North America. InTrust (www.intrust.org) provides regular news and advice to theological schools in North America, working closely with the Association of Theological Schools. The Lilly Endowment of Indianapolis, through its department of religion, has facilitated a number of studies on the topic, including Taylor and Warford[173] and Smith.[174] On the international front, OCI (www.overseas.org) has conducted a number of conferences and workshops on governance in theological institutions in Asia, Africa, Europe, and Latin America. Hardy devotes a chapter to aspects of governance in theological education as taught in the first five years of such conferences.[175] Blackman also attempts to approach governance from a perspective of Majority World nonprofit organizations.[176] An explicit exploration of governance in the Middle Eastern perspective is being pursued by Costa and Kassis.[177]

A small body of descriptive work exists, focusing on the composition of boards of theological schools in North America. Schwartz surveyed 220 theological schools and provides data on board composition, size, structure, and function.[178] Wheeler provides a more recent survey of characteristics and composition of boards of theological schools associated with the Association

---

171. E.g. W. L. Baumgaertner, "The Theological Trustee's Testament," *AGB Reports*, 31, no. 2 (1989); J. C. Gies, *The Good Steward: A Guide to Theological School Trusteeship* (Washington, DC: Association of Governing Boards, 1983).

172. Taylor and Warford, *Good Stewardship*.

173. Ibid.

174. Smith, *Entrusted*.

175. Hardy, *Excellence in Theological Education*.

176. Blackman, *Organisational Governance* (London, UK: Tearfund, 2006).

177. N. Costa and R. Kassis, *Fann al-Hawkamah al-Rashedah: Daleel li-Najah al-Mu'assasat* (The Art of Good Governance: A Guide for Successful Nonprofit Organizations). (Beirut, Lebanon: Dar Manhal al-Hayat, 2012).

178. M. P. Schwartz, *Results of a National Survey of Theological School Board Characteristics, Policies, and Practices* (AGB Occasional Papers), (Washington, DC: AGB, 1994).

of Theological Schools.[179] In addition to the data gathered by Schwartz,[180] Wheeler analyzes board members' financial contributions to the institutions they govern and draws the conclusion that board members must assert higher levels of ownership of these institutions.

Very little attention has been given to the history of seminary governing boards. Aleshire[181] and Lewis[182] both approach this question in very broad terms, tracing elements that have influenced the development of seminary governance in the United States. While Marsden[183] and Ringenberg[184] give some attention to the role of governance in the secularization of Christian education institutions in America, their focus is on Christian universities. Marsden's history of Fuller Theological Seminary provides a useful historical account of the role of a governing board in negotiating a rapidly changing environment and outside threats in the 1960s.[185] Miller explores the function of governance over several decades at Nazarene Theological Seminary (Kansas City) and concludes that the board played an institution-shaping role secondary to powerful presidents and external denominational bodies.[186] Highsmith's exploration of governance at Southern Baptist Theological Seminary (Louisville) tells of an institution that largely sealed itself off from changes within its supporting denomination.[187] Highsmith recounts how outside political action to take control of the board ultimately led to major changes in the seminary's work. Both works share a stress on the influence of external actors on the seminaries.

Two analytical works, both doctoral dissertations, seek to analyze issues of governance. Patterson studies elements of board effectiveness, determining

---

179. B. G. Wheeler, *In Whose Hands: A Study of Theological School Trustees.* Auburn Studies No. 9. (New York: Auburn Theological Seminary, 2002).

180. Schwartz, *Results of a National Survey.*

181. Aleshire, "Governance and the Future."

182. G. D. Lewis, "Governance: What is it?" *Theological Education* 44, no. 2 (2009).

183. Marsden, *Reforming Fundamentalism.*

184. W. C. Ringenberg, *The Christian College: A History of Protestant Higher Education in America* (Grand Rapids, MI: Baker, 2006).

185. Marsden, *Reforming Fundamentalism.*

186. W. C. Miller, "The Governance of Theological Education: A Case Study of Nazarene Theological Seminary, 1945-1976" (Unpublished doctoral dissertation), Kent State University, Kent, OH, 1983.

187. D. T. Highsmith, "The Board of Trustees as Institutional Change Agent" (Unpublished doctoral dissertation), University of South Carolina, Columbia, SC, 1999.

that effectiveness is highest where board members have the greatest ability to understand the institution's mission and purpose as well as broader trends in both theological and general education.[188] Patterson laments that "few board members are trained, or even inspired, to reflect theologically, particularly in the context of the post-modern world."[189] Patterson's work underscores the themes of the broader literature, indicating that an ability to understand and interpret a changing environment is critical. Patterson employs quantitative survey methodology in the study.

Ochola provides a rare exploration of governance in non-North American theological schools.[190] Ochola explores values and aspirations held by board members and faculty members of theological schools in Kenya, determining that there is considerable difference in these two groups' understandings of theological education. The different ideas reflect divergence between internal and external views of the school. Ochola's recommendations include the call for increased training for board members in the area of strategic planning and relationship to external stakeholders. Ochola's work employs a qualitative approach, using structured interviews and content analysis. While the study surfaces many useful points, the broad nature of the approach and the limited number of institutions (two seminaries in Kenya) may limit the applicability of the findings. Both Patterson's and Ochola's findings underscore the importance of an ability to dialogue within diverse learning communities if theological education institutions are to thrive.

Conclusion and Key Questions

The literature on theological education, as discussed above, is one of calls for renewal. Theological schools remain generally slow to change while demonstrating remarkable durability. In recent years, innovation in theological education, particularly in the Majority World, has gathered pace, with an increased sense of clarity of purpose rooted in holistic mission, transformational education, and a prophetic role. It has also become clear

---

188. Patterson, "Theological Boardsmanship."
189. Ibid., 93.
190. J. M. Ochola, "A comparison of values and aspirations of the members of the board of trustees and of the faculty at two theological schools in Kenya" (Unpublished doctoral dissertation), University of Southern Mississippi, Hattiesburg, MS, 2001.

that theological schools are profoundly human ecosystems, where the fabric of human relationships has much to say not only about how the schools is run, but also about what is learned. Increasingly, literature on nonprofit and educational governance has suggested the importance of governing boards moving beyond the fiduciary role to engage in strategic and generative thought. In addition to traditional understandings of fiduciary oversight and guarding and advancing institutional mission, the governing board is critical to the institution's ability to understand and respond in a relevant way to its environment. Based on this understanding of innovation in theological education and a broadened governance role, this study explores the intersection of governance and questions of relevance in theological schools in a variety of cultural contexts. This study observed the governance and leadership of four institutions in Asia, the Caribbean, Eurasia, and South America. It pursued a qualitative approach and focused on the following three research questions:

1. What characteristics contribute to effectiveness of theological school governance?

2. How does the cultural setting of theological schools relate to characteristics that contribute to governance effectiveness?

3. How do governing boards employ insights from internal and external relationships to enhance governance effectiveness?

Through observation of actual practice, this study seeks to better understand how governance is actually taking place in some leading institutions.

4

Listening to Theological Schools and Their Experiences

Within the community of Majority World theological education, discussions of governance have multiplied and deepened in recent years.[1] A general consensus seems to have emerged that *governance matters* to the flourishing of theological education. At the same time, I observed two significant problems in most conversations about governance in Majority World theological schools. First, many presentations and discussions latched onto Western approaches to governing boards, most notably the Carver method, with little thought to how these approaches might (or *might not*) cross cultures.[2] Second, the conversation often seemed to lack substantive reflection on what was *actually* happening in boardrooms of seminaries around the world. This question of what is *really* happening gave rise to this study, a desire to listen in a carefully structured way to the work of governance

---

1. One of the leading centers for this discussion was Overseas Council, which conducted several workshops on the subject of governance as part of its *Institutes for Excellence in Global Theological Education* in the late 1990s and 2000s. Manfred Kohl, long-time Vice President of Overseas Council, had a particular interest in this area and presented many sessions on governance in Institutes, as well as working with dozens of boards of theological schools around the world. In many ways, my own interest in this topic emerged from these activities. Unfortunately, there has not been a significant amount of overlap between these conversations and the broader and deeper conversation and research on governance in North American theological education.

2. When the question of cultural appropriateness did arise, it tended to emerge in a zero-sum sort of way, rather than in a way where the merits of western approaches could be contemplated in dialogue with the contextual realities.

in Majority World theological schools, particularly to theological schools that were perceived by their peers to be practicing good governance.

Because of the diversity of governance function in Majority World theological schools, this study attempted to gain insight from as wide a sample as possible. Available time, language skills, and financial resources made it necessary to delimit the sample of institutions surveyed. It is estimated that there are well over six thousand Protestant theological schools in existence worldwide.[3] These institutions exist in nearly every nation, taking very different forms based on political, social, denominational, and other variables. This study of necessity focused on only a few of the thousands of theological schools in existence.

The study employed careful, structured listening to and observation of theological schools and their work. In technical terms, a research methodology called structured grounded theory was employed.[4] This methodology was chosen in part due to the relative lack of descriptive or theoretical work on governance in theological education outside of the North American context and the relatively limited state of such work in North America. The project pursued a series of structured interviews with participants in the governance process at four theological schools in Asia, Eurasia, South America, and the Caribbean. In addition to interviews, the study also examined historical documents, including board minutes, and structured observation of the work of each theological school and its board. Additional details on the methodology of the study, especially how the institutions were selected, are included in Appendix A. Interview protocols that guided interviews and observations are also included in appendices.

---

3. J. Ferenczi, *International Directory of Theological Education* (Chicago, IL: American Theological Library Association, 2001). This directory is now hopelessly outdated. It always suffered from a poor definition of what constituted a "theological education" in the first place. More recent attempts at a directory can be found at http://www.evangelicaltrainingdirectory.org/ and http://www.globethics.net/web/gtl/directory.

4. Qualitative research methods are, in my experience, not well known in the world of theological education, yet present a powerful opportunity for examination of and improvement of our work. The literature on qualitative research is immense. My work in structured grounded theory was guided by Corbin and Strauss (*Basics of Qualitative Research* [Los Angeles, CA: SAGE, 2008]); Cresswell (*Qualitative Inquiry and Research Design: Choosing Among the Five Traditions* [Thousand Oaks, CA: SAGE Publications, 2007]); and Marshall and Rossman (*Designing Qualitative Research* [Thousand Oaks, CA: SAGE Publications, 2006]), and informed by intercultural communication theory such as Hall (*Beyond Culture*) and Hofestadt (*Culture's Consequences*).

Limitations of the Study

This study was limited by a number of factors. First, it focused on only a few institutions which are not fully representative of the global whole. The researcher addresses this limitation by consulting with organizations such as ICETE, OCI, the Association for Biblical Higher Education (ABHE), and ATS in the selection of institutions to be studied, drawing on these organizations' expertise to identify institutions that provide the greatest potential for other institutions to benefit from the lessons learned.

A second limitation of the study was the researcher's leading role at the time in an organization, OCI. This position led to the expectation that the researcher would have a well-developed relationship with likely research subject institutions. This could be perceived to be at once an asset and a potential limitation. It was perceived as an asset in that the researcher has preexisting relationships with many seminary leaders. The potential for limitation existed primarily due to OCI's role in providing funding to theological schools. This was perceived to be a potential impediment to full disclosure during the research process. At the same time, the disruptive potential of this limitation was perceived to have lessened in the past decade, due to OCI's increased focus on training. This limitation was lessened by the fact that OCI is frequently invited by theological schools around the world to consult and train on subjects of board governance and other matters.

A third limitation of the study related to the researcher's North American identity. Influential work in sociology, anthropology, and other disciplines has questioned the ability of researchers from more economically and politically powerful contexts to truly understand the discourse of post-colonial or marginal societies.[5] In the context of this study, the researcher was both an outsider in other cultural contexts as well as the representative of a national group that has traditionally held disproportionate power and influence, especially in Majority World institutions of higher education and particularly theological education. While it was impossible for the researcher to set this limitation aside completely, careful attention to communication and negotiation of entry was given in order to help to limit the liability. Intentional

---

5. E.g. E. Said, *Orientalism* (New York: Vintage, 1978).

efforts to build rapport,[6] the researcher's "careful deployment of the self,"[7] and use of ethnographic techniques[8] were employed to further alleviate this challenge. Recent work in the field of anthropology, while assenting to the challenges that Said and others have pointed out, affirms that meaningful research can occur in the presence of the correct attitudes and procedures.[9]

A fourth limitation of the study related to the interviewing of persons of considerable influence. Theological school presidents, and especially board chairpersons, are often highly respected, elite members of society. As such, they are often extremely busy people and difficult to access. Once issues of access are overcome, interviews with elites can be difficult in and of themselves, as elites are often more concerned about preserving face and presenting a good image of the institution(s) they represent. While the researcher did not encounter difficulty in obtaining access to these elite subjects, careful attention was given to drawing on the wisdom of research in the area of interviewing elites.[10]

The Institutions

This study involved four theological schools in Asia, Eurasia, South America, and the Caribbean.[11] Two were English-speaking, one was Portuguese-speaking, and one was Russian-speaking. Three were broadly and explicitly interdenominational programs drawing students from a variety of evangelical

---

6. J. P. Spradley, *The Ethnographic Interview* (New York: Holt, Rinehart, and Winston, 1979).
7. Marshall and Rossman, *Designing Qualitative Research*, 77.
8. M. H. Agar, *The Professional Stranger: An Informal Introduction to Ethnography* (San Diego, CA: Academic Press, 1980).
9. E.g. J. Borneman and A. Hammoudi, eds., *Being There: The Fieldwork Encounter and the Making of Truth* (Berkeley, CA: University of California Press, 2009).
10. E.g. Marshall and Rossman, *Designing Qualitative Research*; T. Odendahl and A. M. Shaw, "Interviewing Elites," In *Handbook of Interview Research*, ed. J. F. Gubrium and J. A. Holstein (San Francisco, CA: SAGE, 2001); K. J. Delaney, "Methodological Dilemmas and Opportunities in Interviewing Organizational Elites," *Sociology Compass* 1, no. 1 (2007); W. S. Harvey, "Methodological Approaches for Interviewing Elites," *Geology Compass* 4, no. 3 (2010).
11. The original scope of the project envisioned inclusion of six-seven institutions, including at least one in Francophone Africa. I had also intended to include one institution in North America and one in the South Pacific as a means of comparison. Ultimately, time limitations made this impossible. I especially regret that lack of an African institution in the study sample.

churches. The fourth was a denominational seminary wholly owned by a large denomination yet accepting students from a variety of backgrounds. All offered programs at the graduate level (in the North American sense). The institutions ranged in age from 17 years to 55 years.

Because of the confidentiality of the institutions surveyed, citations will be handled using coding. Each of the four schools will be referenced numerically (S1, S2, S3, S4). Individual interviews will be cited using the school number, an interview number (I1, I2, I3, I4), and the position of the person being interviewed. Observations and minutes will also be cited using school numbers. In a few cases where it is deemed appropriate due to sensitive input, only the school number will be cited.

S1 is an 18-year old institution located in the capital city of an Asian country where Christianity has centuries of history, yet composes only a small minority of the overall population. S1 trains more than 650 students in a variety of programs ranging from certificates to master's degrees. Instruction is offered in several languages. The seminary is broadly interdenominational and serves students from a range of evangelical churches in the country. During his visit, the researcher observed a well-attended board meeting that took place on a non-Christian religious and national holiday from breakfast time through early afternoon. The researcher also interviewed the board chairperson, who has served with the school from its inception, as well as the CEO, who had served in his post for more than ten years. In addition, the researcher interviewed a faculty member serving as interim academic dean and the head of the department of development. Minutes from the previous three years were examined. Since no printed history of the school exists, the researcher reviewed Annual Review Documents submitted by S1 to OCI since the late 1990s. These annual reports provided background on the historical development of the school. The researcher spent three days on the campus of S1 in January 2011.

S2 is a 55-year old theological school located in the heart of a major South American city. Over five hundred students are enrolled in the school's various programs, ranging from continuing education programs to master's degrees. S2 is a denominational seminary, belonging to one of the larger denominations in the country and maintaining ties with sister denominations around the world. Although the school is denominational, students come from a variety of backgrounds. Like many schools in South

America, S2 is non-residential, serving students primarily from the expansive metropolitan area where it is located. All instruction is offered in Portuguese. The researcher conducted four interviews during his visit with the CEO, the dean, the director of development, and two long-serving board members, including the chairperson. Because of a logistical challenge, the interviews with board members took place together and a significant amount of this time was spent in exchange between the two members, therefore yielding less data than had been hoped. The researcher also observed a well-attended board meeting that began in the morning and concluded over a late lunch. In addition, minutes from the past three years were analyzed. Since no written history of S2 exists (with the exception of several paragraphs on the school website, which were analyzed), the historical background of the institution was explored at length over dinner with the president and his wife on the first night of the visit. The researcher visited S2 for three days in March 2011.

S3 is a nearly 20-year old training institution located in a secondary city of a post-communist European nation. S3 trains 346 students in a variety of programs up to the master's level. In 2002, the institution took on the name "Christian University" in order to stress broader offerings, although the majority of students continued to study in primarily theological disciplines. All instruction is in Russian. Full-time residential programs (Russian: *ochnye programmy*), which at one time composed all course offerings, now constitute a very small portion of students, with most involved in modular studies (*ochno-zaochnye programmy*). S3 has a strong relationship with a denomination but exists as an interdenominational school, drawing students, faculty, and board members from several denominations. The researcher observed a well-attended board meeting and interacted informally with board members over meals and other social gatherings. He also conducted interviews with the CEO, the board chairperson, the development director (who previously served both as CEO and chairperson), and the academic dean. Minutes from the past three years were reviewed, as was a five-page written history of the university, produced in 2005. Analysis of data revealed a very strong set of concepts that resonated across all interviews, observations, and documentary reviews. The researcher found that the conceptual similarities and even vocabulary similarities across the various inputs were strongest at S3. I spent three days on the campus of S3 in April 2011.

S4 is an exclusively master's-level institution serving the Caribbean region. The school recently celebrated its 25th anniversary. S4 was founded as a graduate studies center aligned closely with a bachelor's-level denominational seminary. Although the two institutions were once led by the same person, they have grown apart through the years and now have separate administrations. S4 trains 143 students in a variety of graduate programs. All instruction is in English. The institution is explicitly interdenominational and is owned by a regional body. The vast majority of students study in programs not centered on traditional theological disciplines. Plans are in place to transform into a university. The researcher conducted four interviews, including the long-time chairperson, the CEO, a long-time staff member who now oversees the development division, and the head of finance. In addition, he attended and observed a board meeting that took place on the S4 campus. The board meeting included only four non-staff members of the board. Others were absent for a variety of reasons. Minutes of varying formats from meetings over the past three years were reviewed. Since no printed history of the school exists, the researcher reviewed Annual Review Documents submitted by S4 to OCI since the late 1990s. These annual reports provided background on the historical development of the school. The researcher spent three days at S4 in May 2011.

Summary of Results

The nature of qualitative research is such that the task is never complete. Like all qualitative researchers, the writer acknowledges the influence of his own worldview and categories on the analysis. Despite this, the qualitative research process has surfaced a number of emergent categories that are firmly grounded in data at multiple schools. These data help to bring an answer to the first research question, namely *what characteristics contribute to effectiveness of theological school governance?* Although a myriad of themes and concepts can be found in data from individual schools, six predominant categories emerge that are expressed in some form in each of the institutions studied. These categories influence in a significant way the exercise of governance authority within the communities of the institutions studied. It is my contention that these six categories serve as foundation stones of effective governance in theological education. It is not a simple checklist, but rather a complex interrelationship among the various elements that ultimately contributes to effectiveness. The six categories are:

1. The development of **a community of trust.** Although this category emerged most clearly in S2, it is present in some form in all four institutions. This category suggests that presence of a fabric of relationship and trust (or lack thereof) within the institution and a sense of commonality in accomplishing the task of mission. These usually expressed themselves in respect for and trust of leaders (especially CEOs) and board. An equally important aspect was expression of trust and support *by leaders* for their staff, faculty, and board members, *across the fabric of the community.*

2. The presence of **alignment.** Closely related to community of trust, above, this idea was strongest at S3. This category indicates not only the presence of trust and relationship, but also the interaction of various people and structures within the educational institution in a unified pursuit of mission. This expressed itself in unity between the perceived needs of the context, the explicit academic curriculum, as well as the hidden and null curricula.

3. The presence of **strong, enabling leadership.** This builds on points 1 and 2. In each case, the "system" of alignment of the various parts of the organization was in all cases dependent on a strong, enabling CEO figure. It was not merely the presence of strong leadership, or even strong, enabling leadership, but rather the exercise of strong, enabling leadership in an aligned community of trust.

4. The presence of **a shared commitment to education that transforms.** This was expressed through at least three key concepts: a commitment to worldview change in students, a commitment to empowerment of students as agents of gospel change in lives, communities and societies, and a dedication to the unity of knowledge, belief, and actions in the educational process. Although these categories are firmly grounded in the data, the terminology used is drawn from a number of theoretical works, including

Bosch,[12] Mezirow,[13] Freire,[14] Cranton,[15] and Hiebert.[16] Again, the relationship of this category to 1, 2, and 3 was mutually reinforcing.

5. The presence of a **reflective and responsive interaction with the surrounding community/society.** Although this category emerged most clearly in S1, it was visible in a significant way in all four institutions, evidenced by awareness of and concern for broader social and cultural issues, presence of interaction with a variety of both direct and indirect constituents of the theological school, and expression of influence of this awareness and concern on the forms of education and administration practiced by the school.

6. Finally, the data revealed **the importance of planning for the future, especially for succession.** This category emerged most strongly in S4, where categories of transformative education, trust, and responsiveness were present, yet stymied by a lack of alignment among the various parts of the institution. This could be traced in large part to a prolonged transition from a long-term leader through an "interregnum" to the present leadership. The danger of such a transition was also present in S2.

The following six chapters will take each of these major themes in order. Each chapter will draw heavily on "the voice" of the schools themselves in the form of primary data gleaned from interviews, documents, and observations during the research visit.

---

12. Bosch, *Transforming Mission.*
13. Mezirow, *Transformative Dimensions.*
14. Freire, *Pedagogy of the Oppressed.*
15. Cranton, *Understanding and Promoting Transformative Learning.*
16. Hiebert, *Transforming Worldviews.*

5

A Community of Trust

The language of manufacturing and production has crept into discourse concerning mission in general, including the world of theological education. The focus on numeric measures of success, often expressed in the number of "decisions" or "conversions," has left a lasting imprint on the church.[1] This influence has found its way deep into the world of theological education, particularly in broad thinking about "leadership development." I have, in the course of my career, been involved in several projects that have tried valiantly to ascertain "leadership needs" in a given part of the world in terms of a number of people needed at various "levels of leadership." Conversations and projects around the development of theological faculty in various disciplines (and increasingly, sub-disciplines) tend to focus on slotting the person with the right degree into the right slot. These are undoubtedly useful and even necessary exercises.

My concern arises, however, in that such exercises *can* result in a narrow and reductionistic understanding of institutions and the educational process. A focus only on the constituent *parts* of an institution can lose track of the ethos and values that unite the whole. This concern is echoed strongly in the literature on theological education that expresses concerns for the hidden or implicit curriculum.[2] This concern also arose in the institutions considered in this study. Each of these institutions was much more than a sum of individual

---

1. This is a complex subject in mission as well as in Christian philanthropy. Increasingly, the conversation has turned a bit away from a focus *only* on numerical measurements of conversions or people trained to one that takes seriously growth of discipleship and the eventual positive social impact of the church. In many ways, these changes have been grounded in the work of Bosch (*Transforming Mission*).
2. Cf. Shaw, *Transforming Theological Education*.

parts; they were chiefly and essentially *communities of trust*. This category emerged most strongly in S1 and S2. Although this category was present as a significant theme in S3 and S4, I will focus primarily on the context of the Asian and South American institutions. This community of trust proves essential to another major category emerging from the data, *alignment*, which will be taken up in the following chapter and draw more on S4 and, especially, S3.

The presence of a *community of trust* was a foundation stone of governance effectiveness in the theological schools explored in this project. Three of the four schools demonstrated the presence of such a community of trust in a variety of ways. Even the fourth school, which was emerging from a significant and painful period of transition, displayed both the presence of such a community in the school's past and a desire for the reestablishment of this community in the future. The community of trust evidenced itself in two important and interlocking ways in each school. First, there was a strong respect for the positional and authoritative power of the board, the CEO, the management team, the faculty, and the staff, all in their own respective positions. It was understood that the board held the final juridical and governing authority over the institution. It was generally understood as well that the CEO was empowered by the board with full authority to oversee the administration of the school in the light of board oversight. Second, there was a fabric of trust that transcended the power or authority of any one position. With the partial exception of S4, the schools did not display meaningful tension between the CEO, management team, board, and faculty. Rather, there was a respect and trust expressed in each of these institutional body parts to accomplish their tasks, relying on other parts to complement them. The suggestion of the presence of a community of trust in these places does not mean to imply an idyllic relational state. Every school provided interview data that suggested frustration existing between various parts of the institution. This frustration, however, was generally productive in nature, leading to conversation or even conflicts that helped to propel the institution forward. This idea of a community of trust aligns well with several frameworks/themes in the literature on theological education and governance, including the idea of theological schools as ecosystems and the human aspect of life in theological schools. It also affirms the strong focus on relationships in governance present in the work of Scott[3] and Stahlke,[4] among others. It also aligns markedly with the discussion of governance in theological education in Aleshire.[5]

S1 – "A Community from the Beginning"

The category of *community of trust* emerged strongly at S1, appearing in interactions with the board, CEO, management, faculty, and staff. This expressed itself in a strong sense of community, expressions of and actions based in humility on the part of leaders, and general climate of dignity and respect. While there was clear respect for the unique functions of each role, people in various positions within the institution related in ways that are at once biblical and institutionally effective. A strong sense of community was repeatedly visible on the campus, from the free and convivial interaction of the board with staff members during a pre-meeting breakfast to the observed groups of students mingling with professors and staff members during break times. This appeared to be a function both of deliberate management action to create such an environment through policies and personal leadership influence that set the tone for such an atmosphere, as well as a genuine spirit of bottom-up community. The two appeared to the outside observer to be mutually reinforcing elements that gave S1 a strong sense of cohesiveness and congruence. Reflecting on what sets S1 apart from other organizations in the country, the chairperson said "We have to demonstrate the body of Christ in every Christian structure, the church and parachurch. The board must demonstrate the body of Christ. The faculty must demonstrate the body of Christ. We can't have parties fighting" (S1–I2 chair). There were numerous indications that this ethos had been present from the inception of the organization.

A strong sub-theme of respect and humility on the part of leadership emerges at S1. Although this was visible and perceived from the executive leadership, it was also evident in a number of ways regarding the board and board leadership. The board chairperson, reflecting on his own role, spoke

---

3. Scott, *Creating Caring and Capable Boards*.
4. Stahlke, *Governance Matters*.
5. Aleshire, "Governance and the Future."

of the large number of capable leaders who are in place at this school, both in the board and in executive leadership. This presence of a large number of capable leaders allows him to focus on issues of guarding the ethos of the school and assuring its responsiveness to context. "If we didn't have capable leaders, I wouldn't have been chairperson in fact, because I wouldn't have been qualified to be chairperson" (S1-I2 chair). Asked further about his role in preparation for the meeting, he shared that "I have photographs of all the board members where I pray. I pray for each. I ask that God would help us to come up with right decisions. I suppose the only preparation I do is praying. Everything is done by these people" (S1-I2 chair). This humble and trusting approach to leadership is perceived from staff members as well. During an interview, the development director stated:

> It's difficult not to be excited by the ethos and personalities of the leaders. I report most directly to [the CEO], but also each and every member of the council. What I've learned most is the humility of spirit. They are able to move with different types of people and at different levels. Their passions have inspired me tremendously. (S1-I4 development)

This sub-theme of humility was abundantly clear during the board meeting itself when the board and members of staff and management joined together for a breakfast. During the tea break, almost all of the conversations in the room included board and staff together, not huddles of board and staff in separate conversations. Honored leaders such as the CEO and chairperson were the first to join in such conversations, with the chairperson engaging in conversation with secretaries and servers. This was also visible in the minutes, where the single most frequent category of minute involved questions of personnel and staffing, whether appointments, dismissals, care for current staff, or honors.

Although the interview data from S1 demonstrated the concern for empowerment and dignity among board and management members, board meeting observation data also demonstrated amply ways in which this vision is carried out in the daily life of the school through the exercise of care for staff, faculty, and students and for the surrounding community. Both the minutes and the board meeting observed showed evidence of deep concern on the part of the board for the just and fair treatment of staff members.

Perhaps the most compelling case was a subject of considerable discussion at the observed board meeting, relating to the pending retirement of an aged, long-term staff member who was for health reasons no longer able to serve. Concern was shown not only for fair treatment of the employee, but for what this treatment would demonstrate to non-Christian members of the surrounding community. This seemed to be a moment of deeply biblical and countercultural witness, demonstrating to the internal and external community the value of a human life. The minutes gave evidence of a gift given to another departing long-time staff member, helping her to settle near her children in a Western country. Another significant demonstration of this was the formal photograph of the board meeting, which the researcher understands is done at each meeting. The photo was not a formal, posed picture with the chairperson seated in the center, as would be customary. Rather, it was a rather informal, slightly raucous gathering of all the board members, guests, and staff members in the corner for a commemorative photo. Even the man who prepared food and tea for the group was included, standing next to the respected chairperson.

S1's pursuit of empowerment and dignity sets up a visible tension between a deep desire to be part of and responsive to an Asian context that is their own while at the same time speaking truth against cultural norms that are deemed to be counter to biblical teaching. The board minutes and observation of the board meeting indicate that S1 places a very high value on ceremony and especially on honoring those who serve well. Significant attention is given in the minutes to the importance of graduation and other ceremonies at the central as well as extension campuses and the value and benefit of the presence of board members to those events. Great care is given to show honor and respect to those who are completing their work on the board. This deference and value for ceremony is something that is at once resonant with the local culture and with biblical values. At other times, S1 takes a much different approach, as discussed above. In both their program structure and educational methods, the school is willing to question long-held social norms and beliefs if they are deemed to be in contrast to the Christian life, yet all of this is deployed simultaneously for the good of the nation. This interplay was also visible in the board meeting around the role of the chairperson, who arrived approximately one hour into the board meeting after an overnight flight. Although the chairperson took pains to avoid drawing unnecessary attention, he was promptly served a cup of tea by a staff member. This productive tension between respect for leaders and those same leaders' humility in the exercise of their duties further illustrates the ongoing nature of this process.

A final sub-theme at S1 in the area of community and relationships was the presence of a strong and capable team and a spirit of teamwork and trust. Even the founding of the school, as recounted by the chairperson, occurred only when a team embraced the vision for the school. Previous attempts by individuals to begin a school had failed. The beginning of the school, according to the chairperson, "was very fellowship based . . . it was unusual all of these people coming together and saying *yes*, we need it . . . amazing cooperation within the body" (S1-I2 chair). This was also born out in S1's 1997 report to OCI at the inception of the partnership between the two organizations. "There has been an amazing demonstration of how Christ unites diverse peoples exhibited in the [S1] community. This is a much needed witness to a strife-torn community of how the kingdom of God can unite people" (Annual Review Document, 1997). This spirit of working together at the board level remains strong, as this self-perpetuating board continues to seek people of competence, character, and respect who can ably represent a diverse constituency. This was visible in the conversation observed during the board meeting, which focused on serious topics, insights from board member's own lives and experience, all interspersed with storytelling and a spirit of humor. A spirit of trust continues between the management, especially the CEO, and the board. The word "camaraderie" appeared several times in observation field notes. Reflecting on his relationship with the board, the CEO said, "I have learned the value of reporting the good and the bad . . . [so] that they trust what I am saying is not filtered" (S1-I1 CEO). The same spirit of teamwork has strengthened among the management in recent years. During his interview, the CEO shared that:

> The greatest joy I think is coming to a place where I feel that our leadership team is more or less complete, something that I have been working on since I started, but never felt we got all the right people in the right positions who know what their task is, so I used to have to double up, and the stress level was very high. (S1-I1 CEO)

Yet today, the sense is that the competence of the management and faculty team is high. Reflecting on this point, the chairperson stated "A lot of our thinking, for example, [a faculty member] whom you know, he's a genuine thinker . . . these kinds of people will really influence the direction of the school a lot" (S1–I2 chair). The development director echoed this. "The in-house faculty [are] so diverse, from professor [a term applied to an elderly and highly respected faculty member] to, well, everybody else . . . I see that they continue to bring in fresh ideas" (S1–I4 development). To an outside observer, this spirit of teamwork and trust was evident throughout the institution and clearly serves as a strong foundation for their work.

S2 – Community Forged through External Pressure

The historical context of the development of S2 has heavily influenced the current shape of the school as well as the leadership style and practices of the CEO. S2 was founded fifty-five years ago with heavy involvement and support from a North American sister to the national denomination to which S2 belongs. This post-war period was a complex one in evangelical history with emerging tensions between fundamentalist and more neo-evangelical streams of thinking. Both streams were at various points present and dominant in the history of the institution; however, this tension came to a head in the late 1980s when a CEO of more fundamentalist approaches was appointed to lead the school. This new CEO was appointed only part-time and continued to serve in other positions. The current CEO was at the time of this appointment serving as dean, and due to the newly appointed CEO's frequent absences, continued to give day-to-day leadership to the school. After several years, the tensions of this leadership became too much and the current CEO/then dean left S2 to pastor a church in another part of the country. Interviews with both the current CEO and current board members who served at that time confirmed that the early 1990s saw a rapid decline and stagnation of S2, with a steep fall in enrollments, deterioration of the school's valuable property, and overall disenchantment of staff and faculty (S2–I1 CEO, S2–I4 board). The school entered into a period of deep crisis.

At this point, the board of the school, whose members were appointed by the larger governing body of the national denomination, realized that S2 had entered into a terminal spiral if the situation did not change dramatically.

The current CEO, who was at the time pastoring elsewhere, was respected among the board members, staff, and faculty of the school at the time due to his decade-plus of leadership as dean and faculty member. He was called back and appointed as CEO of the school. Both he and two board members at the time recalled a conversation in which the board said to him "you need to run the school; we don't know how" (S2-I1 CEO, S2-I4 board). He accepted the role under certain conditions. In his words,

> At that moment, I was honest with them, and I said "listen, if you see that this institution is not starting to function the way it should, just fire me, and don't keep talking behind my back." So, we have to develop a relationship of trust; if you don't trust me, please let me go, don't continue in a relationship where we don't have trust. (S2-I1 CEO)

At this point, the newly appointed CEO set out to "establish a leadership that is trusting and sustainable" (S2-I1 CEO). The situation began to change and the school has continued to grow and mature to its current state. Other data from interviews, observation of the board meeting and the culture of the school, and review of minutes suggested that this trust is a central feature of S2. An enormous (though not unquestioned, as discussed later) trust is placed in a capable, proven leader who has overseen growth of a strong institution. Although such CEO-centric models are not uncommon, S2 may differ from others in that the CEO does not dwell easily in this trust and continues to submit himself and his plans/vision to scrutiny from the board and input from his team. The CEO himself describes this as "a relationship of trust that has to do with the history we've built through the years" (S2-I1 CEO). This atmosphere of mutual trust forms the bedrock of the organizational culture of S2.

Data suggest that there is a strong relationship of trust that undergirds the governance relationship at S2. The CEO and his senior staff seem to have a deeply trusting relationship, and the board demonstrated repeatedly a willingness to support the CEO in his work, even when major and potentially unpopular decisions were being made. The board is generally seen in terms of "support" for the work of the management team. Neither the board nor the staff seemed to feel a strong sense of the board's ability to contribute meaningfully to original ideas or conversation. Rather, their role was a fiduciary one, one where the staff members report, albeit very openly, and in turn get the full support of the board. This situation has proven remarkably effective over the course of a long and successful presidency. Yet it is unclear that such dynamics can survive a significant change in the system, especially a pending leadership transition as the CEO nears retirement. Because of the combination of the CEO's well-deserved stature with the board and the broader community and the board's relative lack of involvement in bigger issues, this retirement poses a potentially destabilizing challenge. Asked about this potential challenge, the CEO recounted several steps that have been taken to think about succession/successors. He indicated, however, that the board had shown little interest in this topic, deeply pleased with the current state of affairs. While the presence of a strong and abiding trust relationship in the governance of S2 was visible, so were growing concerns about how this might outlast the current CEO's administration. Although the CEO of S2 was not depicted as a man who intentionally gathered power to himself in an authoritarian way, he has, nonetheless, clearly gathered unto himself an enormous amount of respect and influence bred in the context of proven leadership through difficult situations. While this trust has proven durable, serious questions arise when the dynamics shift in transition. This vulnerability in the face of inevitable transition appeared to be the key challenge facing S2 in terms of governance.

Conclusions

Trust was the first and perhaps the primary building block of governance effectiveness in the schools studied. Most of these institutions had experienced a crisis period in their organizational life. In each case, a profound lack of trust was interwoven into this crisis and often remained as a pervasive shadow on the organization for years. This was also visible in the structure of the various boards. Although their background, method of appointment, and means of function differed, the boards of S1, S2, and S3 all demonstrated a bond of trust. This suggests that while structures are important, the culture of human bonds that indwell these structures is far more important to assuring governance effectiveness and broader productivity of theological schools. In many ways, a community of trust provides a meaningful foil to an increasingly conflict-ridden culture. Patty cites a Eurasian church leader, pointing to the increasing challenge of trust in an environment of anger and disinformation.

> There is lots of confusion among young people. There are lots of conflicting values, lots of propaganda that they believe. They are casualties of the information war. Young people are becoming overwhelmed. They don't know whom to trust. Unfortunately, they might trust someone who has power, resources, and means.[6]

Although this quote is specific to the contemporary Eurasian context, it has resonance on a global level. In times of increasingly angry and pugilistic public discourse, the theological school has an opportunity to be not only a source of information, but a sort of example of an alternative community. Elements of this were visible at each of the schools concerned, and it seems to me that these are embers that need careful tending in order to give light and heat in dark times. This presents yet another opportunity for theological school board members to exercise Middleton's concept of boundary spanning, helping to assure not only the proper and legal structures, but also the presence of a community of trust as a foundation stone of effective theological education.

---

6. Patty, "A View of Theological Education," 23.

6

Alignment of the Parts

The previous chapter discussed the presence of a *community of trust* as a foundation of effective governance, particularly at S1 and S2. This involved a united vision, a strong sense of humility and respect, and a focus on dignity and empowerment in each community. In both cases, this sense of community was forged through the experience of building an organization together, often through considerable adversity.

While the community of trust refers to the individual and communal relationships and respect within the context of an explicitly Christian community, the category of alignment refers to the congruity of the administrative actions of the various units of the educational institution. Such an alignment revolves around the institution's explicit and implicit values, as well as a shared commitment to its vision and mission.

This alignment expressed itself in terms of a common commitment to accomplishing mission, drawing on the strengths and skills of various parts of the institution – board, CEO, management team, faculty, staff, and potentially students. Yet alignment goes beyond respecting the various gifts of different sectors. It is evidenced in the congruity of their different actions in governance, general administration, academic administration, and community life. It is evidenced in the *coherence of the overall of life of the school*. This concept arose from and was most clearly expressed in data from S3, where language of "seeing what God is doing" expressed a commitment for ultimate coherence of the school's mission with God's work in the world. Beyond that, it was given expression in a strong desire to see the administration of the school mirror in its activities and values the same humane values that were pursued through the formal curriculum. A wholesale integrity was being sought between the explicit, implicit, and null curricula and in the entire life of the school. The category of alignment also suggests a concern for the broader context and its questions and commitment to responsiveness to those concerns through both formal academic programs and the broader work of the institution. This aligns well with some of the literature on theological education, including Groome,[1] Cannell,[2] and Shaw.[3] It also aligns, again, with the approach to governance of theological schools suggested by Aleshire, particularly his call to "allow information to flow freely."[4]

This category of alignment of the parts arose most strongly in my research at S3, in the Eurasian context. Yet it is a theme that is strongly present in each of the four schools. The interplay between the CEO, the board, and faculty, and the administration was critical to this alignment in each case, although the way in which this played out differed from place to place. This chapter will look especially at the role of the board in "protecting" or "buffering" the organization, especially at S2 and S3. The next chapter will take up the role of the CEO, which in each of the four cases, was critical.

S3 – Rallying around Mission

A key theme at S3 was the alignment of the entire institution around themes of holistic, transformative education. There was considerable acknowledgment that *how* the institution goes about its daily life and administration is as important, if not more important, than *what* is taught in the classroom. There must be absolute integrity between what is perceived from the outside and what constitutes reality on the inside. Reflecting on the situation in the school before his term began, the CEO stated:

> I would also say that the main thing was in my opinion, there was a large amount of attention put on external relations; everything looked great from the outside. There was attention to reports, there were representations (*predstavitel'stva*), there were often prayer meetings . . . students didn't come late to meetings. Students were *never* late to classes. Now students are late. But it

---

1. Groome, "Wisdom for Life."
2. Cannell, *Theological Education Matters*.
3. Shaw, *Transforming Theological Education*.
4. Aleshire, "Governance and the Future," 18.

> became clear to me that this was all built on firm discipline that caused people to hide, that caused people to act a certain way, but lacked internal change . . . I am also in favor of discipline, but this has to be the result of internal processes; otherwise you have obedience without change. This was confirmed when there were several difficult situations among students, difficulties in families or other issues, and these revealed that there just wasn't enough of a foundation (*osnovanie*); everything looked good, but the true knowledge of God (*poznanie Boga*) wasn't there. (S3–I1 CEO)

This integrity came across in interview questions focusing on how S3 was perceived to differ from other organizations in society. According to the chairperson, S3 differs in that,

> There is a strong team of like-minded people (*edinomyslikov*). This is a very strong quality. I think that this is important. So that people are not simply engaged in their own affairs (*dela*), but rather that they are working together. What else? I think that there is also a more open atmosphere here than other institutions. You can do your work in other organizations, but I think here there is a strong relationship with other people. It is possible to see life. Many workers live here on the territory of the campus. This gives opportunity for fellowship. (S3–I3 chairperson)

Such references to unity and integrity in community life were common throughout the interviews, and also appeared in cursory observations of S3's daily life. There was considerable evidence of strong attempts to live out the philosophies and ideas of alignment. The frequency with which this theme arose in both formal and informal conversation was further evidence to the centrality of this question in community life.

The concept of alignment arose in conversations and observations across the organization. While it was clear that the leadership at both staff and board level embraced the idea of alignment in both theory and practice, it became clear that the management played a dominant role in developing and implementing this idea, with the board serving a broader, guarding role. While it was clear that board members were acquainted with the internal realities of S3, this awareness was primarily at the level of *values*. Discussions of both proposed new programs and a proposed new tuition structure revealed that the board deferred largely to the staff in terms of the technicalities of these questions, but expressed concerns in how these initiatives might affect the broader mission and sustainability of the institution. Data generally revealed a degree of ambiguity regarding the board's function and role, its interaction with staff, and even the appropriateness of the idea of board governance to the context. Although this ambiguity concerning roles was a persistent theme, a theme of the board as guardian, enabler, or supporter of leadership initiatives arose consistently. More than at other institutions, the board's role in the overall financial sustainability of the school arose as a persistent theme.

Staff feedback indicated a high degree of respect for the board, both as individuals and as a group. It was clear from both formal and informal interaction that relationships between board, staff, and faculty are strong and go beyond formal roles to personal relationships. There was a distinct lack of clarity, however, regarding the role of the board and the board's performance of that role in pursuit of the overall success of the institution. S3 was the only school in the study where questions arose about the suitability of the board governance model as a contextually appropriate form of administration. One of the staff members reflected on his understanding of the role of the board at length:

> But this is difficult for me to judge... I understand that this [board governance] is a Western model, yes, that was recommended to us as a university. "You must have a board." This is a Western model, it is not what we have in our culture, and we may not even fully understand the role of the board and what it is supposed to do, and the people on the board don't fully understand what they are to do, because at the end, this is not our model of administration (*upravlenie*). It is more like a democratic form, but who should choose the members of the board? Who chooses them? The rector? Now it seems that rector chooses them. [Our president] invites to the board . . . it is not a democratic form. Perhaps it needs to be more like the American system, where there is a big body . . . and they need to choose the board from among themselves and delegate their authority (*polnomochie*). For us it isn't like this, it is artificial (*iskusstvenno*). We don't have that larger body that chooses. In general, I don't have an

answer to the role, since I don't fully understand it. I don't fully understand how it functions in our society. For us as a rule there is a person who is a leader who says what to do. There is a change in corporations. They are building in a Western model. They have investors and boards. They all work toward the end of increasing their money and profits. The board works for the investors, representing them and their money. For us, we've not had that. For me, this is a big question. It is good to see your research, to see how to build the right model of administration (*upravlenie*). (S3-I4 dean)

The fundamental revelation here is of a deep level of ambiguity concerning both the role of the board and even the appropriateness of the board governance model in the context. As the interviewee points out, a more centralized, authoritative model of leadership is prominent in his culture and in many others around the world. Although many of the *forms* of governance have been imported from the West, they remain in a state of continual contextualization. The overall data – including other portions of this interview – did not suggest a desire to pursue a more "traditional" form of autocratic, single-leader governance or a wholesale rejection of the board governance model. Rather, the data reflected a continual concern for appropriateness of the governance model. This was visible in the final portion of the observed board meeting, when the board of S3 engaged in a discussion about their role in a particular situation, which concluded with a decision to review the statutes and by-laws governing the work of the board at the next meeting. Such desires for review and deepening understanding of roles and responsibilities were also expressed by the chairperson in his interview. "We of course have the constitution (*ustav*) for the board, but we need to clarify what we expect our members to do. I think that this is important for the university. There needs to be a greater responsibility" (S3-I3 chair). These data from S3, and to a degree from the other schools, suggested that the question for a "right model of administration" remains a critical central question.

A key phrase arose in several interviews when staff members used variations of a phrase describing board members as "people who understand what we are doing" (S3-I1 CEO; S3-I4 dean). This phrase and accompanying data suggested the import of board members understanding both the vision and the values of the organization. Understanding of the vision, in many cases, seemed to refer to the board's ability to understand, act upon, and bring support to the vision of the management team. One interviewee reflected on perceived differences between members of the board in their ability to understand the vision of the staff. Some, he noted, were better able to do this. He also pointed out that these board members are more capable of bringing necessary financial support to allow these dreams to be accomplished. Another staff member stressed the centrality of management in casting vision and the board's role in defending and supporting it.

> We have an internal, small team that is developing, dealing with both big and little questions, and the board defends this team. Defends in what way? In relation to communication with external constituents, churches, denominations, so that this network was tied together; it seems to me that this doesn't exist often in boards. (S3–I2 development)

This same staff member continued that as the institution has grown more complex, the board members' role has become more detached, more affirmative in nature.

> Now with the development of the university we often see that they are merely *for* something. When we suggest a new master's program, new social projects, other new programs, they merely say "ok," "go ahead," etc. . . . They are more willing to evaluate a proposal, to think about dangers, perspectives, positive aspects, but they are less willing to propose initiatives or take initiative. They are more likely to evaluate, rather than to motivate or stimulate. (S3–I2 development)

This kind of support, however, is invaluable to the team as they execute the vision:

> We receive support for initiatives that all the same are forming here, not in the board, but here in the university. And when we receive this support we can do what we need to do with greater bravery, greater authority . . . beginning new programs, going to the churches, conducting seminars, knowing that all these efforts are supported by key ministers." (S3–I2 development)

As S3 has developed and become a more complex institution, data suggest that the role of the board has become one of affirming and defending the overall vision of the leadership and the vision this group casts.

Although the need for board members to understand the vision of the institution, cast primarily in recent years by the management team, a strong theme was present of need for understanding and willingness to preserve values. Reflecting on the role of the board, the chairperson stated:

> I think that the board needs to understand values, to understand, share, and seek to achieve these values. The board must ask what we can do so that these values, this mission, are accomplished. We need to understand the big idea, the main mission that is taking place in the institution. We can also cultivate these values. We can remind the staff (*sotrudniki*) of this. We can be sure that the programs of the university respond adequately to these values. (S3–I3 chair)

The importance of board understanding both of vision and values was reflected in a comment by the CEO:

> In general, our board has a good composition, they support us. They are a great help to us. They help us when difficult issues arise. I respect our board, they are wise. They are familiar entirely with our values, with what we do. This is important. They are able to present us in front of others. (S3–I1 CEO)

Overall, the board of S3 seemed very eager to engage in such work and an overall commitment to the mission, vision, and values of the institution. The observed meeting included considerable discussion of the need for deepening board members' understanding of roles. The fact that this discussion took place with relatively full participation at the very end of a day-long meeting further indicated board resonance and sense of responsibility for the mission of the institution.

Although this commitment to values and vision appeared to be strong and getting stronger, ambiguity about the role of the board appeared in several areas. At several points in the observed meeting it seemed that staff, board members, or both were in general agreement about direction but were unsure how to proceed exactly. In presenting changes to the modular programs to the board, the dean spent considerable time listing plans, many of which were already in place. He concluded his remarks by asking, "how do you find this idea in general?" (*kak vam eta idea v tselom?*) (S3 observation). The board then proceeded to give meaningful input, yet the general framework of the conversation was clearly established by the staff, potentially limiting space for board engagement. Other situations during the observed board meeting that demonstrated that the board, at times, had difficulty making hard decisions or overcoming disagreements among themselves. In considering a potential new academic program, some board members clearly wished to affirm the program, while at least one had significant questions about its sustainability. The issue was not decided, with the CEO stating that he would follow up with board members. Interaction between the researcher and members of the management team of the school several months after the observed meeting affirmed that the issue had been resolved through written communication with and among board members. A final situation concerned the potential increase in student fees for the coming academic year. After a substantial amount of discussion, including useful board member input on economic realities in their churches, it was clear that there was again a divergence of opinion. At this point, the CEO suggested a compromise solution that was immediately and unanimously adopted. These situations together seem to indicate that the board is willing and able to give input, but at times struggles to make this input unanimous and definitive. In several cases, it appears to have fallen to the CEO to reach a final solution to the problem either in the meeting or in subsequent communications.

The research visit to S3 occurred at a time of considerable financial stress in the organization. Perhaps because of this, questions of sustainability and financial matters figured heavily in board discussions. A considerable amount of thought was given, at least in terms of questions, regarding how to sustain the program financially in the medium- and long-term with continued decrease in overseas income. More than in other schools, the leadership of S3 seemed to have an understanding of the role of board members as assuring that financial resources were in place to support the vision and mission of the program. Speaking from the perspective of the development department, one staff member said that there is continual hope that the board will do more to connect them to necessary funding within their context. "This is a dream in every educational institution that someone was concerned about finances, meaning thinking about this from the perspective of representatives of the church or denominations in the board" (S3–I2 development). The CEO spoke more openly of this failure, although ascribed the failure to contextual factors more than failings of the board individually or communally.

> The board doesn't take full responsibility. It isn't because they do not want to, but we have a specific historical situation, they can't carry it – they don't have the kind of financial and human resources to take this full responsibility on themselves. Of course, we have taken from them good advice. They are mostly senior elders [*starshye presvitery*], our local [regional leaders], president of [a key denomination], etc., very high-level people. But they are not able to take on full responsibility. This is my own understanding. (S3–I1 CEO)

Conversations during the observed board meeting suggested that the board members had a growing awareness of this issue and realized that the long-term sustainability of the institution will come from its relationship to local constituent bodies, including the churches they represent. Yet this assumption of full responsibility, including financial responsibility for the institution's mission, continues to develop slowly.

S1 – "According to our Ethos"

Although data from S1 demonstrate clearly that the institution is not averse to changing policies or practices in order to accomplish its mission, it is also clear that the school runs with a strong awareness of its guiding values, principles, and ethos. In reflecting on the history of the institution and some hard decisions made at the board and management level, the CEO repeatedly used the phrase "going back to principles" in describing how difficult decisions were reached. Describing the role and function of the board, the development officer stated that the board is "always about going back to basics, keeping it simple, not getting cluttered. What I find council doing is making us, the students, everyone, looking at what [our school] is, what does it mean to serve the church, who, what, why, how?" (S1–I4 development). The chairperson also pointed to this role of the board, and specifically to his role as chair. "Now I see the board's role more as ensuring that the school runs . . . according to our ethos" (S1–I2 chair). He went on to say that his particular contribution arises from his role as a theologian, working with the academic committee of the board and the broader community to assure the school's theological integrity. Reflecting on the chairperson's role, the development officer remarked "when our chairperson speaks at our annual meeting, it sets the tone for the direction where the seminary is going. Just looking back I see how he keeps bringing us back to basics – the Word and people" (S1-I4 development). This concept of coming back to the basics, of returning to the basic questions of who, what, why, and how surfaced repeatedly, suggesting that S1 is an institution that is at once in constant, creative dialogue with its society while maintaining a firm grip on its grounding values, ethos, and principles.

This strong concern for values, ethos, and principles also expressed itself in a desire to see these worked out in action. There must also be integration of unity of belief, knowledge, and action. This is expressed in comments about the need for "balance" (S1-I2 chair) or the need for "emphasis on what we do" (S1-I1 CEO). Reflecting on the environment and the mission of the school, the chairperson shared "the church talks about power, evangelism, but not so much about character" (S1-I2 chair). Further developing the idea of how this is pursued in the academic program, the CEO stated:

> Our hope is that on one hand we will be providing books and information and Bible knowledge, and on the other hand a person who can lead churches and organizations with these values so these will be taught in our classes – the integration of our faith, works, spirituality with action things like that. That is the whole. (S1-I1 CEO)

When asked practically how he pursues this in his classroom, the CEO continued:

> I stray; I don't always stay with the content that I am always trying in my teaching. Even when I am teaching Hebrew, Greek, I will try to bring in these relationships, of holiness, of society, sometimes I might take a class break but basically talk about something that happened last week or something that was headlined in the newspaper, because I like how Paul says in the Bible how you learn the Word and the World. This is something we keep saying to the students: you must be a student of the Word and a student

of the World. You must have the newspaper and the Bible. These are little sound bites they pick up. (S1-I1 CEO)

The board minutes and the observation of the board meeting also indicated a strong concern for integration in discussions about the publication of quality theological materials on conflict resolution and concern over the shape and form of teaching in the extension centers. Ultimately, the chairperson expresses this concern from the board level, stating his desire to see "a seminary [that] could produce pastors for these churches that would have a balance of the social, the personal, evangelism, etc." (S1-I2-chair)

S2 – The Board as a Buffer

The experience of S2 in Latin America shed light on an important board role that is rarely mentioned in Western literature, namely serving as a buffer between the leadership of the organization and the surrounding environment, including some hostile forces within that environment who may have divergent values and/or vision for the institution. The history of S2 is outlined in chapter 5, providing background to some of the challenges the CEO and board of S2 faced. The foundation for this kind of protective buffer is trust. The board must trust the CEO, and the CEO must in turn be able to be challenged by the board and, in a different way, faculty and staff. Such a trust is not forged quickly or between any group of persons. Reflecting on challenges of governance in theological schools and institutions in general, the CEO of S2 pointed to the *longue durée* of his relationship with his board and team.

> It's a relationship of trust that has to do with the history we've built through the years. One of the differences is that the other presidents are new to the position. They've not had the chance to build this history. They are very effective people, and I always try to help them, but they haven't had a chance to build that story over a long period. (S2-I1 CEO)

It is this relationship of trust, in his view, that allows for truly productive work. Other options are less desirable. Reflecting on the broader situation in his country, he shares the following forms of governance that he sees:

In some cases, the employee has to do what the board decides. But in other places, you find this development of trust. For example, the school in [another city]. The director of that school is treated as an employee that has to have production according to what the board expects. And then there is the president of the seminary in [another part of the county]. He has more freedom. But there is a third possibility. They think that if they share too much with the board about the administration, the board will start interfering. ... [Some other boards are merely] supporting what he is doing. That is the case of the seminary in [another state]. There are some people in the leadership of the [local denominational leadership in that state] that do not like too much the leadership of the school ... So in that case, the board is the kind of board that functions to protect the school. In that paradigm, the leadership of the school just presents a report of what they are doing, and they support it. The fourth possibility is, the board doesn't know what the leadership is doing and the leadership doesn't know either. The school in [yet another city] has that problem. No one knows what they are doing. (S2–I1 CEO)

The CEO makes an important contrast here between a school where the board acts as a protective buffer on the basis of deep trust and knowledge of the school and a school where the board acts as a protective buffer based on very limited knowledge and blind trust of leadership. This depth of trust, according to the CEO, makes all the difference.

The concept of the board providing a protective buffer to the CEO and the school has arisen several times in S2's history. In the early years of the current CEO's appointment, some tensions remained within the denomination regarding the fundamentalist conflicts of the past. As the CEO requested, the board evaluated him on his record and his results, and in return defended him against these outside critics, whose voice diminished as time went by. This protective buffering again became an issue in recent years, when the leadership of the school, led by the CEO, made the decision to pursue accreditation through the Ministry of Education of the national government, an approach that remains contentious among theological educators in this country today. Describing this experience and others, the CEO relates,

Alignment of the Parts 123

> When we had to do accreditation and we were facing that process, many people didn't think at that moment that this was something important, something we had to do. . . . Also, on different occasions, I had to deal with the leadership of the denomination. Before the accreditation, another challenging time was when we were trying to change the constitution in order to be able to open the school for other denominations. At that moment, we had to deal with the conservative side of the leadership of the denomination and tried to help them to see the importance of opening the doors to other denominations. (S2-I1 CEO)

In this case, the board provided not only support to the CEO in this decision, but also active participation in the process.

> The main support that we received, significant support, was especially when we started the accreditation process with the government. The government requires from the board a very concrete participation in the school even the government sees the board as a group of people that really provides support to the school; for the government, it is important that the board is close to the school, helping and supporting the leadership for the school, not something distant. The significant support we received was when the commission came, the board was there; they expressed full support and readiness to help in any way possible. (S2-I3 development)

Staff members reflecting on the role of the board also raised this protective buffer role. The development officer stated that "the first challenge they have regarding the board is to convince them that they are going in the right direction regarding these challenges" (S2-I3 development). The board cannot simply be taken for granted. As in the accreditation case, they will want to be sure that they are supporting the right thing. The dean, reflecting on a similar question, however, stressed appreciatively that the board, "supports us in major decisions" (S2-I2 dean). Some of this was visible in the observed board meeting, as the board members quizzed the CEO on decisions regarding several contracts with outside agencies. While the board ultimately acceded to the management desires, the board clearly desired to be informed about the decisions and the potential implications of such an approach.

Despite these significant moments in the organization's history when the board has weighed in on major decisions in order to give sufficient support, interviews and observations suggest that, in general, the majority of the strategic thinking of S2 is performed by the staff. Reflecting on the role of the board, the CEO stated:

> Since most of the members of the board are pastors, they don't have too much time to spend discussing issues, thinking about the future; they just hear the reports. The leadership team is the group that is making plans and sharing these with them. Most of the time our team gets together, they do the planning and the projection, and present it to the board, and most of the time the board just says go ahead. (S2–I1 CEO)

Data suggested that this situation grows both out of a desire not to engage in a kind of micromanagement that the board has fallen into in the past, as well as the board's lack of full awareness of the inner workings of the school. Speaking to the former, the development director explained that, from his perspective, "The contribution to the school from the board is very superficial, because they do not want to interfere in the day-to-day decisions or things that are done at the school" (S2–I3 development). This commendable desire not to engage in micromanagement was evident across the S2 data. At the same time, the observation of a board meeting indicated that, in general, the board was very minimally informed on many matters of the school's life, such as the current state of S2's struggling music program. This was clearly, at times, a frustration to the staff. Speaking of the challenges of the music program, the dean reflected:

> It would be good for the board to be closer to the leadership, day by day. That would allow them to be more aware of what is going on here, what are the dreams and challenges, what are the future steps that should be done, and even, since most are pastors, to involve their pastors more in what is going on in the school. (S2–I2 dean)

The fact that the board is composed of pastors of denominational churches seemed to be referenced as a point of potential input or boundary spanning, if only such input could be gathered in a productive way.

This tension between too much involvement and too little real knowledge of the situation, alongside the clear role of the board in providing a protective buffer for the school and its leadership during major decisions, contributed to a considerable amount of input on the need for the board to be made fully aware of realities. Reflecting on the role of the board, the CEO reported on some recent changes in board structure that have allowed the board to focus more explicitly on the work of S2 and not some other denominational schools in the same region that had previously fallen under the board's responsibility. Before this reform, time simply was not adequate: "We had a way that the board was functioning was that I had 15–30 minutes to share with the board how the school was doing. But I need at least 2 hours with them in order to do a proper report how things are doing" (S2–I1 CEO). Not only was time an issue, but the CEO at times felt a need to go deeper with the board on an issue than the board itself was willing to go at first, in order to assure support.

> I discussed this with the board and I said that we need to make a change regarding this. The president of the board said no, no, we don't need to make a change, we just need to listen to you and this is enough for us. Then I went back to them and I asked them to gather as a task force to study this situation. (S2–I1 CEO)

This tension was also visible during the observed board meeting. Discussions arose pertaining to some subcontracted issues within the organization. During the discussions, several board members made statements to the effect that "this is a management decision, you need to make the decision and we will support you." The CEO, however, continued to circle back over the issue. This was seemingly in a desire to assure that the board fully understood the situation at hand and was in turn willing to provide a protective buffer if and when these decisions proved politically difficult. Reflecting on why he brought several of these sub-contracting issues to the board, the CEO stated, "I prefer the board to be part of this decision" (S2–I1 CEO). Reflecting on this process, the development director opined that most boards are quite distance from the day-to-day life of the institutions they govern. In such situations, it falls to the "staff to work to *make that distance short* [emphasis added] to help the board to understand and see in which concrete ways they can walk with the school and help the school in this process of growing and expansion" (S2–I2 development). This desire to keep the distance short between staff and board, although visible elsewhere, seemed especially important in the presence of an understanding of the board serving as a protective buffer for the school and its leadership.

Conclusions

If trust is the first building block in the foundation of governance effectiveness and fruitful theological education, alignment of the parts was a clearly adjacent stone, relying deeply on trust, but carrying it to the next level of assuring, through appropriate structures, the coherence of the organization's various parts. This was in many ways the embodiment of the community to trust. Not only was there the presence of trust, but this trust was enabling to the community to accomplish something meaningful together. In a world that is increasingly complex, with an ever-growing number of conflicting messages, the ability of theological school board members, leaders, and faculty to build on trust through building and maintaining strong community alignment stands as a critical task. Much like the presence of trust, the theological school's ability to maintain alignment in their inherent diversity has a powerful potential to speak loudly to the surrounding context, both inside and outside the church.

7

Strong, Enabling Leadership

In chapter 1, I discussed at length the challenges of leadership facing the church and broader society today. If a theme emerged with absolute unanimity across the institutions studied, it was the importance of leadership at the CEO level. All four CEOs shared some common traits and values. All were "strong" leaders, but all realized that they could accomplish far more in working in an enabling way with a team. This presence of a strong yet enabling CEO appears to be an essential element of effective governance. Although all four observed boards clearly took their work of governance and final authority very seriously, it was equally clear that all four relied to a very heavy extent on the competence of the CEO and his team. The generative thinking that has propelled adaptation and development in each of these institutions has generally arisen from the management/staff level and been supported and encouraged by the board. Often, the board has been an enabler or provider of a protective buffer when such innovations were bold or politically sensitive. This paralleled in many ways the governance function of "legitimacy" as defined by Abzug and Galaskiewicz.[1] Three of the four CEOs showed a high degree of influence over the board in its activities, usually through carefully inserted and crafted "rudder" statements or remarks that propel the work of the board forward without assuming authority over it. This kind of interaction produced something that Brown would call relationally strong boards.[2] The careful nature of these statements, complete with occasional inflection of humor, suggests that they are tools employed well in the high context culture[3]

---

1. Abzug and Galaskiewicz, "Nonprofit Boards."
2. Brown, *The Imperfect Board Member*.
3. Hall, *Beyond Culture*.

of most of the institutions observed. Interestingly, this consideration of the CEO role, while frequent in the literature on governance, is not as widespread in recent literature on theological education.

In a similar way, the "strong CEO model" discussed here is also an enabling role, one that draws heavily on the strengths of a surrounding staff and faculty, and seeks to enable and give wings to strengths in this team that the CEO himself or herself may not possess. Perhaps most importantly, the type of CEO observed in each of these schools was the type who understood his (the four leaders in this study were all male) fundamental need for others in order to fully accomplish the vision and mission of the institution. Individual approaches to this varied, with the CEO of S3 demonstrating the strongest enabling role of all. S3 also appeared to be the school most ready for a leadership transition, although none is planned. The characteristic of a strong, enabling CEO does not denigrate or lessen the import of the board. The CEO's enabling role toward the staff in most observed cases also extended to the board as well through careful efforts to provide the board with necessary information, to help staff to speak in language the board could understand, and through careful, respectful steering of conversation. While data affirmed the critical nature of the board to overall institutional function, *it also made clear that the board is only part of the overall picture of effective governance.*

S3 – "De-centered Leadership"

The leadership patterns exercised by the CEO and the management team of S3 were striking. A phenomenon that the researcher came to describe in field notes as "de-centered leadership" seemed to be at work. Although the CEO of the institution was very clearly in charge and highly effective in stewarding both the work of the staff and the board, his leadership style was at once authoritative, yet empowering. This leadership theme appeared in the broader administration as well. Although the difference between this leadership style and that utilized by previous leadership arose in every interview, the staff showed considerable ability to take a *longue durée* perspective, pointing out the ways in which the institution has been stitched together by diverse people over the course of its life. Both formal and informal interactions suggested a strong commitment to fellowship and building of community in a way that is resonant with the educational values discussed above. Overall, there was a consistent theme that the research described in field notes as "people matter." All of this worked together to produce what appeared to be a durable community structure that is seemingly the most amenable to peaceful and effective leadership transition of the four institutions studied.

Although the current CEO of S3 had been involved in the school since its founding and had served as CEO for most of this time, he had been absent for several years to pursue doctoral studies in the West. All interviewed staff members pointed to his departure and return as key moments in the life of the institution. One reported this change as follows:

> When I came here in 2006, there was a change of rector. [One man] was here, then [another]. And then [our current CEO] came back from studies. There was a kind of formation of the team, a reformation of the old team. I think that this was the most serious change in the life of the university. The various leaders interpreted the mission of the university differently. You don't just simply read this, it's a matter of interpretation, and each rector did it slightly differently. Each had their own perspective and vision, and from the perspective of the workers, this influenced the climate of the school, the mood of the team, our relationship to one another, the relationship between the team and the students. (S3-I4 dean)

Reflecting on this same period, the current CEO recalled:

> One of the difficult moments was when I returned after studies the last time, during that time a different team had formed with a different understanding and it was difficult to adapt. I didn't want to make drastic changes, and at the same time, I knew change was necessary. It was difficulty. The first year was especially difficult. The first thing that struck me was a big gap between students and staff, an abnormal thing. There were students, there were staff. It seems to me that the staff wasn't properly serving the students. It even seemed to me sometimes that they were chiefs or commanders [*nachal'niki*]; this was difficult to see. I would also say that the main thing was in my opinion, there was a large amount of attention put on external relations; everything looked great from the outside . . . Not just this, but a kind of cruelty that

> diminishes people, that in the end does not develop respect or trust in him. (S3–I1 CEO)

This reflection helps to point to some of the leadership values that define S3 today. Perhaps most explicit was the linkage between leadership styles and behaviors and the relationship of this to the formation of persons in an educational institution. Again, these data show the strong linkage of all aspects of the institution to the overall goal of holistic formation of leaders.

A key theme arose in several interviews of the importance of creating an atmosphere that is favorable for formation. Reflecting on his views of leadership, the CEO noted:

> There are several components [of leadership] . . . the first, which I stress always is the creation of an atmosphere [*sozdanie atmosfera*] – an atmosphere of mutual understanding [*zaimoponimanie*], of acceptance [*priniatie*], of love, *because in such an atmosphere people can develop correspondingly*. The second, although this is really a first, although I always say it second, it is receiving a defined vision and carrying out this vision . . . I would probably stress these two. The first encompasses sensitivity [*chuvstvitel'nost'*], knowing what God is doing, seeing the strengths of people . . . In this time, we have a strong team, by comparison, with other churches or denominations. In these other organizations, there is such a concentration of people. We have a very strong team. This can be both strength and weakness. In strength, this leads to independence, we know ourselves what to do. In this, the board helps to maintain a balance. It helps us constantly to move forward. (S3–I1 CEO)

Other staff members mentioned this positive "atmosphere" as well. Reflecting on his favorite part of his work, the development director stated:

> My favorite part . . . I think that it is dialogue/discussion in which we participate, thinking about new ideas, when we think about valuable questions, with people who are talented and who have strong positive motivations. All of this happens in a positive atmosphere. (S3–I2 development)

This has in turn led to a kind of creativity that has influenced the shape of the school and its programs through the years. In the words of the dean:

> We aren't afraid to experiment with new forms. Our churches are an open space [*ploshchadka*]; there are no strict written rules that it has to be this or that; there is the idea that there is a person and there is a ministry. . . . (S3-I4 dean)

This atmosphere of openness, understanding, and acceptance has facilitated a creativity that is helping the institution to address some of its pressing challenges.

The CEO displayed behavior in the observed board meeting that further demonstrated the idea of creating an atmosphere of mutual understanding, as well as a climate of productivity. Much like his counterpart at S1, the CEO of S3 was very much in quiet control of the board meeting, constantly observing its progress and trajectory and inserting comments when appropriate to steer it in the right direction. The very level power dynamics of the boardroom enabled this. All participants in the board meeting, including board members, staff, and guests, sat around a large oval table which had been set with numerous snacks. Although the chairperson opened and closed the meeting and the CEO played a key role in facilitating the day's events, the general atmosphere was one of openness and lack of hierarchy. While it was clear that some of the members of the board were highly respected, input was given by all. At several points, the CEO interjected what the researcher labeled in field notes "rudder statements," or insertions in the conversation that clarified or moved the conversation forward. For example, during the academic dean's report, the CEO rather forcefully interjected, requesting the dean to elaborate and clarify a key point about program transitions. While the dean's report had been clear for an internal audience, the CEO clearly sensed that for an external audience (board included), the point was confusing. Another frequent example was the insertion of points of humor in the conversations, at some times self-deprecating humor. This seemed to be an overall mark of the CEO's leadership. These and other CEO insertions helped to guide the conversation through the agenda. It was noted that the CEO's role became more central as the day progressed and the pressure of time and necessity of decisions began to build.

A theme that arose frequently in the S3 data was the willingness and ability of the current team to exist at once within formal, hierarchical structures and at the same time to step out of these roles in the interest of aiding the overall team and mission. The CEO reflected on this in the following way:

> There are also places where peoples' natural gifts and abilities come out. So we have people who work formally in one area, but step a bit into another, simply because he or she has a kind of calling. This is a type of teamwork. I should say that this is what I want to see; I'm not sure what is in reality. (S3–I1 CEO)

Reflecting on the past, the dean affirmed this ability to step out of formal structural responsibilities in order to accomplish the common good.

> Everyone was to do only what was their job. There were very strong borders and frameworks. This led to the feeling that everyone does his own thing, there was no sense of unity *(soobshestvo)*; this is my thing, don't mess in it. That form I personally did not like. It is effective in certain areas. Now we are trying to find a balance between official jobs and this sense of commonality. We see that sometimes in the official organizational chart there is a position that because of lack of funding doesn't exist. This is where you have to go beyond. When I came, it was not written that I'd have to do certain things . . . that I'd have to engage in technical questions, that I'd have to set up tables and chairs. I'm the dean. But, others help me, we help one another. We go and come and help. The general work that we do is done together. (S3–I4 dean)

These statements and others gave strong shape to a balance between a sense of purpose (expressed here as *tselenapravlennost'* or orientation to a given purpose) and the attendant creation of a strong community (*soobshchestvo*). It was because of the shared sense of importance and the shared sense of vision imparted by leadership that people were willing to step out of necessary hierarchical boundaries in order to help respected co-workers achieve common goals. This sense of community was present even in the board meeting, where informal fellowship after the board meeting and over meals revealed a strong sense of commonality.

S2 – "Centralizing Leadership"

The leadership of the current CEO of S2 can be seen in two directions, one downward on the organizational chart toward management and staff, the other upward on the organizational chart to the board. Senior staff members who were interviewed have generally worked with the CEO for a long time, more than a decade, and clearly demonstrate a respect and appreciation for him and his leadership. The dean described her working relationship as follows:

> You can talk about it. If I do a wrong thing I can say I'm sorry. This is a good thing among all the people who are here. This is a good thing, we are able to make mistakes . . . this is good for [our school], this is very important. My daughter is working with a company in [another city] and she doesn't have this kind of relationship with her bosses. This is good here, because we can speak, [the CEO] and I, not in all things we think the same way, but I will do it, and sometime after he can say to me, okay, you made this decision, it was a good decision, if you'd done it like I wanted to do it, it would not have been good. This kind of relationship is very important to do a good job. (S1-I2 dean)

The director of development, who has also been deeply involved in administration of the school, describes the working environment as follows, as distinguished from his perception of other institutions:

> The main distinctive for me is that in comparison with other organizations that have a hierarchical structure, we have a more integral, interdependent structure. It's not that each one or each section functions in an isolated way, they interdependent, each one for each other. With a small group of people, we can manage such a big institution, because we have this exchange, this sharing of resources, sharing of responsibilities between each member of this institution . . . We also try to draw from other organizations and companies in the secular world, ideas or concepts that they use and implement in the way that they manage the school. We are a learning organization, trying to draw from others outside

the Christian world and apply that to the way we operate here. (S1–I3 development)

The CEO is clearly regarded as the central authority of the organization, but the leadership culture remains one of empowerment. In an informal conversation following the formal interview, one of his colleagues described his leadership style as "centralizing leadership" (*liderança centralizando*), as if to suggest that the various activities of the institution draw energy from and revolve around him in an atmosphere of productivity and balance.

The unusual spirit of trust at S2 was forged throughout the period of the CEO's leadership, based in large part on the perceived successes of S2 during this time. It seems that members of the community feel very satisfied with the current vision and accomplishments of the seminary. Although the *person* of the CEO is clearly perceived as critical to the institution, it is his *vision* for the institution that has enabled it to grow and that has served as a foundation for trust.

This centralizing leadership function can also be seen in the CEO's relationship to the board. The board meeting took place in a classroom, with the board chairperson and the CEO sitting at a table in the front facing the other members, staff, and guests, who were seated randomly among rows of chairs. Although the chairperson opened the meeting with a word of greeting, the agenda/discussion was almost completely led by the CEO with the chairperson playing only a minimal role, although it was clear that when he spoke, people listened carefully. The conversations observed were hardly passive in nature. The board members all showed interest in and willingness to raise questions. It was striking, however, that although there was a prepared agenda and book of bound reports totaling over one hundred pages, the conversation did not seem to follow this agenda. Rather, it moved from point to point. One of the staff members, sitting near the researcher in the back of the room, when asked if this was a typical board meeting, responded that it was indeed. "This is a group of people talking to [the CEO]" (S2 observation). Just as it appears that the staff members tend to draw energy from and revolve around the CEO, it seems that the board members, as well, tend to see him as the central figure of the school and understand their role, for the most part, in supporting and enabling him.

S1 – "A Great Sense of Freedom"

This theme of enabling leadership was strongly tangible at S1, including not only the CEO, but the enabling and encouraging work of the board itself. The S1 board is composed of a diverse set of people, including key religious leaders, pastors of large churches, a respected university professor, and Christian leaders from leading Christian families. Yet the observation showed that the power dynamics of the boardroom were very flat. It was clear that the board members knew and respected one another and there was no sense of conflict in the sense of personal animosity. In evaluating the situation, the dean stated that interaction between board members and staff is not unusual outside of the confines of S1, since the Christian community in the country is a "kind of a small village" (S1-I3 dean). The development director agreed, contrasting to boards in other organizations: "I think that they are unusually ... approachable. It doesn't matter how you fit in. They don't think in terms of hierarchy. Every member of the council has been approachable and friendly" (S1-I4 development). Continuing on the unique strengths of [our school] and its board and leadership:

> Compared to institutions out there in [our country], there's a great sense of freedom in working at [our school]. People's strengths are encouraged. It really is a learning institute ... not just the students, but the faculty and everyone is encouraged to learn. [Our CEO] and the council are themselves learners and appreciate that. I think also that [our school] is different that there is a greater culture of appreciation of what we do and who people are. Even people's personal lives and what they are going through. This is very different from corporate culture where it is very cut and dry and mechanical. (S1-I4 development)

Although the learning orientation and approachability of the board was a recurrent theme, appreciation was also expressed for the board's and management team's ability to get things done. In the words of the CEO, "the board are looking at meeting real needs rather than simply going on with what we have" (S1-I1 CEO). A staff member echoed appreciation for their ability to be bold and accomplish things. They have "the ability to turn dreams and visions into something tangible, to translate it into that makes a lot of sense to me and keeps me very excited" (S1-I4 development).

Another powerful sub-theme was the critical role of the CEO in the cultural elements described above and in the organization's overall perceived success. The S1 CEO has been involved with the school since its inception and has served in his current position for more than ten years. Described by chairperson as a "self-starting leader" and "one of the most competent leaders . . . in the country" (S1–I2 chair). Interviewed members of the staff pointed to the CEO as the predominant starting point for change. "From my vantage point, I see it being initiated primarily by [the CEO]. He's always filled with big ideas and visions. He's never content to just let it be because it is fine. I see him being one of the prime people who initiates it and follows it through . . . sees it happen." This leads to a "constant feeling of movement, rather than stagnation . . . [with] visionary people coming and wanting to work in partnership" (S1–I4 development). The CEO himself reflected on the ability to take risks, and to be backed by the board in these risks. He spoke especially of his decision to appoint a female dean who has proven herself extremely capable in a broader culture and church culture where such appointments were not the norm as well as the launching of a development department, another unusual feature in institutions like S1 in this culture. It was clear that the CEO played a significant role in the orchestration of the board meeting, from assuring that a well-organized agenda and report was given to all by his assistant to assuring that the staff reports followed a compelling and logical format accessible to outsiders. Perhaps most importantly, the CEO was deeply involved. The researcher's observation notes included the following: "[The CEO's] eyes are continually moving, looking around him, watching the conversation and its dynamics" (S1 board meeting observation). He frequently gave short bits of input to steer the conversation along toward accomplishment of the agenda. It appeared that the CEO was indeed a linchpin of the function of the board, both enabling them to do their job better and in turn being enabled to run the school effectively.

Conclusions

One of the more glaring commonalities across these four different schools was the presence of a certain kind of leadership. I have used the term "strong, enabling" leadership to title and organize this chapter. At the same time, I have avoided the term "servant leadership," despite my deep appreciation for the rich and transformative stream of thinking that has emerged from Greenleaf's seminal work.[4] While it would be legitimate to argue that servant leadership was at work in each of these cases, or, in other words, that principles of servant leadership had influenced these leaders, something else was also at work. These institutions and their leadership demonstrated a synthesis – a *productive* synthesis – between *strong* leadership that knew where the community needed to go and *enabling* leadership that realized the leader could not drive the community there by fiat alone. I found an echo of what I have in mind in Patty,[5] describing the challenges and opportunities facing theological education in Central and Eastern Europe.

The following is a quote from a Russian theological educator:

> In Eurasia, the predominant thinking is Byzantium with hierarchy and authority of tradition. At the same time, the second paradigm is informed by the invasion of Western way of thinking with democratic, individualistic values. The standard approach is to choose one way or another . . . It seems that one of the innovations most needed is how to blend those two worlds, because going just one way or the other will not work.[6]

This quote, which I believe demonstrates continuity with the kinds of leadership I saw exercised in these institutions and elsewhere, points to the ongoing need to think about leadership, not simply as a product of a Western "leadership industry," but as effective thinking about what it takes to bring about change amidst the complexities of various contexts. The quote above points to the great need for more thinking about how various leadership values – present whether we acknowledge them or not – interact.

---

4. Greenleaf, *Servant Leadership*.
5. Patty, "A View of Theological Education."
6. Ibid., 11.

8

Reflective Responsiveness

Sometimes, reading older literature about theological education, it seems that one is reading about an activity that takes place in complete isolation from the rest of the world. At times, this is a splendid sort of isolation, evoking the best of ancient or medieval monastic life and fervent pursuit of truth. At other times, it seems a frightful dislocation from the crazy, messy world we all live in. I believe that this tension – a tension between very good things – is at the heart of much of the debate about theological education. As the review of literature on theological education in chapter 2 shows, the relationship of theological education to its environment and its *missional* role in this environment has become a central element of understanding theological education, especially in the Majority World. The four institutions studied all exercise this in varying ways.

No institution exists as an island. All theological schools are influenced by broader explicit and implicit societal trends, both inside and outside of the ecclesial world. Data from this study suggest that the ability of these schools to see, interpret, make sense of, and proactively relate to a changing external environment is a critical characteristic of overall institutional effectiveness and specifically to governance effectiveness. All four schools demonstrated a profound, organization-wide curiosity about, awareness of, and care for broader trends in church and society, from concern for developments in majority religious communities in Asia to developments in the secular education sphere in South America to the continuing challenges of family life in the Caribbean. This responsiveness was evidenced across the organizations, from the board to the CEO to faculty and staff. Repeated evidence suggested that this commitment on the part of the CEO of the institution was especially important. *The data even suggest that the CEO is the linchpin in developing and nourishing such a culture of responsiveness.* Board members at all schools clearly shared these concerns and attempted in many cases to draw lessons from their observation of the surrounding culture into their work as board members, a classic case of Middleton's concept of "boundary spanning." The main role of the board members in each of the institutions appeared to be a support for and encouragement of pursuit of responsiveness by the CEO, faculty, and staff of the institution. Again, this characteristic resonates deeply with much of the recent literature on theological education, particularly in its calls for greater interaction with context.[1]

I define reflective responsiveness as an awareness of and curiosity about both the immediate and broader context in which the school operates, as well as the broader context of the Christian church as it relates to non-Christian society. Theological education in this understanding cannot be purely abstract knowledge, but must engage with truly local issues – social, cultural, political, economic, etc. This foundation stone of responsiveness unified the institutions despite their different histories, geographies, and contemporary institutional realities. Reflective responsiveness built upon the community of trust and the alignment of the institution and its structures around values and extended the institution beyond its walls into the broader community. This idea of reflective responsiveness relates closely and deeply to the idea of transformational education, which will compose the subject of the next chapter. This chapter will focus primarily on S4 and S1, with a brief mention of S3, although this theme was present in all four institutions.

S4 – "Christianity Must Go More Than Skin Deep"

The theme of responsiveness was strong at S4. This is visible not only in the interview data, but also in the historical reports that were examined. The current CEO showed an especially nuanced view of the potential of S4 to assist in meeting several long-term challenges in Caribbean society, especially regarding family:

> Family, as you know, is a major issue, has been for two centuries. Certainly after the emancipation in the 19th century, we were provided the opportunity to renew the society; we haven't made

---

1. E.g. Dharamraj, "We Reap What We Sow"; Suazo Jiménez, *La función profética*.

any progress. We still have the same statistic of children born in conditions less than stable for the family. I'm sure you know that this is a major issue. In Sunday's newspaper there was a major story on children at risk, which is based on interviews with people involved in the care for children and people tracking the state of human trafficking. It is really alarming. This is where you begin to create stability, by dealing with children, both in family situations as well as those in state care, of which the numbers are growing. So family, leadership is one issue, which needs a lot of attention, family is another. (S4–I1 CEO)

At the same time, S4 functions in a context with a long Christian tradition and nations where vast majorities of the population affiliate to Christianity. Yet despite this strong tradition, impact has not been what it should be. Real impact "has to do with leadership, it has to do with vision, it has to do with laying out the kind of society that we need to be for the good of all, the way in which [our country] could provide leadership for the rest of the Caribbean" (S4–I1 CEO). Other staff members echoed this assessment of both the realities of Caribbean society and the potential role of the church and the school.

> The challenges are in the whole society; we are known to be a corrupt society, and we are known to be a violent society. There has been an increase in the murder rate to five a day. There is a civil unrest. We live in that kind of milieu. I am conscious that the Scriptures tell us to live with sobriety in this present age. And I think the church has not responded to this call, to live righteously, soberly in the context of what is. We've settled in, rather than changing it. (S4–I2 development)

The chairperson agreed with the need for greater influence of Christianity in "a superficially Christian nation":

> Christianity must go more than skin deep. What extent can the church challenge and how can [S4] help the church to challenge secularism and new ideas that are taking root in society, and saying that the ideas are bogus, and here's why they are ... They [churches] should be able to call on us for research, for counseling, for information, for training. That's a weak area. I don't know who's doing that; it's a wide-open gap. (S4–I4 chair)

In this way, various leaders show an awareness of the vast needs of their region and demonstrate a similar desire for S4 to play an important role in equipping the church for ministry in such a society. This value seems to have been strongly present from the beginning of the school and remains a core of the belief in the school's potential today.

S1 – "Keeping His Finger on the Pulse of the People"

The theme of responsiveness resonated across interviews, board minutes and meeting observation, and institutional history at S1. The institution showed a repeated and deep-seated concern for awareness of and responsiveness to their unique Asian context in contemporary time. This commitment to responsiveness, however, exists in strong harmony with an equally deep commitment to the institution's values, ethos, and theological beliefs. As discussed below, these two play out in creative tension in many facets of the institution's life. This concept surfaced repeatedly in regard to the educational process offered at S1. This process must be able to empower students for active ministry, must result in substantive worldview change, and must facilitate a unity of belief, knowledge, and action.

S1 showed both capacity and passion for the pursuit of reflective responsiveness. Speaking of violence in society, the dean spoke of the need:

> To build that kind of inner humanness with the full dignity of knowing that we are being restored to the full image of Christ, that we are created in the image of God, that we aren't someone's pawns or minions or cheering squad. We are blessed with a beautiful country with amazing resources. When he gave this land to us with all these resources and position in the world, with all this lovely weather.... What on earth are we doing with all this? We are killing each other and hating each other.... Because of the ethnic conflict we have brought in ... courses that directly address these issues of war and peace and what is Christian responsibility in the civic sphere, in the public square, about politics, about public ethics, helping our students for the first time to talk about things that their churches don't necessarily talk about and to look at the Scriptures and find out what is

government, what are Christian responsibilities in a loosely existing democracy? (S1-I3 dean)

This type of feedback was common. It showed a deep discontent with the status quo in broader society, often expressed in stark terms. Yet despite the intractable nature of many of the problems, each conversation was also filled with hope that the Christian church, though tiny, could make a real difference.

All the interviewees, when asked about what S1 can contribute to church and society, mentioned in some form the need for the training of laity who can make a difference in all sectors of society, rather than a more narrow focus on vocational pastoral training. This foundation stone of S1's identity is itself a deeply responsive approach.

> They were trying to get lay people theologically educated to go into the world. This has been another sub-theme that has gone right through our training. So we have a lot of students whose dream is not vocational Christian ministry. That's why we have evening classrooms. [Our city] is a place for this kind of people. We need lay people. I guess these are things we've thought about. (S1-I2 chair)

This theme is also visible in historical documents. In 1999, S1 stated their vision as such: "The [S1] community will be used of God to produce men and women who ensure that the history of [our region] will read differently in the 21st century" (Annual Review Document, 1999). In a similar way, both the chairperson and the CEO pointed to the ability of S1 to respond to its context by its explicit decision to offer training in vernacular languages, in order to empower people unable to study in a more dominant language. Reflecting on this decision, the CEO credited the board: "I think that the people in that stage of the board were very missiology sensitive" on the language issue (S1-I1 CEO). The ability of the school to serve growing charismatic churches also emerged as an issue of responsiveness. "A lot of our faculty are non-charismatic. Most of our students are charismatic," coming from churches that are attracting many of the influential people in society, along with the poor. "I'm very keen that we are a school open to this, that's where God is working, that's where the movement is" (S1-I1 chair). At times, issues such as this have led some in the Christian community to charge that S1 is "held captive to the local church" (S1-I1 chair), yet this is seen by the school's leadership as a positive thing. This responsiveness was repeatedly visible in key decisions that have been made by board and leadership regarding the mission as well as the structure of the school, including decisions about the time of day when courses are offered, the languages of instruction, and elements of the curriculum.

This awareness of the outside world and its impact on the work of theological education was visible not only in broader programs and structures, but also in the lives of individuals in the seminary. The development officer, reflecting on highlights of her service with S1, stated "This constant awareness of what does this have to do with [our nation]? This might work somewhere else, but does it work here? How can we adapt it? This kind of question is always buzzing around" (S1–I4 development officer). The CEO was described by his chairperson as an innately curious man:

> He is one of those people who reads his newspaper and asks what does the Bible say about this? He's very engaged and aware of what is going on. He's the kind of guy who writes letters to the newspapers on national issues. He asks the driver of a three-wheeler [taxi]... keeping his finger on the pulse of the people. It's great to have a person like that who is always asking the question 'what does this mean for the church?' (S1–I2 chair)

This curiosity was even described at the level of the board. The chairperson reflected on the board's role by saying, "Let's talk about how we run our meetings. There's a lot of social, theological, and political discussion that goes on in our board. In other words, we're trying to be sensitive to what is happening in the country. And that will make its way into the policies of [our school]" (S1–I2 chair). Or in the words of the CEO, "People on the board are looking at meeting real needs rather than simply going on with what we have" (S1–I1 CEO). This input, perhaps as much as any gleaned at S1, demonstrates how an inherent curiosity and concern for the surrounding culture has shaped the institution.

For S1, questions of responsiveness to context and the outworking of these questions on the basis of the institution's values, ethos, and principles led to discussion of the educational process itself, both in terms of the formal structure of the curriculum and in the pervasive hidden curricular assumptions about what truly matters in the educational process. In this way, it built very much on the foundation stones of a community of trust and alignment, and began to build a bridge to education that transforms, further linking these into a coherent whole. In the words of the dean, "These students are getting more than information here, really their perspectives are changing" (S1-I3 dean). S1, from the time of its founding, has not been interested in isolation, or even splendid isolation. Rather, This commitment to instilling in students both the institution's core values and the responsiveness that drives the institution were evidenced in ongoing concern for empowerment and dignity, worldview change, and unity of belief, knowledge, and action.

S3 – "Saturated with Mission"

S3 also demonstrated a strong sense of reflective responsiveness. Evidence of this concern for the broader needs of society is evidenced frequently in minuted board discussions. At one point, one board member stated:

> We must focus on the needs of society. We speak more about the needs of the church. It is more creative to think about *mission*. What do pastors think of the preparation of missionaries? Everything in the university must be saturated with mission. [We need to] think more about the world. (S3 minutes, 15 April 2008)

This same responsiveness was visible in the minutes on more modest factors as well, such as the suggestion that serious attention must be given to the geographic realities of their particular region, where people were scattered over a wide geographic area with the majority living in small- and medium-sized villages. Care must be taken to assure that training does not lead graduates to simply abandon these villages for larger cities where opportunities for a better lifestyle are great (S3 minutes, 29 Sept 2008). This responsiveness has taken the form of new programs and initiatives through the years. According to the dean:

> In the last few years, we created new programs, new opportunities. In the last three years, we've had five new programs, no six, over the last three years. Yes, this was a lot of work. But it was positive change. Until this time there were just three standard programs. This was the first attempt to do something more flexible (*bolee legkaia*), mobile, for the churches . . . these *programs arose out*

of the sense of what God is doing [emphasis added]. We look carefully at what God is doing, at the realities of life, and seek to apply. (S3-I4 dean)

This attempt to respond to what God is doing through educational programming is a theme that arose repeatedly throughout the data from S3, ranging from the orientation to questions people were asking in the uncertain atmosphere of the early 1990s to the challenges of geographic space and demography in the early twenty-first century.

Conclusions

The idea of reflective responsiveness is hardly novel. Discussions of responsive theological education in the context of twentieth-century theological education often begin from Karl Barth's call to hold the Bible in one hand and the newspaper in the other.[2] John Stott spoke frequently and passionately about this need and this spirit of cultural engagement suffused the 1974 Lausanne Covenant and, arguably, much of the architecture of global evangelical theological education. This conversation often came into productive dialogue with the growing missiological field of contextualization. Despite the length of this conversation, data from these institutions suggests that there is still far to go in terms of adjusting the structures, cultures, and curricula of theological schools to be more dialogical with the challenges of their ever-changing contexts. Patty contributes two voices on this subject, the first from Bulgaria, and the second from Russia.[3] Both go beyond the simplistic statement that much of theological education in this region is drawn from Western models and continue on to seek both roots and solutions:

> We copied and pasted the model of training of the US and Western Europe without thinking, and we didn't pay attention to some of our contexts like Islam or Orthodoxy. We needed to contextualize, but we actually didn't understand our own context!
>
> Theological education in Russia and Eurasia has covered basic ground of theology, history of theology, missiology, and so

---
2. For a discussion of the genesis of this quote, see http://ptsem.edu/Library/index.aspx?menu1_id=6907&menu2_id=6904&id=8450 (accessed 30 Mar 2015).
3. Patty, "A View of Theological Education."

forth. It seems that we are not yet getting deeper into linking the knowledge of theology and biblical texts with our current and unique context. A new phase is needed, one that is more reflective, more analytical, more dialogical in our culture. We need to take it from Western textbooks to our real situations.[4]

Both point to an issue that resonates with the data from various institutions: theological schools do not struggle with a lack of information, or even with lack of local expertise and thinking on theological subjects. The gap is often in the tools to both understand the local context and in the ability to apply theological thinking from various perspectives to these contexts. The institutions studied suggest that progress is being made, as the research of MacLeod affirms.[5] An increasing ability to achieve and maintain responsiveness will be at the heart of effective governance and leadership of theological schools in the coming years.

---

4. Ibid., 14.
5. MacLeod, "Unconventional Educational Practices."

9

Education That Transforms

Broader higher education, technical education, as well as primary and secondary education have been deeply impacted by the Industrial Revolution. It is hard to escape the industrial elements that permeated much educational thinking in the late nineteenth and early twentieth century. At the risk of oversimplification, education was a path for masses of people to acquire knowledge in order to become economically productive in a manufacturing society. Knight opens his volume on educational philosophy in Christian perspective by pointing to the tendency of twentieth-century American educators to focus more on the "how" than the "why" of education.

> America has been making an unrelenting assault on technique for more than a century ... The very word "progress" has come to be seen in terms of new methods. ... Educators have been concerned more with motion than progress, with means than ends. They have often failed to ask the larger question of purpose.[1]

In many ways, the tension between this approach and more classical educational philosophy remains in much of our educational discourse today. This American fixation on technique has filtered far beyond national borders. Has this impacted theological education? If so, in what ways?

It is my sense that this industrial approach to education has deeply influenced the development of theological education, although the historical roots of that are tricky and require further thinking. Some models of theological education, driven by the acquisition of cognitive knowledge, are often framed in the language and terminology of classical approaches

---

1. G. R. Knight, *Philosophy and Education: An Introduction in Christian Perspective* (Berrien Springs, MI: Andrews University Press, 2006), 4–5.

to education, with appropriate usage of terminology like moral formation and character development and, perhaps most pervasively, "head, heart, and hands." Yet curricular models of theological education have almost always placed the greatest amount of emphasis on the head, or the acquisition of academic knowledge. The discussion of recent literature on theological education in chapter 2 seems to show that there is increasing unease with this approach. The emergence of an understanding of theological education as mission and, more recently, the idea of the prophetic or transformative role of theological education, suggests the emergence of new possibilities. The evidence gleaned from data in this study suggests that all four schools studied are taking *education that transforms* very seriously.

S1 – "Blowing Their Minds"

This theme of education that transforms was especially pronounced at S1. It emerged in the form of concern for outcomes of the educational process that lead to worldview change, often described as "changing perspectives" (S1–I3 dean), "creation of mental growth," (S1–I3 dean), and even "blowing their minds" (S1–I2 chair). S1 does not exist merely to convey information or to train skills, but rather to produce the kinds of leaders who can make a difference in line with the vision of the theological school. Reflecting on this in the classroom, the dean described his teaching a course on the environment:

> And when they realize, my word, this is God's creation. This means something to Him. And when our relationship with Him is restored, we must treat this world with great respect. This is a way that we demonstrate how God is reconciled to His creation and helping their churches reduce the pollution in their area, all kinds of things, projects they come up with, something they have done, projects for their dissertations, to see how wide and deep and meaningful our existence is as Christians in this world, not to see this place as merely an airport lounge, but to see this as our home and to see heaven as a renewed creation as a new heaven and a new earth, but that this will pass away but it will be renewed. It's not going to be consigned to annihilation. It's all good. It's just very strange, it's a bit disappointing that none of

my other courses have created this kind of mental growth. (S1-I3 dean)

Another important reference to perspective change and worldview growth is expressed in the school's explicit desire to see greater understanding of the breadth of the church and a greater commitment to the overall body of the church. Speaking about S1's goals, the chairperson said:

> My dream for [our school] would be that . . . our curriculum would be such, and the life here we have would be such that they will be evangelicals with principles. For example, one of the phenomena that we've been confronted with are the independent churches. . . . For some reason, God seems to be using these independent churches to win a lot of people to Christ. There are a lot of possibilities of people falling away, of casualties, of young workers being crushed. [Our school] has attracted a lot of people from independent churches. My dream would be that in coming to [our school] they would learn that there are other sincere Christians apart from their own, that there would be an appreciation of other Christians. Less propensity . . . to do things that will hurt another church. That's happening a lot. A lot of hurting of churches in a desire to grow. The body of Christ becoming more the body of Christ. That is one thing I want [our school] to do. (S1-I2 chair)

S1 does not desire merely to affirm the beliefs of students that they possess upon entering the school, but rather to form their thinking to better reflect S1's values and ethos.

This idea of education that transforms often expressed itself in terms of empowerment and dignity. The term empowerment was used frequently, as were such terms as "nudging the church" (S1-I1 CEO), helping those with "very little identity, very little to be proud of" (S1-I2 chair), and "seeing ourselves as an amazing network of leaders" (S1-I1 CEO), among other expressions. Empowerment encompasses a broad understanding that goes beyond simply equipping students with skills, knowledge, and dispositions necessary for ministry. It also includes the idea of calling on Christians in all walks of life to act boldly in all spheres of society. It seems to draw in some ways on the thinking of Freire.[2] This approach, while not unique to this Asian country, is deeply influenced by what was frequently referred to as the "politicization" of life in the country, where the perception has grown, even among Christians, that the only political leaders really matter and have any meaningful influence. This broader cultural phenomenon, together with the minority status of Christians in the country, has led to a kind of apathy. Speaking of S1's role, the CEO stated "this is how we are positioning ourselves. Rather than cursing the darkness, empower people who exercise leadership . . . from homemakers to business-executives . . . just challenging people to make a difference where they have influence" (S1–I1 CEO).

The sub-themes of empowerment and dignity also were clear in many board decisions that have been made through the years. Not least of these is the decision in the school's early history to offer training in vernacular languages at the degree level. Since those able in English generally come from more affluent backgrounds, this decision for vernacular offerings has opened the doors for study to poorer Christians. In the words of the chairperson, "right from the start, we wanted to have a seminary that reflects the nature of the body of Christ as a society where there are no class distinctions" (S1–I2 chair). This has become increasingly important as church growth has accelerated among poorer classes. Again, in the chairperson's words: "It is the poor who are coming to Christ, the poor who have very little identity, little to be proud of. They aren't even proud of their religion." Addressing the need for empowerment, the dean painted the following picture of his vision for their students, including a broad awareness that,

> I'm his [Christ's] child and I do not fear you and I will stand for what is just and will to the utmost of my power be sure that my neighbor is also safeguarded. To build that kind of inner humanness with the full dignity of knowing that we are being restored to the full image of Christ, that we are created in the image of God, that we aren't someone's pawns or minions or cheering squad. (S1–I3 dean)

This vision of overcoming a "sense of helplessness in looking at our society" (S1–I1 CEO) animates the work of the institution, from inspiring

---

2. P. Freire, *Pedagogy of the Oppressed* (New York: Continuum, 2000).

public communications in national newspapers by S1 leaders on societal issues to the means of formation in the classroom, helping to form in students a sense of their ability, despite their background or social standing, to be agents of godly influence.

S2 – "Teologia Reflexiva"

A concern for education that transforms is woven deeply in the fabric of S2's identity. According to the CEO's telling of the institution's history, S2 was founded for "reflective theology" (*teologia reflexiva*). This has more recently been expressed in the language of holistic formation that encompasses the whole person. In the words of S2's website answering the question "who are we?" (*Quem somos?*), they state:

> Our work is not limited only to academic aspects. Our attention is also focused on research and reflection (to know/to reflect – *saber/refletir*), as well as considering practical ministry formation (to do – *fazer*), affective formation (to feel – *sentir*), relational formation (to live together – *conviver*), and more than that, the formation of character (to be – *ser*). (S2 website – accessed 23 Feb 2011)

The language of holistic learning and transformation arose often in the data. The school is infused with the idea of making a difference. A first level of this has been the consistent desire to reach beyond their own denomination. Reflecting on turning points in the school's history, the development director stated "one element I see as influencing change is the fact that [the CEO] came on board as president of the school, when he came to the school, he came with a vision that the school should be an influence not only to the [our denominational] world but to the church in general." He continued, however, that the holistic focus continues to motivate him and his colleagues:

> What excites me is the possibility that the school has to train people to make an impact in society, people who can make a difference, a change, in society. That's something that we do here and it's a great possibility for us, and it's something that excites me, to train people to make a difference. (S2-I3 development)

Several discussions pointed to the rapidly changing educational and ecclesial context of the country and the region, and the need for adaptability. As the expectations for pastoral leadership and the shape of the worship service shift away from traditional forms and structures and more toward the worship experience itself, there is a perception of less desire for in-depth theological training. This has led to the closure or near closure of many of S2's sister schools in the country. Yet S2's sensitivity toward rapidly changing needs and their focus on providing accredited degrees that are accessible not just to vocational pastors but also to lay people has allowed them to continue to flourish. In the words of the CEO, one of their clear goals is to "show the theological institution could be sustainable in the long run, and also could be strategic for the future of the church" (S2–I1 CEO).

S3 – Shaping the Image of the Minister

Much like S1 and S2, S3 showed a strong desire to see their educational process provide more than simple content to students. Rather, S3 exists to respond to needs of church and society by its "calling to help beginning ministers to form a Christian worldview, to receive deep knowledge in the area of Holy Scriptures, to obtain the habits of building and strengthening relationships, as well as to define one's calling and further ministry."[3] Although knowledge is clearly a critical component, interviews revealed that the inclusion of "formation of Christian worldview" is not listed first accidentally. Rather, this desire flows deeply into every aspect of the institution. From the beginning, S3 has sought to offer transformative education. S3's written history opens by describing the situation surrounding their founding: "Many people were drawn to God, tired of spiritual coldness and desiring to find answers to many different questions" (S3 history). In a broader context where the evangelical churches had by political necessity limited their concern only to their internal church life, this desire to help the spiritually hungry find answers to life's many questions represented a step outside of the norm. Yet as young Christian leaders worked in the new environment, they found that "they began to deal with problems of which they were previously unaware" (S3 history). This led to a desire to see S3 "shape the image (*obraz*) of the

---

3. School website, accessed 21 November 2011.

minister in light of a biblical worldview for the spread (*rasprostranenie*) of the kingdom of God in contemporary society" (S3 history).

Interview data readily revealed a clear theological vision for the school, rooted very much in the idea of knowing and following what God is doing, and this clearly undergirded both the explicit and the hidden curriculum of the institution. Despite the strong concern for the questions of broader society and the need for responsive mission, S3's leadership team was unanimous and univocal on the centrality of spiritual need. Reflecting on an earlier statement to this effect, the dean stated:

> I want to be clear that there is nothing wrong with social projects; they are all important part of the church, but more important is this need, when people know their need for God and when he is the center, then these other things will come, a human has this connection to God and submits to him and listens to him about what needs to be done. (S3–I4 dean)

The chairperson, who also serves as an official in the denomination most closely associated with the school, put it like this:

> I think that a great need today is for devoted (*posviashennikh*) leaders, ministers. In society, the problem is values. There is a very low moral/spiritual value today. This is something that needs to be a response of the church. I think of [our country] ... people don't value honesty, principles; they think of position, they think of power. They don't think of spiritual values. This is a problem. Of course there are many others as well – narcotics, children without parents, divorce, alcoholism. But all of these grow from values. People don't have the right understanding of God and his principles. All these other things emerge as consequence. (S3–I3 chair)

Continuing on the theme of worldview, the development director, responding to a question about the biggest needs he sees in society, stated that the fundamental problem is one of worldview. "People live according to their own worldviews, the way that they were formed improperly" (S3-I2 development). Putting this discussion of worldview into the broader frame of the evangelical church context, the CEO affirms this commitment to helping people to understand how it is that they see the world and why it is that they believe what they believe, rather than standing blindly on tradition.

> For many churches... there remains the problem of the influence of traditionalism, which continues to influence. I am not against traditions themselves. When people like this or that, that doesn't bother me. But some stand on traditions and live through them. I see that some places the church preaches a tradition here, but everyone lives differently. This is a kind of "[our national] syndrome," a kind of dualism, where we all know that there is a certain law, and yet we know that no one observes it. We all know it's there, but we all do differently. This is also in the culture of the church. (S3–I1 CEO)

This commitment to worldview change is given flesh in the educational programs of S3. The leadership of the school is committed to seeing these kinds of changes occurring in their students through a transformative educational experience that unites knowledge, skills, and dispositions. "We aim to prepare ministers with a biblical worldview, formation of the personality (*lichnosti*) of the person, formation of the *whole person* [emphasis added], his theology, his character" (S3–I4 dean). In the words of the CEO, "education is the changing of the paradigm of thinking, to implant a biblical worldview. This is our founding purpose. We do this with the church" (S3–I1 CEO). The dean, when queried about the most rewarding part of his job responded:

> The most visible part where I can see the results is in the class, to see the response (*otklik*) of the students, when I hear them disagree with me, when I see what is happening inside of them, this gets my emotions. This is, of course, difficult, but I like this part. (S3–I4 dean)

This concern for the educational and its transformative character was also evidenced in the observed board meeting. During the report of the academic dean, the issue of how new modular programs are being taught in order to take into account that students have less time for one-on-one interaction with professors than would have been the case in more traditional residential education. The dean took up this question, responding that rather than changes to content, S3 has sought to change the methods of teaching and to help their faculty learn new modes of assessment. The board expressed support for this approach and affirmed the necessity of such modular programs, but continued to encourage the administration to watch this carefully. In the words of one board member: "one needs to try, but one also needs to prove" (*nado pytat'sia, nado probovat'*) (S3 observation). Overall, the data suggested a strong commitment to transformative education on the part of all members of the community.

S4 – True Engagement

There was also strong coherence in the data regarding S4's potential to contribute to social transformation through its educational programs. Although all indicated that there was room to grow, there was strong evidence of the continued development of a holistic educational vision that empowers, results in worldview transformation, and unites knowledge, beliefs, and action. Reflecting on the history of the institution, one staff member suggested that this has not always been the case, but has rather been a product of the institution's maturation:

> There has been a discernable shift in our philosophy over the years. I remember in the earlier years the emphasis was on academic excellence. Gradually I noticed that our purpose was to bring change as a result of the work we do to society more generally. So this has been a shift in philosophy and I'm very happy about that. (S4–I2 development)

The CEO also charted a vision for education that transforms. Reflecting on some of the challenges facing Caribbean society and the types of education required, he advocates for "true engagement."

> At the end of the day, that is what transformation is going to take, true engagement. Through learning and struggling with issues and coming up with the right kind of leadership to try to vision how to deal with these issues. Of course underlying all of this is to be informed by the Bible, Scripture, and a theological base, how that informs our life and our actions. So I'm looking for more experiential models that engage the whole student and help them to get their hands in the field. (S4–I1 CEO)

Another staff member, reflecting on how S4 relates to societal challenges, held that the school is responding, but must do more:

> It is responding, the counseling program . . . there is more of a need in our schools for guidance, counselors . . . [Our school] is addressing some of these through our counseling program, but I believe, too, we need to have more programs for pastors or church leaders, leaders in the church, persons in the church in leadership positions, maybe Sunday school programs, programs that can empower our Sunday school teachers. (S4–I3 administration)

The theme of how S4 must do much more to achieve this vision was strongly present in a number of comments. Several members of staff, including the CEO, used strongly worded statements to describe the changes that still need to be made:

> I think that the graduate school is very academic, and it teaches from texts that are available, most of them are available texts. What is taught in the US is taught here. It is very textbook oriented. We produce people with degrees. We follow the rules. We are very academic people. There's a transformation that needs to take place that is not now taking place. In every academic course there is the application of theory and practice, and somehow we have to get our students doing real research that will inform their learning and the outcomes of their education. We need to be more directive in how we design our classes . . . we are primarily an academic institution, and we've got to change if we want to survive as a graduate school. (S4–I1 CEO)

Another staff member was equally strong in his call for further educational changes:

> These things are about the curriculum and your mission statement and training people for transformation of both church and society; it is included in both the statements and the curriculum, but my sense is that the school itself is not doing a lot of transformational work. It is not itself a faith community, *it is not able to model what we teach* [emphasis added]. This is why I like the . . . model of experiential learning; it helps people to

learn in their own social and community settings. [S4] has not been able to do anything outside of the task of teaching; learning has an experiential side of it.

When asked if S4 has the *potential* to accomplish this, the same staff member responded as follows:

> Yes, yes, yes! We are surrounded by inner city communities . . . we don't have to go very far. But somehow schools generally see themselves as preparing people to go out and do it, when I think there has got to be a blending of the practice with instruction. (S4–I2 development)

This common belief in transformative education and the potential of S4 to accomplish this suggests a significant convergence of values among at least some staff and faculty members. This continued belief in potential appears to be propelling the institution forward, in spite of significant challenges.

Conclusions

This study did not set out with a plan to look at educational approaches or curriculum of theological schools. Yet questions about governance effectiveness in each case led to discussions of curriculum and educational programs. Each of the board meetings observed devoted a significant amount of their time to thinking about the curriculum and educational approaches of the seminaries. This was the largest area where Middleton's concept of "boundary spanning" was employed, as boards thought about how existing or proposed academic programs related to the broader context of the seminary. Board members, for the most part, rather explicitly did *not* come at this as insiders, but rather as outsiders – pastors, business leaders, or other believers in broader society. In general, it was my sense that these conversations were productive. It is likely conversations of this sort – seeking to better align academic programs and educational ethos and praxis with the needs of the surrounding context – that will compose a major task for boards of theological schools in coming years. Helping theological school board members and academic administrators to have these conversations as productively as possible may constitute an area for meaningful external consultation.

10

Planning for the Future

A final characteristic of governance effectiveness was a *concern for the longue durée*[1] *of the institution, especially in terms of succession planning.* In all of the institutions, there was a good understanding of the historical context of the institutions and how different passages in their organizational history had impacted their present and future realities. Several of the schools, especially S3, showed a particularly strong awareness of this. In all of the schools, it seemed that awkward or unplanned transitions were the single greatest threat to the presence of the other characteristics mentioned above. One of the observed schools is just emerging from a long, awkward transition that has had considerable effect on the school's ability to accomplish its mission. Another school is approaching a retirement that could usher in an even more challenging situation. While it is clear that a strong, enabling CEO is essential to governance effectiveness, it is equally clear that the board must take seriously what might happen in the absence of such a leader. It seemed relatively easy for the observed boards to place a large amount of trust in the work of the CEO and his team. While this contributed to effective governance, this cannot lead to complacency. Although none of the observed boards appear to have engaged seriously in succession planning, the overall data suggest the absolutely critical nature of this exercise for good governance in any kind of organization. The need for succession planning aligns well with the literature, especially Aleshire,[2] McKenna,[3] and Costa and Kassis.[4]

---

1. A French term, meaning roughly "long term," that arose in historical studies, stressing the importance of long-term historical processes in understanding individual events.
2. Aleshire, "Governance and the Future."
3. McKenna, *Stewards of a Sacred Trust.*
4. Costa and Kassis, *Fann al-Hawkamah al-Rashedah.*

S3 – "It Has Been Small Steps, Some Larger, Some Smaller"

An interesting theme that arose in the data from S3 is an ability of the staff to quickly reflect upon and evaluate the institution's past, including past leadership, in a way that clearly pointed out differences of style and substance yet in an a way that showed strong respect. This revealed a strong sense of the *longue durée* of the organization. Perhaps even more importantly, it revealed a high value on the role of individual leaders, but an even deeper ultimate reliance on the purpose and mission of the institution. This continued a theme of humility that emerged throughout the S3 data. The dean gave voice to this concept in his reflection on changes from previous CEOs. "Each had their own approach, their own contribution (*vklad*). In the long-term perspective, it's probably not all that important" (S3–I4 dean). Reflecting on high points and low points of organizational history, the CEO made the following evaluative statement. "But when I look over the whole 20 years, it has been small steps, some larger, some smaller" (S3–I1 CEO). Such an expression of the importance of small steps that compose an ultimate contribution of a group of people committed toward the same ends resonated strongly at S3. No one particular time or leader was held up as being ultimate, although the individual contributions of many were held up as an important part of a broader story.

In contrast to S2, the issue of leadership succession in the sense of what comes after the current CEO did not arise in any of the conversations at S3. One member of the management team previously served as CEO in the school's early history and several other members appeared to be qualified to step into such a role if this were necessary. Overall, power appeared to be held very loosely and information shared very broadly with the management team. Management team members interviewed seemed to have a strong sense of empowerment in their individual areas. They also seemed to have a deep awareness and appreciation for the atmosphere that allowed this empowerment. If liabilities were visible, they were present in the sense of being short-staffed and under financial pressure. While staff at every level appeared to be willing to go above and beyond the call of duty in service of mission, the stresses on senior leadership were visible. This question arose even in the board meeting in the contemplation of potential remedies to assist the leadership. Overall, S3 showed a strong sense of sustainability in at least two ways. First, although the CEO and other key leaders clearly played critical roles, the atmosphere was such that succession could take place if it became necessary. Second, the organization from board to leadership to staff appeared to be in serious dialogue with issues of short-, medium-, and long-term financial sustainability, all rooted in a common understanding of vision and mission.

S4 – Transition

In contrast to the other three schools that took part in this project, all of which were experiencing fair degrees of stability, especially in terms of leadership, S4 appears to be at the conclusion of a long transition process from the previous CEO through a period of interim leadership to the present CEO. Data suggest the enduring nature of the institution's core founding values, although there is clearly divergence on some lesser issues such as specific program offerings, relationship to a nearby institution, and the relationship between the various parts of the organization. There is also strong evidence of continued belief in the potential of the school by the board, leadership, and staff. Despite this belief in potential, the data suggest that the school remains in a transitional period where there is an absence of complete alignment between board, the CEO, the management team, and the staff. There is evidence of a potential lack of alignment within the board itself regarding some key issues. This overall lack of alignment appears to give rise to frustrations and potential conflicts at all levels. At the board level, observation data and minutes suggest the presence of significant potential for strategic and generative thought, yet this input appears to be stymied by differences of opinion and approach, the lack of follow-up, and glossing over significant questions. Overall, S4 demonstrates many of the same commitments and structures found in the other three schools, yet *transition toward alignment* remains a central and controlling concept here. The fundamental issues of commitment to holistic education and responsive interaction are present. The desire for a community of trust and alignment also appear to be present. S4, however, remains in transition, moving slowly toward the kind of alignment that will allow for more robust institutional function. The data strongly suggest that this potential will be realized in the near future.

The extended transition at S4 requires that a bit more historical background be presented. S4 was founded twenty-five years ago by a regional evangelical association to serve as a graduate center for theological education. The school was the vision of a long-serving missionary in the Caribbean who in turn recruited the previous CEO (a national of another Caribbean nation). The current chairperson was initially involved in the governance of the nearby denominational seminary and has been involved with S4 since the beginning, serving for many years as chairperson. The chairperson and other key leaders were and remain very close to the previous CEO who has since accepted a teaching position in another country. The former CEO remains the president of the regional evangelical association that owns the school. When he departed the CEO position approximately five years ago, his successor, who was resident in another part of the world, was unable to assume the role for a year and a half. This gave rise to what was commonly referred to as the "interregnum" when a long-time academic dean gave interim leadership to the school. The current CEO assumed his role approximately two and a half years prior to the research visit. The former interim CEO departed soon after this to assume a pastorate in another Caribbean nation. Data suggest that all parties have worked tirelessly to bring about the best possible transition, even if their work has not always aligned well or pushed in the same direction. There appears to be an extraordinarily strong commitment on the part of all parties to S4 and a strong belief in its potential for influence in the church and society of the region.

The person of the former CEO, although not present during the research visit, figured significantly in interviews as well as the minutes of the board. The data suggests that the former CEO played a linchpin role not dissimilar to that of the CEO of S2. It is clear that the former CEO played a critical role with constituents, donors, the board, and the staff, and was well respected by each group. The minutes indicate repeatedly a concern for "re-energizing the donor base," often through engaging the former CEO to call on donors (S4 minutes, 27 Feb 2008; minutes, 3 Jul 2010). The minutes also suggested that a number of key supporters of the institution struggled to continue their support in the absence of the former CEO, especially in the interim period before the appointment of the current CEO (S4 minutes, 2 Feb 2008). The data suggest that the former CEO was relatively successful at aligning both board and staff around mission and had an established and productive *modus operandi* with the board chairperson that helped the two to navigate leadership together. The chairperson reflected on the former CEO as follows:

> [The former CEO] was a good president . . . [an] aggressive fundraiser; I think the board tended to ride on his back in respect to his achievements. Now that he has left there has been an interregnum and slippage . . . so that support for the president and for all the other ideas that are emerging are the sort of things that the board could be more involved in. (S4-I4 chair)

Staff interviews also suggested that the former CEO played a kind of "linchpin" role in the organization. A staff member, reflecting on the role of the former CEO, remembered him as follows:

> One of the things about [the former CEO] was that he listened and then he came up with ideas, and I have been able to see my footprint in some of these changes. When something was good, he would use it. The members of the leadership team had input into the shaping of the philosophy of the institution. We were formally part of the mission statement and the vision statement, and so I've appreciated the fact that these things can be done from above but as a leadership team was able to put this together through lots of dialogue. (S4-I2 development)

These comments in context did not reflect negatively on the new CEO, who was universally seen as a highly competent, visionary leader. It was clear, however, that the era of the former CEO was marked by a kind of system of broad governance and administration of which he was a linchpin. The interregnum and transition that followed clearly disturbed this system that had endured for two decades. S4 and the individuals that compose its leadership, board, and staff appear to have not yet fully recovered from this disruption. Individuals, although still firmly committed to the values and potential of S4, seem to be struggling to find new ways to interact in a new system.

Data suggest coherence regarding the potential impact of the school in the Caribbean region. The values of holistic ministry and education surfaced in all four interviews. At this level, there appears to be a strong alignment of values. At another level, however, especially in terms of how these values take the form of programs and administration, there is considerably more divergence and even potential conflict. Another point of commonality is the essential nature of S4 for church and society in the Caribbean. Variations of the phrase "no one else is doing that" were heard in all four interviews, and this same sense of the unique position of S4 was also present in the observed board meeting. This belief in the essential nature and potential of the school, however, did not necessarily reflect immediately in agreement about how to address specific real challenges. The vision and potential of S4 as evidenced in interviews will be traced below, stressing coherence in this vision. This will be followed by perceptions of change in values over time and current examples of dissonance regarding the future of the institution.

Despite significant coherence on potential and values, the data also revealed significantly different visions for the future of S4. As suggested, these differences were not so much matters of values, but rather of different tactical approaches to the many challenges confronting the institution. Reflecting on this, one staff member suggested that "we need to go back to our values, this will guide us" (S4–I2 development). The dissonance regarding key issues facing the school was not immediately evident to the researcher during the visit, but rather appeared first through careful analysis of the minutes, and second, through a re-examination of interviews. Since some of the issues had potential to cast a negative light on friends and fellow members of the S4 community, it was clear that interviewees were very guarded in their input. A consistent pattern began to emerge, however, suggesting a tension between near-term fixes to critical challenges and long-term sustainable solutions that would allow the institution to reach its full potential.

The concern over too much focus on the short-term issues at the expense of the long-term was most visible in a staff interview. The problem was described as follows:

> You see, I don't know that the board has that [visionary] model in mind. The board is interested in the bottom line, how to finance. I don't see the board as *visionary* [emphasis added]. I see them carrying on an official function. I don't get the sense that they are looking at the future of the organization. (S4–I2 development)

The CEO raised a similar sentiment by saying "The only danger we have is not paying sufficient attention to forward thinking." He continued "[S4] is in its 25th year. At 25 years of age you look back and some things worked well, some things did not work well, you've got to make adjustments. *You've got to make adjustments* [emphasis added]" (S4–I1 CEO). In contrast, input from the board chairperson suggested a strong desire to deal with short-term sustainability issues. Responding to a question of what he would most like to see, he responded: "What I'd like to see is financial viability" (S4–I4 chair). This tension, while visible to a degree in the interviews, was most pronounced in the minutes as well as during informal interaction during the research visit. This appeared several times in conversations about which academic programs should be continued and strengthened. Some were clearly favored for their ability to immediately bring in students, and therefore resources, while other longer-term solutions that may prove more viable were not as widely supported at board level. A specific episode in the minutes showed an instance when the chairperson wished to aggressively pursue one program that was believed to be financially beneficial, while another board member encouraged the need to listen to and incorporate the CEO's long-term plans (S4 minutes, 14 Oct 2008). This tension between short-term and long-term questions was merely one facet of what appeared to be a lack of alignment among various parts of the organization.

The CEO came to S4 from a successful career in student ministry. He brings a strong background in the humanities and social sciences in addition to theology, and is deeply aware of the realities of the Caribbean context. In the 21 November 2008 meeting, he outlined his vision for the school, with a special focus on clear communications (both internal and external) as well as vision for the future. Although this vision was endorsed by both the chairperson and several other board members (S4 minutes, 21 Nov 2008), the vision document did not appear in further minutes. Reflecting on his view of the S4 governance, the CEO called for a "non-interfering" board:

> I have a very sort of narrow view of what the role of the board is and should be. I think that the board has important but limited functions; I prefer a board that is a non-interfering board, that is a governing board, that lays out policy, that directs the CEO and approves budget, and supports the institution. . . . I would like the board to take that agenda, but also to be ambassadors of the school and bring support. It is not healthy in my view for a board to interfere in making decisions that have to do with the administration. (S4–I1 CEO)

He advocates board oversight but at the same time calls for a leading role for the CEO, who will ultimately oversee implementation of any board policy:

> The CEO has to have some influence. In a sense, it's his board. It's the board he relies on, the board that supports him, and the board must protect him, and he must protect the board as well. But who influences more, it's hard to say. You must have a board strong enough to say no to a president, but that means the board must allow the president to say no as well. But equally I think that the president must have sufficient strength to say that this is the wrong direction. There has to be that dynamic interaction between the president and the board. (S4–I1 CEO)

The relationship between the CEO and the chairperson is especially key:

> For me the key issue, really, is the relationship between the board chair and the president, because there may be a case where the president or CEO gets along with most of the board, but not with the chair. . . . They must be able to work together with each other. The chair is going to provide leadership for the board, must understand the president, and must be able to guide the president, and the president must be able to lay out his vision in a way that the chair understands . . . That has been a critical issue for me, the relationship between the chair and the president. The other members of the board must maintain good relationships . . . the board is only, mainly effective when it meets in session. You may have individual members with good advice, etc. No matter how great or wonderful their advice, no individual should be influencing the president in a particular direction without consent of the board. That's why you have a board; the board has to work together. (S4–I1 CEO)

The key theme here is one of trust – trust between the CEO and the board, trust between the CEO and the chairperson – an overall network of relationships that allows the school and its vision under the CEO's leadership to be accomplished. The data suggest that S4 is not yet fully aligned on this account.

The viewpoint from the staff regarding governance process differs significantly. The finance officer expresses appreciation for the board's

Planning for the Future 169

expectations for financial reporting and commends the "high-level professionalism" of its members (S4–I3 administration). As in other schools, the network of informal relationships between board and staff members through church networks, etc. is quite close, so informal interaction between staff and board is commonplace outside of the confines of S4. It is clear that there is a high degree of mutual respect. However, it is also clear that there is some sense of disconnect from the work of the board. One staff member stumbled into an awkward position in an interview when the interviewee referenced an upcoming organizational transition that was then realized not to be public knowledge. While the researcher was already aware of this transition from discussions with the CEO and the chairperson, this revealed some tension regarding communications. It was clear from this and other informal interactions that staff sometimes feel a sense of distance from decision making.

> There is very little exposure to the board. They meet at night when we are all gone. Board matters aren't really shared unless there is a policy that the board has initiated, and then we hear from them. I don't know if it's the nature of boards that they should maintain a distance from the rest of the organization, but that's the reality. . . . One of the things I find is that we have members of staff who feel left out because they don't know the people and the basis on which decisions are made. And so I find that there are a few employees who are detached; they do their job function and go home and leave [S4] behind. (S4 interview)

Circling back to the perception of shortsightedness on the part of the board and relating that to this idea of leaving the staff feeling disempowered and detached from decision making, the same employee continued:

> [S4] is perpetuating an institution . . . I really want to see that school rising to be the force for good in society that I know it has the potential to be. But a board . . . it doesn't matter how much time they spend on issues like economic challenges, in fact the focus on the negative forces has robbed us of the dream and has caused us to make counter-productive decisions because we have no clear values, no dream, so we respond to the circumstances, and that is why. *We need to come together. We cannot accomplish*

> anything that is going to be helpful unless we have a vision that goes beyond the realities of our situation [emphasis added]. That's where my heart is for the school. But a lot rests with the board. That board doesn't think in this way. I don't know what their job description is, but they see themselves as responsible for the efficient working of the organization, and that mindset perpetuates the past, it doesn't affect the future. So the question is can we change the mindset, or must we change the board? (S4 interview)

The kind of synergy and sense of "coming together" around common vision that so distinguished data from S3 seems markedly absent at S4. While there remains a strong sense of commonality of values, comments such as these suggest that there is considerable space between various parts of the organization.

S4's board chairperson has brought considerable continuity to the significant transitions the school has experienced in the past five years. While he was very much a central part of the system that existed under the previous CEO, he also has had a long relationship with the current CEO. As he nears retirement, it is clear that he is considering his legacy. His first goal, as articulated earlier, is to see the institution in a financially sustainable position. Another goal is to see the board more engaged in its work, especially in the area of providing financial resources. He would like to see,

> A greater sense of the input of the board members, who have great gifts to give to this situation. What one can do in a one-day meeting . . . is not very effective, quite frankly. [Two board members] are in the private sector Hall of Fame. They've aggressively articulated their Christian position and provided returns for their shareholders. I'm not sure that we are using them enough. In terms of how we make use of them and our overseas people is not as much as it should be. I think that part of it is transitional. (S1–I4 chair)

He continues, stressing again the financial responsibilities of overseas board members:

> I think that a tradition of more aggressive support of the president is emerging. This is where the weakness of the organization is.

> We don't have as much input from the overseas people. They come once a year to graduation, the next day board meeting, and are gone the next day. I think that somehow we have to change that in terms of a level of responsibility that we want to develop … [I may need] to say to the board members "there's what I want you to do over the next six months, either raise money or do this … given them duties, etc." This should be pursued. (S4–I4 chair)

The chairperson's concern for financial stability was also revealed in an episode recorded in the minutes following presentation of a rather gloomy financial report. The chairperson suggested that the financial realities suggested the necessity of considerable change in the organization. The dean responded in agreement, yet argued that these changes should not be pursued without planning, but should rather be carefully aligned to the perceived further development of the school. In short, any potential staffing changes must be done so as to preserve strength in areas that would be core to the future, and perhaps more marked in areas that were perceived to be less core (S4 minutes, 24 Apr 2011). This tension between short-term fixes and long-term sustainability is a common challenge for every board member and leader. Such tensions seemed to be especially strong in S4 as it continues through this transitional period.

The form and structure of the board of S4 differed slightly from other schools investigated. As an institution owned by a regional evangelical association, the S4 board is not self-perpetuating, but rather appointed by this owning body. It also includes more members from outside the region than any of the other schools (both S1 and S3 had one missionary resident in the region; all other members were local or regional). The inclusion of overseas board members appeared to be closely linked to these members' ability to raise or provide funds for the operation of the school; however, both the chairperson and the CEO pointed out that their participation was very low and highlighted this as an issue in board development. The low attendance at the observed board meeting (four non-staff members) seemed slightly anomalous when compared to attendance records for other board meetings as recorded in the minutes. The lack of participation and attendance was noted several times in the minutes as an issue of concern (cf. S4 minutes, 21 Nov 2008). Other steps have been taken recently to strengthen governance function.

Realizing the inability of the board to conduct true governance through an annual meeting, the board recently appointed a committee consisting of local people who now meet monthly to review the affairs of the school on a more regular basis. This body in turn reports to the full board its activities. Another issue that appeared was the highly varied nature of minutes, both in form and content. While some of this may relate to the transitions of leadership, there did not appear to be a consistent style or length to the minutes of meetings. Minutes ranged from more than ten pages for one meeting to two pages. The observed meeting revealed a relative lack of engagement by the board members present. One member engaged very little in the conversation until the end of the meeting. Minutes also reveal that a majority of minuted board member input came from three members of the board.

The observed meeting together with the reviewed minutes revealed a considerable amount regarding the function of the board. Although both sets of data revealed input, this was what the researcher came to label in field notes "popcorn" input or "low-level" input. One especially notable factor was a significant amount of time (nearly twenty minutes in the observed board meeting) spent on correcting and approving board minutes of the previous meeting. One board member in particular seemed to take this matter very seriously and pointed out several considerable errors along with a number of more stylistic issues. The minutes reveal that meetings often include a significant number of annotations to minutes of the previous meeting. There were also several examples of board members dwelling at length on particular decisions or policy issues with relatively little forward movement toward a decision. Examples in the observed meeting included lengthy discussions of the venue for an upcoming celebration (especially concerns regarding parking) and discussion of a statute of limitations for students who withdraw and then return to finish their degree (a concrete policy proposal already in operation had been brought to the table by the dean). The focus on this type of input, however, should not be seen as board members' inability to contribute more widely and deeply. Toward the end of the observed meeting, the researcher was requested to share briefly about his interactions with theological schools and particularly with boards of theological schools around the world. This 25-minute conversation demonstrated that the present board members were deeply capable of engagement. Discussion of the researcher's brief presentation among board members was participatory, lively, and filled with potentially generative questions. The minutes reveal several other situations when similar input from outsiders or from staff members generated significant thinking or "brainstorming" about issues critical to the school.

Several pieces of staff input also seemed poised to generate productive discussion. During the observed board meeting, the dean presented a recent study completed by the faculty on characteristics of S4 students of the present and future. The study raised many potentially critical questions. The study was, in fact, a response to a specific request from the board for such a study in the previous meeting. However, the discussion of this study and its results was not long and quickly moved on to other agenda points. At another point, the minutes reveal a brainstorming session that raised a number of critical and promising issues; however, there was little evidence in the minutes of follow-up or follow-through on these issues. As in other institutions, it appears that the majority of generative work arises from the staff, with the board responding. One staff member suggested that recent developments in the education program were very much staff-initiated: "We began to see that beginning to emerge in the thought process, in our strategic planning. It was not a board-initiated thing. It was out of our interaction at the leadership level" (S4–I2 development). Other evidence of this was found in the minutes, as the dean reported to the board on recent interaction with a person with broad experience in theological education and the staff's subsequent interaction with stimulating questions resulting from this exchange (S4 minutes, 21 Nov 2008). The data are clear that generative thought and strategic thinking are at work in S4 at the level of staff. Indications suggest that the board members are also qualified to engage in these kinds of critical questions. Despite this ability, there appears to be a disconnect between the perceived need for this kind of thinking, the ability to engage in it, and the actual function of the board. Data suggest that this is due in part to the focus on short-term financial issues, rather than long-term sustainability issues.

Conclusions

A common aphorism states that those who do not know history are bound to repeat it. Organizational history and its product, organizational culture, are deeply embedded in educational institutions, in ways that are both explicit, known, and celebrated, as well as in ways that are implicit, tacit, and unacknowledged. It is my sense that there has not been enough historical work done on the history of theological education and theological schools in the Majority World, especially younger, evangelical institutions. It is my hope that the future will yield more work of the sort of historical work that has enlivened and expanded the understanding of the history of theological education in North America, as discussed in chapter 2.

At the same time, the four institutions studied here all had strong command of their histories, although little had been written. In one case, the CEO drew an elaborate and detailed and *enlightening* diagram of the institution's history on a large napkin at a dinner the first night of my visit. At another, nearly every interview referenced the school's historical development in some way. At another, somewhat contested versions of history played a part in many discussions. In each case, consideration of the *longue durée* helped to put contemporary issues into context and proved to be especially important to generative conversations in the boardroom.

All four of these institutions had points of considerable and commendable strength. Unlike some of their peers, none appeared to face a crisis that would threaten their continuation. Challenges were, for the most part, more quotidian. Yet all demonstrated the importance of thinking about succession planning, as all four relied heavily on a capable CEO. It is this challenge that presents perhaps the greatest and most immediate test of effective governance, especially in those institutions that will face CEO retirement in the short- or mid-term. While the community of trust and strong alignment among boards, CEO, management, and faculty was admirable, it cannot become a matter of complacency.

11

Four Institutions in Summary

The four institutions observed in this study differed significantly in their geography, denominational background, and organizational culture. Yet the themes discussed in the previous chapters emerged in related ways across all four institutions. Below, I will summarize key themes for each of the four institutions and how they contributed the overall theory that is presented in the following chapter.

School 1 (S1) – Responsive Interaction

Although wide-ranging data from S1 revealed many insights into the work of governance in the institution, two particular concepts were especially evident and well developed. First, throughout its history, S1 has shown a commitment to responsive theological education that empowers students, strengthens their Christian worldview, and unites in them belief, knowledge, and actions. These conceptions arise from a diverse stream of inputs found in interviews, observations, historical documents, and minutes. The frequent mention of the theme of empowerment, in particular, resonates strongly with a church overwhelmingly composed of poorer members of the population, itself existing in a minority status within broader society. Second, a spirit of unity and teamwork, evidenced both in the school's multi-denominational approach, its open relationship with churches, and its internal teamwork and relatively level power dynamics, arises as a strong conceptual theme. This concept in particular suggests that the work of governance at S1, while resting clearly in the oversight and fiduciary responsibility of the board, is understood as a broader community task of thinking, casting and sharing vision, dreaming, and refining together as board, faculty, management, and staff. This conceptual theme surfaced strongly not only in formal input of interviews and documentary evidence, but also in observations of the life of the institution. Reflecting on the experience, the researcher wrote "There is very little that seems to be able to be called typically [representative of this national or regional culture] about this board. Everyone I asked said that they weren't typical at all" (S1 – observation notes). Data suggest that governance forms exercised at S1 are less determined in their distinct regional or cultural form and are more distinguished by their interaction with their surrounding culture. This conception of continued, multi-point, dynamic interaction between the educational institution and its context in a variety of relational forms begins to suggest a broader category of responsive interaction.

School 2 (S2) – Community of Trust

Three predominant concepts arose at S2 that resonated across interviews, board minutes and meeting observation, and limited access to institutional history. First, there was overwhelming evidence of the importance of the presence of a long-term, strong, bold, visionary leader who had wielded an enormous influence on the organizational culture and programmatic vision of the educational institution. Although evidence was strong that S2 is a very CEO-centric organization, data also revealed that part of the CEO's input has been creation of an enabling culture that has given significant space to other leaders. Second, the data showed an understanding of the board as a buffer or protector of the organization against external threats to its being or reputation. Although the board, in general terms, placed an enormous amount of trust in the president and his management team, it was clear from the minutes and narration of the organization's history by multiple parties that the board had on numerous important occasions stepped in to assure the rightness of a path being taken or to provide the necessary protection in the face of a risky or controversial decision. The presence of such leadership patterns and the development of a protective buffering function by the board have allowed the school to function to this point in a network of strong, trusting relationships. Finally, the data suggested the liabilities and dangers of succession in such a situation of strong trust in a capable long-term leader.

This appeared to be a significant emerging threat for the institution. Again, these conceptions were not unique to S2, although the historical experience of the institution in its cultural context and its denominational nature heavily influenced their development.

In summary, data from S2 reveal many things about the exercise of governance in this institution. Some of these, such as the importance of holistic education, echo data from S1. They also share a strong sense of community. Two key concepts, however, distinguish S2. The first is the presence of a long-term, very capable, and broadly respected CEO who is deeply identified with the identity of the institution. S2, in comparison with S1, is a more CEO-centric institution, although the leader has succeeded to a degree in building a similar team environment. The second key concept is the idea of the board serving as a protective buffer to the institution, providing it with legitimacy to its constituency, even at times when difficult or unpopular decisions have been taken. This ability to provide such a protective buffer has not arisen through statutes or other formal dictates, but has rather arisen over the course of two decades through the formation of a community of trust between the board, the CEO, and the staff. The preservation of this community of trust requires the careful exchange of information with the board so that the board members feel capable of supporting major decisions. The data reveal that this remains an imperfect process. Overall, the specter of leadership succession constitutes a significant threat to the organization, as it has considerable potential to upset this carefully woven community of trust. Again, as in S1, there was little at S2 that could be labeled as particularly "local" or "cultural" regarding the exercise of governance. The focus was rather on the institution's and governance structures' development in dialogue with its context over a long period. Although grounded deeply in the historical context of S2, the idea of the board as protector, enabler, and supporter of a strong, visionary leader, has potential to contribute to a broader category of *community of trust*, which can further inform understanding of governance in theological schools.

School 3 (S3) – Alignment

Three concepts arose at S3 that together form a category entitled alignment, stressing the understanding and pursuit of a commonly understood mission across all aspects of institutional life. First, a number of themes arose around a concept of unity in the educational process. These themes included an awareness of responsiveness to context, a strong commitment to holism, a view of education as a transformative act, and the attempt to bring every aspect of the educational institution, including the administrative structures, into alignment with this vision. Second, a number of themes concerning leadership arose, suggesting a concept of visionary, enabling, somewhat de-centered leadership. Finally, the work of the board in assuring and encouraging fulfillment of mission arose, although some ambivalence was evident about the fulfillment of this potential. Together, these concepts suggest the critical nature of *alignment* in the work of a theological school, including structural alignment of the board, CEO, management, and staff, as well as the deeper and more ambiguous need for alignment around all aspects of mission, both those stated explicitly and those more hidden in the implicit daily life of the school.

Data from S3 builds on and strengthens categories present in data from S1 and S2. The theme of holistic education that unites belief, knowledge, and character was again strong. The expression of this at S3 generally arose in concern for unity between the explicit curriculum and the hidden or null curricula of the institution and an overall shaping of worldview and "alignment with what God is doing." Although this conception of holistic education was strong in the other schools, it was most pervasive by far at S3. The category of responsive interaction was also echoed strongly at S3, stressing the importance of alignment of the institution and its training not only to the needs of the evangelical churches, but also to the questions of broader society. There were also strong echoes of the category community of trust, although S3 demonstrated this in a less CEO-centric way than S2. In S3, this was expressed much more strongly in terms of teamwork, empowerment, and a co-ownership of the mission of the institution. Although these themes were similar, S3 revealed a strong sense of *alignment* of the many parts and personalities of the educational institution. This category revealed itself in a variety of ways, including the strong emphasis on being attuned to what God is doing, assuring the coherence of training and formation with contemporary questions, and very importantly assuring that the school's hidden and null curricula speak as heavily toward their mission of training leaders as the explicit curriculum. The board's role in this process is one of assuring alignment. While there were echoes of the protective buffer idea of S2, S3 existed in a slightly less complicated political environment. Regardless, the board clearly felt an awareness of and a need to protect the undergirding values of the organization. It was clear that neither staff nor board members felt that this was being accomplished perfectly. Reflecting on the process, the board chairperson pointed out that,

> I need to be more in touch with the leadership team of the university, to see the situation inside. I think that I need to find ways so that people don't feel just a formal place here, but know how they can help the university to develop. (S3-I3 chair)

This desire to see the board move from a formal role to one that enabled the university to develop reflected a perceived key challenge to alignment. As the school becomes more dependent on local resources and constituents, such an awareness and feeling of responsibility will become even more critical. In order to accomplish its mission, S3 – and other schools pursuing similar missions – will undoubtedly need to pursue such alignment with even greater purpose.

School 4 (S4) – Transition

Although S4 was the most dissimilar of the four schools observed, many commonalities were visible. At a deep level, S4 shares the commitment to holistic education and unity of knowledge, beliefs, and actions that was evidenced so strongly in S1, S2, and S3. The leadership of the school also showed a deep concern for responsiveness and interaction with the needs of church and society in the Caribbean. S4, however, was distinct in many ways. Unlike other schools, which had not seen a CEO leadership transition for at least five years (most had also had considerable stability in the broader management team), S4 had experienced the departure of a long-time CEO, a long-time dean, and an awkward "interregnum" before the arrival of the current CEO. The sole consistent figure in this transition was the board chairperson, who is himself nearing the end of his active service. The effects of this transition upon the school, its governance structures, and its overall stability were obvious. There was a distinct lack of alignment between the various parts of the institution, including but not necessarily limited to the

CEO, board chairperson, other board members, and faculty/staff. While these groups adhered to many similar values and shared a deep belief in the potential of the institution, their approaches to more concrete questions of institutional development differed quite markedly. Although generative thought was clearly present in staff work and board members demonstrated capacity for such thinking, most board work seemed to be focused on short-term solutions rather than long-term sustainability.

Data from S4 helps to strengthen categories of responsive interaction, trust in community, and alignment in both positive and negative ways. It also suggests, along with data from S2, an overarching category of *effects of transition on systems*, or stated differently, the ability of leadership transitions to disrupt the function of overall governance and administration of a theological school. Data from S4 suggests strongly that a stable system (not necessarily a perfect system) existed under the previous CEO and that the extended transitions of the past five years have undermined that organizational system. It appears that several "systems" have in fact emerged, each one working with overlapping values, yet often at organizational cross purposes. The effect of this has resulted in a distinct lack of alignment which has in turn led to or contributed to significant challenges throughout the organization. The raw potential for the emergence (or re-emergence?) of a well aligned system remains strong, especially in the desire across the institution to see S4 be a responsive institution engaged deeply in questions that contribute to the ministry of the church in broader society. The example suggests, however, the extremely vulnerable nature of such organizational systems and their potential for disruption.

12

Conclusions

This study set out to deepen an understanding of governance practice in theological schools in a global perspective. As such, it investigated the governance process at four theological schools located in Asia, South America, Eurasia, and the Caribbean using a structured grounded theory approach. Analysis of data revealed six overarching categories that were perceived to contribute to governance effectiveness, bringing an answer to the first research question, *what characteristics contribute to effectiveness of theological school governance?* These characteristics have been taken up in turn through the previous six chapters.

To summarize, the characteristics that contribute to effective governance in theological schools include a community of trust, strong alignment, the presence of a strong, enabling CEO, reflective responsiveness, a commitment to education that transforms, and adequate planning for transition. These characteristics did not exist in isolation, but rather in a profound interdependency. Overall, it became clear throughout the study that the observed institutions are a kind of organism where each and every part is dependent on other parts. While the board holds final authority and the CEO is tasked with a central administrative role, the overall effectiveness of the institution is reflected in the warp and woof of the fabric of the institution, with each part playing its role while caring about the maintenance of the whole. The weaving of such a fabric is a matter of careful balance and watchful vigilance by all, especially as the pace of change accelerates. The board's role in this process is special, as this body carries ultimate responsibility for the mission of the institution. Effective governance clearly depends on the effective work of the board. Data from this study, however, suggest that this is not all that is required. The effective participation of the CEO, the management, and to some degree faculty and staff in the process of governance is equally critical. Overall, it seems that a concert of governance is required to assure the overall effectiveness of the institution.

This concluding chapter will take up the two remaining research questions, namely how does the cultural setting of theological schools relate to characteristics that contribute to governance effectiveness? And how do governing boards employ insights from internal and external relationships to enhance governance effectiveness? Following a discussion of these questions in light of data, the grounded theory methodology will be brought to conclusion through the positing of a theory encompassing the overall data that can strengthen the process of governance in theological schools in global perspective. This emerging theory will be compared and contrasted with extant literature on governance. Implications of this theory on theological education and the extant literature on renewal in theological education will also be considered. Finally, areas for potential further research will be outlined.

Culture and Governance

The second research question is how does the cultural setting of theological schools relate to characteristics that contribute to governance effectiveness? This question was the genesis of this research study in many ways. As the researcher interacted with boards of theological schools in various parts of the world, questions arose about the appropriateness of forms like the Carver Model in various cultural contexts. While questions about prescriptive forms of governance persist, the researcher was surprised to find very little evidence regarding specific "cultural" forms of governance. In each of the observed schools, it was very difficult to point to aspects of the governance process that were particularly "Asian" or "Latin American." With one significant exception, board governance did not seem to be perceived by participants in the process as a "foreign" structure, although there were numerous expressions of desire to see the processes of governance become more responsive to the cultural realities of a given place.

The relationship between board governance practice and the culture in which it is exercised is complex. While board governance appears to have developed in many of its current forms in the North American context,[1] it is now widely used in nearly every part of the world. Although the "Westernness" of board governance models did not arise frequently in the data, one significant interview did raise the issue. As discussed in chapter 4, the dean of S3 referred to boards as "Western."

> This is a Western model, it is not what we have in our culture, and we may not even fully understand the role of the board and what it is supposed to do, and the people on the board don't fully understand what they are to do, because at the end this is not our model of administration (*upravlenie*). (S3–I2 dean)

This reference to "our [Eurasian nation's] model of administration" could be approached in various ways, but it appears that in this Eurasian context and many others, the dominant model of leadership and administration would be more focused on a single strong leader. It appears to align with an understanding of high power distance[2] where decision making is more centralized and hierarchical. As the same interviewee indicated later in the same interview, the board governance model, while not a traditional norm in his society, has become more the norm in the corporate and educational worlds. Regardless of the "foreignness" of board governance, this statement surfaces a critical issue in approaching the second research question. While board governance may not be in and of itself culturally inimical, the model is *not fully understood* by many of its participants. This lack of understanding can lead to governance as a sort of vestigial appendage, part of the organism, but not fully functioning. Data suggest that more engagement around the *actual* function of the board in the context of the broader organization could help to deepen its engagement with and function within the broader organizational structure.

As Hall recounts,[3] board governance in the United States arose in and was nourished by the representative, "booster spirit"[4] of the nineteenth-century US. This fundamental idea of boards holding institutions in trust on behalf of their constituencies is not easily understood in many places,

---

1. Hall, "Cultures of Trusteeship."
2. Hofestadt, *Culture's Consequences*.
3. Hall, "Cultures of Trusteeship."
4. D. Boorstin, *The Americans: The National Experience* (New York: Random House, 1965).

including many places in the West. The "foreignness" of boards arose only once in the data, yet vagueness concerning the roles and responsibilities of boards came up repeatedly in each school. The more understandable nature of a model of administration that relies on a single strong leader may be a factor in why a strong, enabling CEO is so critical to effective governance in the observed schools. It may also contribute to the frequency of the role of boards providing a protective buffer to these leaders. It may also explain the consistent and repeated references to frequent interaction in a broader relational way between board members, faculty, and staff members of various schools in personal capacities in what one leader described as the "small village of [our national] Christianity" (S1-I3 dean).

The study did not produce data suggesting the need for an Asian or South American "model" of governance in terms of forms or structures. Data did arise suggesting the need for a more fluid approach to governance that takes into account local leadership patterns. The most compelling data regarding the relationship of governance and context reflected on this issue at a much more fundamental level. Rather than suggesting the need for Asian schools to pursue an Asian form of governance, *it suggested the need for all governance structures to be responsive to their context.* The simple application of governance structures and forms that have arisen in a complex historical relationship with Western culture will not suffice. In some contexts, this may call for the recognition of a *de facto* empowerment of the CEO and his/her leadership team with many of the responsibilities of generative thought, strategic thinking, and perhaps other tasks that may have been conceived in theory as the domain of the board. At the same time, it may call for board members to more explicitly assume their role as counselors to and protectors of the CEO. The critical task of governance effectiveness will rest on both parties: to assure that they are working in concert to achieve the mission of the organization in the best possible way in order to meet dynamic needs of the constituency. *Such a task can only be achieved within a community of trust.*

Although such responsiveness includes an awareness of and adaptability toward local and national cultural context, it is affected even more deeply by the unique immediate contextual and organizational culture of the institution. This was especially prevalent in data from S2 in South America. The denominational nature of this school and its attendant board structure involving appointment by an external denominational body, as well as the complex historical conflict between more progressive and more conservative forces within that denomination, has had an enormous influence on the formation of governance process. The development of the board as a protective buffer arose almost explicitly from this historical context. In a similar way, the governance structures and forms of S3 were very much influenced by the institution's evolving relationship with two church denominations in the context, one of which has historically been a key supporter, while the other (a leading denomination in the country) has at times had a difficult relationship with S3. Rather than suggesting the importance of culturally appropriate forms of governance, this affirms the need for overall responsiveness of the institution and the development of governance forms that are appropriate and able to help the institution to continue to adapt.

One issue arose in the context of consideration of question 2 that requires further elaboration. All four schools share the commonality of having been founded with significant financial support from outside of their context. In some cases, this once approached one hundred percent of overall operating expenses. This has changed markedly in the course of the past fifteen years, with each school now relying to a much greater extent on local forms of income derived from tuition, direct support from local churches or donors, and especially rental incomes and other exploitation of campus infrastructure. In this sense, S2 is a bit of an outlier, since nearly their entire operational budget stems from local resources. The other three schools, to greater or lesser degrees, continue to struggle with the overall implications of this change. Data suggest that the boards of these schools, in particular, struggle to understand this new reality and its implications for their governing role in particular. At S3, this concern for financial resources and support expressed itself in several statements from staff regarding concern for the board acting merely as approval, rather than as an active participant in terms of providing financial support. This was expressed most starkly by the S3 CEO:

> The board doesn't take on full responsibility. In legal sense, it carries it, but for day-to-day [*tekushie*] activities, they don't take on full responsibility. For example, when we say "there is no money," they say "well, okay," and that's all. We have to think ourselves about what to do further. . . . I think that it is a

consequence [*sledstvie*], it is an indicator [*pokazatel'*] of the real situation in the churches. (S3–I1 CEO)

A similar tension was visible at S4, especially in the inclination of some to approach critical challenges by conducting more fundraising in North America while others argued for a more long-range thinking about sustainability of programs in the Caribbean context. This issue of sustainability and its interaction with cultural understandings of governance is likely a common challenge and one that needs to be viewed in the framework of overall responsiveness of an institution.[5]

Governance as Boundary Spanning

The third research question asks how do governing boards employ insights from internal and external relationships to enhance governance effectiveness? This question was designed to shed light on participants' use, explicitly or implicitly, of boundary spanning[6] as a tool for generative thought,[7] with the two considered critical components of governance effectiveness. This question was focused primarily on the exercise of governance by members of boards. The overall data, however, pointed to a broader concert of governance involving a spectrum of people associated with the educational institution. Overall, the utility of boundary spanning and generative thought to the function of the governance process was shown to be very high, affirming the applicability of the work of Pfeffer in the health care sphere to theological schools.[8] The two activities are in many ways embodied in and contribute to

---

5. This issue continues to grow in importance in discussions of majority-world theological education, and theological education more generally. A number of studies in North America have raised significant questions about the financial sustainability of North American theological schools (Miller, Ruger, & Wheeler, 2009; Ruger, & Meinzer, 2014). The Association of Theological School's *Economic Equilibrium in Theological Schools* project (http://www.ats.edu/resources/current-initiatives/economic-equilibrium-and-theological-schools) also looked at this issue in-depth in the North American context. On a more global stage, a collaborative project between Overseas Council, ScholarLeaders International, and three leading theological schools in the Majority World in 2012–2013 shined a light on this issue. This project is summarized and reviewed in Smith (2013) and has given rise to an ongoing effort to better understand these issues. Further research is expected from Bellon (forthcoming) and Ferenczi (forthcoming).

6. Middleton, "Nonprofit Boards of Directors."

7. Chait, Ryan, and Taylor, *Governance as Leadership*.

8. Pfeffer, "Size, Composition, and Functions."

an overall concept of responsive interaction. *These activities, however, were rarely practiced by board members.* In all four observed institutions, greater levels of meaningful boundary spanning and generative thought were taking place at the level of management, staff, and faculty. Board members were clearly aware of the concepts and engaged in both activities, yet at quite low levels with minimal influence on the direction of the institution. The potential and competence for greater inputs from board members was clear, but it does not appear that these tools are embraced as part of board service in the observed schools. A much greater emphasis is put on guarding values, assuring fiduciary responsibility, and acting as a protective buffer.

Boundary spanning and generative thought did not appear to be understood in a primary sense as a role of board members in the observed schools. Although board members expressed a general need for responsiveness as discussed above, data suggest that they tended to rely heavily on staff to accomplish this task. There were exceptions. The chairperson of S1 clearly felt he played an important bridging role to the broader global theological discussion and considered this his main contribution to the governance process. Other board members explicitly brought insights from their professional backgrounds in educational administration (S1, S4) or law (S4). Board members who serve as pastors seemed less able to play this role, as most clearly evidenced in conversations at S2 that drew heavily on a staff member to interpret changes in the worship style at denominational churches. In most cases, board member input remained at a relatively low level, such as input on the parking concerns for a celebration event at S4. In general, the data suggest that there is a lack of understanding of a more generative mode of governance[9] that could draw on this input and channel it into productive ends. Informal interaction with board members, especially over meals, revealed both strong competency and desire to contribute meaningful thinking to the future of the institution. Brainstorming discussions included in the minutes of S3 and S4 further attest to the ability of present board members in this area. A lack of understanding of the role of this governance function as well as lack of time and the perceived absence of deep knowledge of the actual function of the institutions being governed appeared to be three key elements limiting the

---

9. Chait, Ryan, and Taylor, *Governance as Leadership*.

development of this role. Brown's statement that "individual competence can lead to collective incompetence"[10] seems appropriate.

Emerging Theory – A Concert of Governance

Although the six categories elaborated in chapter 5–10 may prove useful in and of themselves to the process of governance in theological schools, it is the goal of this study to elaborate a theory that achieves a more integrative summary, to "pull all of the research threads together to construct a plausible explanatory framework about the experience."[11] The ultimate utility and correctness of this theory cannot be judged by the researcher. As Glaser indicates,[12] the true judge of validity of grounded theory is that it fits the situation and that it works in the eyes of those who engage in the activities described.

Overall, the data suggest that greater effectiveness in board governance need not require the wholesale adoption of Western forms. The beauty of approaching administration from the perspective of a "concert of governance" is that it allows the institution to perform the basic tasks of governance (that is, to assure accomplishment of mission in a responsible and legal way). The concert of governance, however, does not stop here. It allows for an expansion of the understanding of governance beyond an automated, static response to a more nimble administration that allows the organization to remain relationally stronger and more contextually responsive. Such a vision of governance is unquestionably more leader-centric, as are the dominant models of administration in the contexts observed. Leader-centric models are clearly open to dangers both for the leaders who assume such roles, and for the institutions they lead. Casual observation would suggest that quite a few theological schools in the Majority World have experienced the pitfalls of autocratic leadership. *A concert of governance model should not be seen as enabling such leadership.* Rather, a concert of governance calls on the board to invest itself heavily and actively in the appointment of leaders who are able to function under the authority of the board while still drawing on board members' wisdom and buffering. Perhaps even more important, the

---

10. Brown, *The Imperfect Board Member*, xviii.
11. Corbin and Strauss, *Basics of Qualitative Research*, 264.
12. B. G. Glaser, *Basics of Grounded Theory Analysis* (Mill Valley, CA: Sociology Press, 1992).

concert of governance calls for leaders who are able to understand their strengths and weaknesses and are able to bring people around themselves who complement and balance these strengths and weaknesses. *A concert of governance simply will not work with autocratic leadership, as the central call of leadership in such a situation is drawing on and caring for others in the service of organizational mission.*

This approach confirms suspicions about universal models and structures of governance. Despite Carver's pronouncement of the universal applicability of his Policy Model of Governance,[13] there is no magic bullet or perfect form that assures good governance in the work of a theological school. A policy governance framework may assist a board to do better work, especially in the fiduciary sphere, yet true governance effectiveness requires the assurance that the institution is fulfilling its mission and meeting relevant needs effectively. True governance effectiveness must go broader and deeper than the Carver Model and must draw in more voices. The board itself is clearly the critical final authority in the governance process, yet the overall work of governance stretches beyond the boardroom and into the fabric of the institution as a whole, drawing on the insights, talents, and abilities of the CEO, the management, staff, and faculty, as well as the board. This "concert of governance" presupposes the ultimate authority and responsibility of the board. It suggests, however, that in the types of institutions observed in this project, the full work of governance must draw on staff resources as well in an empowering way that aligns all of the parts of the organization to responsively fulfill its purpose. Although the above theory rises from the data, it aligns well with understandings of governance as encompassing more than just board members put forth by Middleton,[14] Chait, Ryan, and Taylor,[15] Eadie,[16] and Freiwirth and Letona.[17]

---

13. Carver, *Boards That Make a Difference.*
14. Middleton, "Nonprofit Boards of Directors."
15. Chait, Ryan, and Taylor, *Governance as Leadership.*
16. Eadie, "Meeting the Governing Challenge."
17. Freiwirth and Letona, "System-wide Governance."

Implications for Governance

The implications of a theory of a "concert of governance" are many. Data from the observed schools suggest that it more aptly and correctly describes the actual function of governance in these institutions than more prescriptive approaches. It also aligns with what appears to be a significant shift in the literature on governance, most clearly evidenced in the work of Middleton,[18] Chait, Ryan, and Taylor,[19] Renz,[20] Eadie,[21] and Crompton[22] that suggest that the true work of governance must at times step beyond the neat "policy model" proposed by Carver.[23] The relationship of the theory of a "concert of governance" will be considered below in the context of the current discussion of governance, especially the tension between models espoused by Chait, Ryan, and Taylor[24] and Carver.[25] The work of Heifetz, Grashow, and Linsky[26] is also be referenced as an important interpretive key.

John Carver's Policy Governance Model has been among the greatest influences on the work of governance in nonprofit organizations in recent decades. Carver's model is quite simple. It presupposes that the board represents the will of the stakeholders (those who benefit *directly* from the organization). This board then appoints leadership (a CEO) of the organization. The relationship between the board and the CEO is then governed by policy. Policy is effectively defined as the definition of boundaries within which the CEO and management have full authority. Policies must themselves emerge from and be coherent with organizational mission/vision and values. These policy boundaries effectively define where the authority of the CEO/management ends.

Carver's model is especially useful in that it focuses boards on the work of governance, rather than management issues. The stress on policy emerging

---

18. Middleton, "Nonprofit Boards of Directors."
19. Chait, Ryan, and Taylor, *Governance as Leadership*.
20. D. O. Renz, "Reframing Governance," *The Nonprofit Quarterly* 13, no. 4 (Winter 2006): 6–13.
21. Eadie, "Meeting the Governing Challenge."
22. L. C. Crompton, "The New Future of Governance," *Board Member* 18, no. 6 (2009).
23. Carver, *Boards That Make a Difference*.
24. Chait, Ryan, and Taylor, *Governance as Leadership*.
25. Carver, *Boards That Make a Difference*.
26. Heifetz, Grashow, and Linsky, *Practice of Adaptive Leadership*.

from mission/vision and values is helpful. It is helpful in defining the limits of board involvement and setting clear lines of authority and expectation. The establishment of policy boundaries gives the CEO/management broad room for action. It tends to help overcome the challenge of micromanagement. The Policy Governance Manual advocated by Carver is unquestionably superior to the practice of many boards, which simply minute decisions that are then easily forgotten or ignored. The weakness of this "minuting" model was apparent throughout this research.

For all of its positive elements, the Carver Model has limitations. Some of these are in the conception of the model itself. The central tension is one of proclaimed universal applicability. Carver is explicit that his model is applicable and must be applied in full in any situation, anywhere, at any time. This statement becomes especially suspicious when cross-cultural interaction is taken into account. Such an approach assumes that the expectations of the governance process are universal and limited to fiduciary oversight. This position has already been critiqued by Diniz[27] and Bradshaw et al.[28] Doubts about the universal applicability of Carver's work fueled the initiation of this study.

Although Carver has been critiqued and studied by several, the most influential alternative model is that developed by Chait, Ryan, and Taylor.[29] Their *Governance as Leadership*, while not explicitly critical of Carver (his work is neither mentioned nor cited), argues that governance studies need to draw more from the lessons gleaned from the study of leadership in recent decades. They present a three-fold model of governance that calls on boards to engage in fiduciary governance (assuring that organizational resources are used in acceptable, responsible, and legal ways), strategic governance (thinking about how to deploy resources in the future), and finally generative governance (thinking about not just what the organization *is*, but what it *can be*). While Chait, Ryan, and Taylor's *fiduciary mode* of governance can be seen as aligning at least in part with Carver's Policy Model, the other two modes, especially generative governance, branch into new territory that is less prescriptive and open to greater cooperation between management

---

27. Diniz, "The Changing Face."
28. Bradshaw et al., *Nonprofit Governance Models*.
29. Chait, Ryan, and Taylor, *Governance as Leadership*.

and board. The authors acknowledge that this creates a less neat picture of governance, but believe that generative thought is necessary. The approach articulated by Chait, Ryan, and Taylor has become increasingly ascendant in North American conversations on governance, and seems to be a central element in the thinking of BoardSource (www.boardsource.org), the leading association for nonprofit board governance in North America, figuring frequently in their publications. Both Scott and Brown also place greater stress on the perceptive and relational nature of board governance.[30]

The conversation on governance can also be enriched by Middleton's concept of "boundary spanning."[31] This concept allows the board to see both inside and outside the organization, and to draw strength from both. Middleton's concept adheres to Greenleaf's definition of trusteeship, namely that "institutions need two kinds of leaders: those who are inside and carry out the active day-to-day roles, and those who stand outside but are intimately concerned, and who, with the benefit of some detachment, oversee the active leaders. These are the trustees."[32] Middleton's and Greenleaf's understanding of the board as a kind of intermediary between the organization and its environment is less neat than Carver's delegation model.[33] Yet it seems to hold greater potential for assisting organizations to adapt to changing environments. It also aligns more clearly with the realities observed in this research project.

While the above works provide useful critiques of Carver's model, it is the theory of adaptive leadership as developed by Heifetz, Grashow, and Linsky[34] that forms the basis of a more fundamental critique of Carver's model that aligns at least in part with the theories advanced by the authors discussed above. Heifetz portrays organizations as inherently conservative places that are resistant to change. Organizations, Heifetz argues, prefer to stay in their

---

30. Scott, *Creating Caring and Capable Boards*; Brown, *The Imperfect Board Member*.
31. Middleton, "Nonprofit Boards of Directors."
32. Greenleaf, *Servant Leadership*, 40.
33. Smith (*Entrusted*) would query Carver's understanding of the board representing the will of the direct stakeholders *only*. He would stress that the role of the board is to hold the institution "in trust" for both its immediate stakeholders and the good of the broader community. Others (cf. Ostrower and Stone, "Governance") have cautioned that Smith's definition of stakeholders may be too broad.
34. Heifetz, Grashow, and Linsky, *The Practice of Adaptive Leadership*.

"comfort zone."[35] Change is not resisted because of an opposition to doing better or any inherent aversion to adaptation, but rather because all individuals and groups within organizations have specific interests and benefits that they are seeking to guard, either explicitly or implicitly. While technical problems (those that can be resolved within existing structures and policies) do not generally challenge these interests and benefits, adaptive problems (those that require more fundamental changes to the organization's culture) are a direct threat. Adaptive changes challenge people's priorities, beliefs, habits and loyalties. Heifetz suggests that adaptive leadership must exercise awareness of these *affective elements* in order to lead people through change.

At this level, the implications for governance are already apparent. Most governance tends to focus on technical changes (what Chait, Ryan, and Taylor would call fiduciary governance). Boards tend to focus on problems and look for a concrete solution. For example, one board observed in this project focused repeatedly on the question "how can we effectively raise more funds" while failing to look at broader issues that have led them to their current challenged state. *Adaptive leadership would approach these challenges differently*, querying deeper levels of the organization and perhaps surfacing more pervasive and more discomforting questions about the organization's failure to obtain significant numbers of new donors. Heifetz' model suggests that while technical problems can be solved internally within the organization, often by management alone, adaptive problems require the participation of stakeholders as well.[36] This aligns well with what Scott calls the need for "capacity for perceiving and responding to complexity."[37] Middleton's and Greenleaf's positioning of the board on the boundaries (and spanning the boundaries) of an organization is helpful in placing the board for this interpretive, perceptive work.

But Heifetz' concept goes further in its utility for governance. Heifetz stresses the critical difference between authority and leadership in organizations. Authority is something that is clearly in existence and given within organizations with clear limits. Heifetz believes that such authority, while essential, can be a force in organizations that can lead to atrophy.

---

35. Ibid., 29.
36. Ibid., 20.
37. Scott, *Creating Caring and Capable Boards*, 10.

The delegation of authority, including that from a board to a CEO, can be expressed as "I look to you to serve a set of goals I hold dear."[38] This can be a positive relationship, based in well-articulated organizational values. Yet Heifetz argues that it is more often a negative structure, wherein "good leadership" comes to be defined as "excellence in executing directions set by others."[39] In short, such structures can *prevent* the exercise of adaptive leadership, which in its essence is poised to raise critical questions about the nature and direction of the organization.

Carver's Policy Governance Model is very clearly an exercise of authority in the way Heifetz defines it. It creates a space for action that is sanctioned by a higher authority with certain vested interests to be maintained. Heifetz is perhaps too quick to assume that authority will be used to protect vested interests, but he is right to point out the fundamentally conservative nature of organizations and their slowness to embrace change. Dynamic times call for dynamic leadership, and Heifetz' conception of adaptive leadership holds considerable promise. Yet his conception of adaptive leadership comes into direct conflict with Carver's Policy Governance Model when it suggests that adaptive leadership requires stepping across lines of established authority and risking telling people what they need to hear, rather than what they want to hear. Heifetz calls this "stepping into the unknown space and disturbing the equilibrium."[40] In effect, Heifetz' adaptive change calls for stepping across authoritative lines, of which Carver's policies could be seen as one, in order to ask provocative questions.

Heifetz' work is infused with a strongly competitive tone. Many of his examples are drawn from major corporations and politics. It regularly references and is even structured around terms drawn from evolutionary biology. He seems to have a very dim view of human nature and a strong sense of individuals' and groups' tendencies to protect themselves and their interests at all costs.[41] Heifetz is right to point out that we all have articulated and unarticulated interests that cause us to resist change. He is also right to point out that authority can curtail innovations. This critique seems especially

---

38. Heifetz, Grashow, and Linsky, *Practice of Adaptive Leadership*, 24.
39. Ibid., 25.
40. Ibid., 28.
41. This approach resonates to a degree with a biblical anthropology. It lacks, however, the hope of redemption or *what could be* that Christian faith can inspire.

appropriate when thinking about Carver's Policy Governance Model. While useful in terms of defining board and management roles and preventing board micromanagement, the Policy Governance Model can also stifle innovation by creating a *cordon sanitaire* of acceptable activity and defining good leadership performance as staying only in this safe area.

The idea of a "concert of governance" presents a tentative beginning point for those attempting to see governance structures enable more effective theological schools and other institutions. Although they possess boards that clearly understand that they hold the final fiduciary authority for the institution, their governing practices in general tend to lean heavily on a presidential figure who in turn draws effectively on a web of interlocking relationships both within and without the community of the institution, especially among senior management. These relationships tend to be indwelled strongly with trust. In this way, the line of authority becomes a bit blurrier, with much boundary spanning taking place. While policies may exist, the boards clearly rely to a large degree on the insights of others within the organizations and, at times, through relationships with broader networks of stakeholders in the community. This dynamic, relational model of governance adheres much more closely to the adaptive leadership discussed by Heifetz and the modes of governance described by Chait, Ryan, and Taylor, as well as Middleton. They reflect models of governance that are inherently focused on institutional development and improvement, as opposed to institutional preservation. Although the Carver Model has unquestioned utility in terms of assisting board process, it lacks this important focus on facilitating difficult discussions that may transcend and ultimately undermine established policies. While a useful tool, the rapidly changing environment in which we live calls for more adaptive modes of governance than that offered by Carver.

Implications for Renewal in Theological Education

The discussion of renewal of theological education over the past three decades has produced a staggering amount of writing, conferences, and plans. As discussed above, these inputs have arisen from a wide variety of disciplinary approaches, including philosophical/theological, educational, historical, and leadership perspectives. The tension between fragmentation/integration is strong throughout the literature. It is easy to read through several decades of such literature and have the sense that very little has changed. The traditional four-fold curriculum remains dominant in most theological schools around the world and theological educators continue to struggle to find appropriate models of integration and responsiveness to the church. It may be that the very *fragmentation of the discussion on renewal in theological education* has contributed to less positive change than many would have hoped. It must be noted that a number of works, including Banks,[42] Ott,[43] Cannell,[44] and Shaw[45] have attempted to bridge between various disciplinary approaches to the theological education debate. Yet perhaps the scale of change is greater than an initial glance would suggest, especially when theological education in a global perspective is considered. Aleshire speaks to both the stability and flexibility of theological schools.[46] Such institutions are remarkably stable and tend to be among the last societal institutions to pursue change. Yet one must acknowledge a certain amount of flexibility as well, since such institutions have proven remarkably durable, often far outliving their counterparts in the for-profit world (one could argue that most higher education institutions, at least until very recent times, have shared this durability). Perhaps the model of change is more one of accretion. Aleshire suggested the following in a presentation to African theological educators: "Theological education changes as a tree grows; it adds rings. If we don't add rings, we won't have the strength or stability to meet the changing winds of the future."[47] This study would suggest that at least some theological schools in the Majority World are intentionally and creatively pursuing a renewal agenda that is seeking to pursue theological education that is more integrated, more deeply responsive to the church, and more administratively nimble, a suggestion affirmed by MacLeod.[48] The experience of the institutions observed in this study may contribute in a significant way to thinking about renewal in theological education.

---

42. Banks, *Reenvisioning Theological Education*.
43. Ott, *Beyond Fragmentation*.
44. Cannell, *Theological Education Matters*.
45. Shaw, *Transforming Theological Education*.
46. Aleshire, *Earthen Vessels*.
47. D. Aleshire, "The Future Has Arrived: Changing Theological Education in a Changed World," presented at the Institute for Excellence in Global Theological Education (4 May 2011) Addis Ababa, Ethiopia.
48. MacLeod, "Unconventional Educational Practices."

The study affirms the importance of seeing theological schools as embedded in and responsive to their contexts. While they retain their ultimate allegiance to the Word of God as revealed in Scripture, they are also sensitive to Walls' conception of both the indigenizing and the pilgrim principles.[49] In short, they are aware of the need to remain affixed to the universal nature of God's work while at the same time allowing it to find dwelling in their own dynamic local context. The category of responsive interaction with the surrounding context suggests that achievement of mission for these schools involves a continual dialogue with the realities of their local and global contexts and a concern for enabling the church to have a vision for nation and society. A staff member of S4 said this well.

> Is there a heart that drives for the people of this country? Don't ever forget that the church exists within the nation. God's people are like a nation within the nation. We have to have that national impact. This has been one of the problems that I see in the church . . . that same lack of a dream for the nation. You cannot be in this business and not dream about the nation. Who are we trying to save? Who are we trying to win? Are we trying to get more members, or are we trying to win the nation? (S4–I2 development)

Although the delimitations of this study did not intentionally seek schools that attempted to pursue transformative education, as expressed in desire for worldview change, empowerment, and unity of knowledge, belief, and action, all four observed institutions clearly shared this category. *This educational approach seems to be a critical element, both encouraging responsive interaction with society, as well as being nourished by such exchange.*

A second implication pertains to the exercise of governance itself. The "concert of governance" as expressed above suggests that governance structures in the observed institutions are fluid. While institutional governance structures vest final authority in the board, the actual work of governance is accomplished in concert with the CEO and the staff of the institution. The success of this fluid relationship relies heavily on a strong community of trust that ties together and aligns the various parts of the institution together. Chait,

---

49. Walls, *Missionary Movement*.

although not speaking about theological schools, adds weight to this point by suggesting that the best governance sees a "problem of purpose, rather than performance" and empowers people to accomplish meaningful work.[50] The observed schools seem to suggest that such empowerment of a concert of governance has allowed them to achieve real and meaningful change. If there is an imperfection, it is the fact that the board often remains underutilized, with members' inputs remaining on a relatively low level. Chait suggests that this too can be enlivened through greater empowerment of board members themselves. "We've learned that the more opportunities board members have to add value, the more value they derive, and the more value they derive, the more likely they will add even greater value. There's a reciprocity to good governance."[51] The continued quest for such reciprocity seems to hold promise for continued positive change in theological schools.

Finally, the theme of integration arises once again, though not as a call for curricular integration or greater alignment of the work of the theological school with the church. Although this study suggests that focus on the mechanics of governance alone will likely not lead to positive change, the overall practice of governance should look holistically at the institutions being governed, including their means of leadership, sustainability, and administration. The data from S3, in particular, suggested the necessity of strong alignment between the institution's stated and implicit values, its explicit curriculum, *and* its community and administrative processes that facilitate daily life. The overall category of alignment suggests that it is the coherence of these various areas of institutional life that can best facilitate true transformational learning. This suggests that while curricular questions and other educational matters should be a subject of governance discussions, matters of community life, the principles undergirding administrative processes, and public relations – all matters critical to the fabric of the institution – must also be discussed by those involved in governance.

The study has demonstrated the importance of both boundary spanning and generative thought in the work of theological schools. It has suggested that staff and management of these institutions, rather than boards, more frequently engage these activities, although board members have clearly

---

50. R. P. Chait, "'GAL' turns five!" *Board Member* 8–11 (2010, March/April): 9.
51. Ibid., 10.

demonstrated both desire and competence to be further engaged in such work. Perhaps the most important implication of this study for the future of theological education is the affirmation that theological schools must remain in close touch with their dynamic environments and contexts and find ways in which they can adjust while at the same time guarding their founding values and principles. This implication aligns well with the emerging theme of the prophetic role of theological education discussed in chapter 2. Board governance, when approached from the perspective of a "concert of governance," seems to demonstrate significant ability to enable the observed theological schools to practice that careful balance of adaptation and preservation. Further attention to harnessing the potential of and empowering board members toward more involvement in the process could stimulate even greater productivity.

Suggestions for Further Research

This study has observed a mere four theological schools in four countries. The concepts and categories discussed above could benefit mightily from further observations. Beyond this numeric and depth possibility, several other possibilities for meaningful further research arise:

1. The initial proposed methodology planned to include schools in North America. This did not occur for logistical reasons. The plan was rooted in a desire to compare and contrast the exercise in governance in Majority World contexts and a North American context where board governance was more historically ingrained.[52] The data referred to in the answer to the second research question suggests that the governance practice observed in several of these schools, especially S3, may align to a degree with leadership models prevalent in the context that tend to favor a single strong leader. In retrospect, this makes the lack of inclusion of a North American institution disappointing and suggests that this could be a further line of meaningful inquiry. Such an engagement with North American theological schools would also draw on the significant resources of

---

52. Hall, "Cultures of Trusteeship."

groups such as the Association of Theological Schools, the Center for the Study of Theological Education at Auburn Theological Seminary, and – perhaps especially – InTrust, whose sole purpose is seeing better governance of North American theological schools.

2. The interplay of leadership style of the CEO and governance in the broadest sense arose as a significant theme. It is clear that the institutions studied were generally quite CEO-centric. While the institutions possessed in at least a superficial form a model of governance that aligned roughly with the Carver Model, the actual dynamics were quite a bit more complex, with the CEO playing a dominant role in the system. This raises the question of how administrative structures (perhaps imported from or influenced by other contexts) cohere with leadership patterns based in the local context. Further exploration of this potential dissonance is needed on multiple levels. At the theological level, further work on Old Testament leadership patterns exercised in the Israelite community may be able to shed light, especially as many Majority World contexts share greater affinity with the Ancient Hebrew world than with Enlightenment world that gave rise to many contemporary models of leadership, administration, and governance. There is also room for significant sociological and/or anthropological research on leadership patterns in an increasingly globalized world where leaders mediate between various cultures on a daily basis.

3. The "concert of governance" suggests a sharing of the governance process. This study did not engage significantly with the broader notion of shared governance involving faculty, although interviews with several faculty members contributed to the theory. This was largely pursued due to a lack of a strong culture of shared governance in most Majority World theological schools. A further study of the role of faculty in the governance of theological schools in the Majority World would be useful.

4. The study noted several significant differences in the methods of board selection. One institution was owned by a denomination and board members were appointed by a central body, albeit with

input from the school leadership. Another was owned by a regional association which appointed board members. The other two had self-perpetuating boards. A further exploration of these variables and especially the role of denominational relationships may shed further light on governance practice.

5. As noted, a governance industry has emerged in recent years, with a seemingly endless number of consultants offering their services to nonprofits and educational institutions. In North America, InTrust focuses exclusively on the work of theological school boards. Internationally, OCI has conducted numerous seminars and training workshops on the topic, and several ICETE-related institutions have engaged in this area of activity. A thorough study exploring the impact of these interventions on theological schools may suggest meaningful ways to improve board governance, especially in terms of empowering board members.

6. The issue of succession and transition as destabilizing elements in the systems studied raises the critical importance of succession planning. Further study of actual experiences of succession and of succession planning would likely be useful.

7. The history of the institutions studied was considered in a very cursory way. It is clear, however, that a deeper historical understanding of the development of Protestant/evangelical theological schools in these contexts would assist in better understanding their realities and potential. A particular focus on the area of intercultural interaction between local church leaders and expatriate funders may be especially helpful in understanding governance. History of the sort exercised by Marsden,[53] observing specific institutions in the broader context or by Miller,[54] attempting to look at theological education as a whole in a context would both prove valuable.

---

53. Marsden, *Reforming Fundamentalism*.
54. Miller, *Piety and Profession*.

Undoubtedly, there are many other promising areas of inquiry that could be pursued qualitatively or quantitatively.

Conclusion

This study set out to deepen understanding of the governance process in theological schools in diverse cultural contexts. The results have illuminated the governance processes in four schools globally and suggest the importance of seeing the governance process as a "concert," where governance is a fluid function centered on the board but drawing in the expertise, skills, and time of the rest of the organization as well. The importance of governance taking place in the presence of a community of trust, organizational alignment, the presence of a strong, enabling CEO, reflective responsiveness, education that transforms, and concern for the effects of transition on organizational systems were highlighted, all in dynamic interaction. The study suggests the limitation of the Carver Model of governance for theological schools and stresses the import of a more flexible and encompassing model that employs both boundary spanning and generative thought in assisting an institution to respond appropriately to its environment while guarding values. The study also suggests the importance of such nimbleness in responding to the environment in the overall agenda of renewal in theological education, affirming that boards must play a key role in this process. Much remains unknown about the intersection of culture and governance. It is the hope of the researcher that this study has shed some light on actual practices. It will fall to colleagues in theological education around the world to test this hypothesis in the light of their own experience of governance.

Epilogue

A Library, a Farm, and a Train Station

A Library

Several years ago, I visited a seminary in South America. This was an older seminary, one that had been founded by missionaries many decades before. Like most properties in this city, a high wall surrounded the seminary compound. Guards patrolled the gate. This was all quite well and necessary given the realities of the city. To have less security would have been foolhardy. As I talked with the then-president of the school, however, he told me about some recent research that he and his team had done in their surrounding community. An informal survey of the seminary's neighbors revealed that the vast majority of them had little to no idea what the seminary did or why it existed. Beyond that, the overwhelming majority had vague but very negative feelings about the seminary.

This feedback rightfully shocked the seminary and its leadership. They were exceedingly well known within the evangelical community in their country, as well as throughout their region. Leaders of the evangelical churches and even international Christian leaders were frequent guests on the campus. Yet their neighbors, some of whom shared a wall with the seminary, had very little understanding and quite negative feelings about them. These feelings were seemingly not rooted in any kind of specific ill will – there was too little knowledge for that – it was rather a vague distrust of the unknown.

The seminary began to explore more about its immediate neighborhood. It learned that a large number of families in the working-class neighborhood sent their students to the local government school. Like many such places, the teachers worked hard with few resources. The lack of a library was repeated over and over again as a problem. How were children to learn to read well if they had no access to books?

The journey continued with the launching of a children's library on campus in a previously under-utilized space. After school, children from the community came onto the campus to take advantage of the availability of a growing collection of children's books. The library became known as a "safe space" in the community and parents began to learn more about the seminary and those who worked and studied there. The seminary repeated the informal research about a year after the opening of the library and learned that the results were nearly inverted from the previous study: the vast majority of respondents had some good idea of the work of the seminary and saw it as a positive influence in the community. *The walls of the seminary had been breached.*

A Farm

In a West African country, a small Bible institute began its work with the best out-of-the-box Western curriculum, drawn from a leading Western seminary. Students were assembled, lined up for classes, and fed content. All along, however, the school's African leaders and some Western missionaries helping them felt that something was not quite right. Thankfully, they had the courage to embark on a number of changes that led to a radical rethink of the curriculum, the delivery structures, and the very identity of the school. Today, it is one of the larger training programs in this part of West Africa, with a diverse set of programs that wed together theological and vocational training.

The problem emerged, however in that the vast majority of the school's students came from rural environments, where the role of vocational pastor was nearly impossible. Nearly all church leaders earned their family's keep through farming, occasionally supplemented by gifts of produce or livestock from members of their flock. Even more critically, the pastors together with their community struggled with life on the edge of subsistence, struggling to make a living amidst increasingly uncertain climate conditions and the lack of sustainable agricultural practice. Watching this reality, the school's leadership could no longer abide the dissonance between what was being taught and the lives of their students. Drawing on lessons from a large sustainable agricultural training community begun by the Catholic church several decades ago, the school's leadership began to develop a second campus on a piece of property in a rural area. The curricular approach of this center for students from rural background would include sustainable agricultural training, as well as a theological education offered in a deeply integrated way. The approach taken was one of inquiry. Not everything worked well on the first try. Yet the spirit of inquiry led to a gradually evolving program that was increasingly fit for its purpose in this West African context. *Theological education in this case was increasingly seen as rooted in the soil of the context.*

A Train Station

Recently, I had the opportunity to visit a seminary in Japan. Through a providential turn of events, the seminary obtained a property within ten minutes' walk of the city's main train station. The central stations in major Japanese cities are universes unto themselves. Not only can you catch a long-distance bullet train, a commuter train to the suburbs, or the city subway, you can also buy a new coat, shop for stationery and books, or dine on any number of Japanese or international delicacies. These stations are, in many ways, the heart of the city and the culture.

The incredibly efficient nature of Japanese train transport makes this seminary accessible within 2-3 hours to the vast majority of the Japanese population. I stood on the roof of this seminary, looking out on the bustle of the neighborhood and the bullet trains passing by every few minutes. The busy docks loomed in the distance, engaged in trade with every part of the planet. Enormous automobile factories loomed further on the horizon, powering the Japanese economy. A major university campus sprawled just a few blocks away. The seminary's leadership did not see their strategic location as coincidence, but rather as a very intentional part of their identity. They understood their role as a sort of train station for the church, a connecting and equipping point. While the seminary offered formal, degreed training programs, perhaps their greatest value was in the more informal programs that served as an ongoing resource to the Japanese church. *The seminary was seen as a crossroads and resource center for the church and the nation.*

Each of these three vignettes – and many others that could be offered from every corner of the globe – present a hopeful future for theological education. None of these innovations or understandings – library, farm, or train station – came from some sort of *sui generis* strategic planning exercise. Instead, most emerged out of the much messier, iterative stew of day-to-day organizational life. The key and common ingredient, however, was an openness to innovation and a keen sense of mission, as well as a healthy dose of willingness to try, succeed, fail, and learn from experience. It is my hope that such bold learning cultures will undergird more and more theological schools globally, leading to ever more responsive theological education for the global church.

Recommended Reading

Chapters 2–3 contains extensive treatment of literature on theological education as well as nonprofit and educational governance, with full references given at the conclusion of the book. The following, however, is a short, annotated list of key works in both areas that I would recommend to all theological educators.

Theological Education

1. Aleshire, Daniel. "Governance and the Future of Theological Education." *Theological Education* 44, no. 2 (2009): 11–20.
2. Aleshire, Daniel. *Earthen Vessels: Hopeful Reflections on the Work and Future of Theological Schools.* Grand Rapids, MI: Eerdmans, 2008.

Dan Aleshire writes from inside the heart of the theological education world of North America in his capacity as Executive Director of the Association of Theological Schools in Pittsburgh, Pennsylvania. I have always appreciated his deep reflection on the task and import of theological schools, his keen sense of the human elements of leaderships, the importance of governance, and his desire to learn from and serve the global church. The two writings above draw on this experience and values. The *Theological Education* article, in particular, is remarkably aligned with some of the outcomes of this research, although I (rather unfortunately) came upon it only after the defense of my dissertation in 2012.

3. Farley, E. *Theologia: The Fragmentation of Unity of Theological Education.* Philadelphia, PA: Fortress, 1983.

This may be the most cited work in the literature on theological education. Its prescriptive value in terms of suggestions for practical change is limited. Its tone, as well as some of Farley's later work,[1] is quite pessimistic. Despite this

---

1. E.g. E. Farley, "Why Seminaries Don't Change: A Reflection on Faculty Specialization," *Christian Century* 114, no. 5 (1997).

and its age, I believe it is still quite useful, along with Kelsey,[2] to excavate some of the philosophical and historical strata of theological education.

4. Suazo Jiménez, David. *La función profética de la educación teológica evangélica en América Latina*. Barcelona, Spain: Editorial Clie, 2012.

This work, based on the author's dissertation at Seminario Teológico Centroamericano (SETECA), is one of the richer recent works on evangelical theological education, drawing on a wide literature base. While valuable first and foremost for its contributions at the global level, it also gives voice to the challenges and possibilities of Latin American evangelical theological education. It is my hope that this work will become available in English.

5. Pohor, R., and I. Coulibaly, eds. *Christianisme authentique en Afrique contemporaine*. Abidjan, Côte d'Ivoire: Les Presses FATEAC, 2014.

This series of essays, arising from a colloquium held at the Faculté de Théologie Evangélique de l'Alliance Chrétienne (FATEAC) in May 2013, presents a bold articulation of a vision for theological education in Francophone Africa and in Africa more generally. It wrestles deeply with the relationship of Christian theology and theologizing and African culture, suggesting the need for ever-deeper interaction. It also addresses what appears to be a fairly pan-African desire for a broadening of definitions of theological education in terms of subject matter.

6. Searle, J., and M. Cherenkov. *A Future and a Hope: Mission, Theological Education, and the Transformation of Post-Soviet Society*. Eugene, OR: Wipf & Stock, 2014.

This work, written by a British academic/theological educator who served a number of years in Ukraine, as well as an Ukrainian theological educator/academic, builds on works like Banks[3] and Penner[4] in articulating a holistic mission basis for theological education in the context of a "church without walls." While deeply relevant to the current context of Ukraine and Eurasia, it has much to contribute to the global conversation as well.

---

2. Kelsey, *Between Athens and Berlin*.
3. Banks, *Reenvisioning Theological Education*.
4. Penner, "Introduction."

7. Theocharous, M. "Not Living on Bread Alone: Theological Education as Prophetism." *Evangelical Review of Theology* 38, no. 3 (2014).
8. Dharamraj, H. "We Reap What We Sow: Engaging Curriculum and Context in Theological Education." *Evangelical Review of Theology* 38, no. 3 (2014).

These articles, first presented at the ICETE Triennial in Nairobi, Kenya in October 2012, charted new territory in terms of the interaction of theological education with culture and context. Drawing on the authors' experiences in Greece and India, respectively, they challenge many assumptions. Dharamraj's work, in particular, not only challenges assumptions, but speaks of practical ways in which she and her colleagues have engaged South Asian culture more deeply in their study of the Bible and theology.

9. Shaw, P. W. H. *Transforming Theological Education: A Handbook for Integrative Learning.* Carlisle, UK: Langham Global Library, 2014.

This work arose out of a number of years of leadership of practical workshops in curricular planning at seminaries around the world and provides a practical, step-by-step guide for theological schools to reflect on their mission and the overall alignment of their institutinos, particularly the area of the hidden curriculum. B. Ott's *Understanding and Developing Theological Education*, originally published in German but soon to be published in English (Carlisle: Langham Global Library, 2015) is invaluable.

10. Greenleaf, R. K. *Seminary as Servant: Essays on Trusteeship.* Peterborough, NH: Windy Row Press, 1983.

This work, which does not seem to have had the attention in the literature that it deserves, was remarkably prescient, seemingly foreseeing many of the turns in organizational and leadership thinking that would come in the following decades. This work is perhaps the most foundational to my study and thinking on theological education. I would recommend it for the consideration of every leader of theological education and theological school board member.

11. MacLeod, M. "Unconventional educational practices in Majority World Theological Education: A qualitative research study." Unpublished manuscript. Indianapolis, IN: Overseas Council, 2013.

This study grew up in many ways alongside my dissertation research during my tenure with Overseas Council and employed similar methodologies. The study and my many conversations with the author during the research, proved foundational to my thinking about theological education and leadership development. Its study of innovation in the context of diverse schools, and particular the fragility of this innovation, continues to inspire my work with Cornerstone Trust.

12. Banks, R. *Reenvisioning Theological Education: Exploring a Missional Alternative to Current Models.* Grand Rapids, MI: Eerdmans, 1999.
13. Ott, B. *Beyond Fragmentation: Integrating Mission and Theological Education.* Oxford, UK: Regnum Books, 2001.

These two works both were critical in the movement of the theological education debates from a diagnosis of fragmentation to a grounding of theological education in the *missio Dei*. They both also contain rich bibliographic reviews and critique of precedent literature and are strong on concrete suggestions for change.

Governance

Greenleaf, cited above, is also an essential work in the governance literature.[5] Aleshire also bridges the two areas.[6]

1. Middleton, M. "Nonprofit Boards of Directors: Beyond the Governance Function." In *The Nonprofit Sector*, edited by W.W. Powell. New Haven, CT: Yale University Press, 1987.

Somewhat like Greenleaf, this work from the 1980s has received more attention in recent years. Middleton's conception of "boundary spanning" by boards was fundamental to my thinking and also contributed to Chait, Ryan, and Taylor's broader understanding of governance. This is a short work that might prove useful to theological educators and boards.

2. Carver, J. *Boards that Make a Difference: A New Design for Leadership in Nonprofit and Public Organizations* (3rd ed.). San Francisco, CA: Jossey-Bass, 2006.

In many ways, this work has joined with others in the governance field as a subtle critique of the Carver method. Despite the weaknesses of this work, it remains invaluable. While governing boards of theological schools must

---

5. Greenleaf, *Seminary as Servant.*
6. Aleshire, "Governance and the Future."

move beyond a simple fiduciary understanding of their work, a move toward micromanagement would be catastrophic. Carver's invaluable clarification of the roles of boards and management and the tool of policy handbooks remain stimulating and useful in considering what the work of boards is – and more importantly – isn't.

3. Chait, R. P., W. P. Ryan, and B. E. Taylor. *Governance as Leadership: Reframing the Work of Nonprofit Boards.* Hoboken, NJ: John Wiley, 2005.

This 2005 work, together with its application and dissemination through BoardSource, has changed the contours of the conversation around nonprofit governance in North America. This is an essential starting point for anyone thinking about governance.

4. Wheeler, B. G. & H. Ouelette. *Governance that Works: Effective Leadership for Theological Schools.* New York: Auburn Center for Theological Education, 2015.

This recent work, which appeared after this manuscript was complete, provides a contemporary view into the governance of theological schools in North America. Based on both quantitative and qualitative research, the study aligns in some ways with key conclusions of my study, particularly the central role of the CEO. It also provides interesting data on the demographics of theological school boards in North America. Overall, it provides a realistic survey of the territory, along with some hope that things can improve.

Appendix A

Statement on Methodology

Six criteria drove sample selection. First, this study explored only institutions that adhere to an evangelical statement of faith, as demonstrated by their relationship with a member body of the International Council for Evangelical Theological Education (ICETE) or OCI. Second, the study was limited to institutions whose primary organizational language is accessible to the researcher, namely English, Russian, French, Spanish, or Portuguese. Third, the study was limited to theological schools that conduct both traditional, campus-based, formal training as well as some form of distance or modular education. This delimitation was established to reflect the "mixed mode" approach that Banks,[1] Cannell,[2] and Aleshire[3] argue will be increasingly prevalent, as the lines between formal and non-formal training blur. Fourth, the researcher sought to include institutions from Africa, Asia, Latin America, the Caribbean, Eurasia, and/or the South Pacific due to the relative lack of data surrounding governance in these regions. The fifth criterion revolved around the institutions' perceived importance and relevance in a region and their commitment to meaningful renewal; the study sought to explore those institutions that are frequently looked to by other theological schools as a source for ideas and best practices. The sixth and final criterion for selection was the perception of positive board function. This study sought to include those institutions whose boards are recognized to contribute to the institution in a positive way.

---

1. Banks, *Reenvisioning Theological Education*.
2. Cannell, *Theological Education Matters*.
3. Aleshire, *Earthen Vessels*.

In the summer of 2010, the researcher approached several outside experts for help in sample selection, based on the six criteria above. Four Overseas Council regional directors (in Asia, Africa, Latin America and the Caribbean, and Eurasia) responded to a brief questionnaire regarding schools in their regions of responsibility that fit the criteria. In addition, the researcher sought identical input from representatives (in each case, the CEO) of ICETE member bodies in Africa (Association for Christian Theological Education in Africa- ACTEA), Asia (Asia Theological Association), the Caribbean (Caribbean Evangelical Theological Association – CETA), Latin America (Asociación Evangélica de Educación Teológica en América Latina – AETAL), and Eurasia (Euro-Asian Accrediting Association). By September 2010, seven institutions had been chosen, together with seven alternate candidates. Complex logistics and limitations of financial resources and – especially – time led to only four institutions being studied.

During the final quarter of 2010, the researcher negotiated entry with the four final candidates. In each case, statements of confidentiality and informed consent were signed. The researcher worked carefully with the CEO of each institution to gain access to appropriate materials in advance of the visit. Between January and May 2011, the researcher visited each of the four participating institutions for three to four days. The researcher requested that the CEO provide a background on members of the governing board, including their tenure on the board, educational background, church background, and professional responsibilities. Additional artifacts to provide a background for the fieldwork, including written institutional history and board meeting minutes for the previous three years were also provided. These artifacts were reviewed prior to the site visit. While on site, the researcher observed a board meeting. The researcher also conducted structured interviews with institutional and board leadership. Interview protocols and other documents guiding observation and analysis, together with further information on the research process, are included in Appendix A.

Full transcripts of all interviews were developed. In two cases, interviews were conducted in English. In Russia, the researcher conducted interviews in Russian and did a full translation of all interviews into English. In Brazil, the researcher was accompanied by a translator who assisted in interviews conducted in both Spanish and Portuguese. All transcripts of these Brazilian interviews were produced in English, with careful attention to and review of the Spanish or Portuguese originals.

Data analysis was carried out utilizing structured grounded theory methodology. This process allows for an iterative process of continuous analysis.[4] The specific methods of grounded theory analysis developed by Corbin and Strauss[5] were chosen by the researcher because of their ability to allow for an iterative, evolving process of analysis that builds on data as it emerges, and because of their strong emphasis on the importance of thought, reflection, and intuition. Corbin[6] stresses the absolute importance of entering fully into the research process through repeated reflection and thinking. "Thinking is the heart and soul of doing qualitative analysis. Thinking is the engine that drives the process and brings the researcher into the analytical process."[7] Stressing the iterative nature of qualitative grounded theory, Corbin stresses the need to develop both concepts (lower-level words that attempt to express commonalities in data) and categories (higher-level organizing principles that begin to give meaning to concepts) that are fluid. "Concepts will be scrutinized against further data and added to, modified, or discarded as the products of analysis accumulate."[8] Following Corbin, analysis began the moment of the first artifact examination, with careful notation of key themes and resultant retooling of protocols and interview instruments. Field notes compiled during and after the site visits further refined thinking, developing initial concepts for further exploration.

Data analysis was conducted using the software tool MAXQDA (www.maxqda.com), a German qualitative research tool. This tool was adopted based on the Corbin.[9] Corbin recommends this tool because of the ways in which it allows the researcher's thinking and intuition to remain at the heart

---

4. Cresswell, *Qualitative Inquiry*.
5. Corbin and Strauss, *Basics of Qualitative Research*.
6. Ibid. Although both Corbin's and Strauss' names appear on this third edition of their text, Corbin writes this edition 12 years after Strauss' death and 18 years after the first edition. A review of the second edition (1998) reveals a book revised to such a degree as to be nearly a different work. Although Corbin retains Strauss' name on the book, it is important to stress that she draws on significant developments in grounded theory, qualitative research, and undergirding issues of philosophy since his death. I have chosen to use Corbin alone at points where I sense that this difference is especially strong.
7. Ibid., 63.
8. Ibid., 187.
9. Corbin and Strauss, *Basics of Qualitative Research*.

of the process, while bringing technological tools that strengthen this process. Rather than bringing rigidity by offloading analysis to computer programs, programs like MAXQDA are important tools that can "enhance the ability of the researcher to search for, store, sort, and retrieve materials."[10] MAXQDA provides a structure for uploading various types of documents, ranging from transcripts of interviews, observation notes, field notes, minutes, historical documents, and even photographs. It then provides a means for reviewing these artifacts and assigning to them codes that begin to describe concepts or categories. Codes are fluid and able to be placed in flexible hierarchy, renamed, or reorganized as the analysis process continues. The central tool of MAXQDA and Corbin's process is the use of extended memos. Memos can range from a few sentences concerning a particular piece of data to lengthy reflections on the concepts emerging from a specific interview or set of data. Over 250 memos were generated as data were reviewed.

The overall analysis process aligns in many ways with other approaches to qualitative grounded theory, including Cresswell.[11] These approaches start from open coding, allowing for formation of initial categories observed during data gathering. Such initial categories seek to identify individual phenomena that either assist or impede the governance process. This then allows for attention to be given to what influences this phenomenon either positively or negatively. For example, early analysis of data accumulated during the first site visit began to show a repeated concern for the realities of the theological school's particular context – politically, linguistically, and socially. This gave rise to a number of specific concepts, such as responsiveness, empowerment, and the unity of belief and action. As these same themes emerged in later site visits and analysis, these concepts gradually gave rise to a broader category of responsive interaction as a critical variable in governance function. These categories, however, were not static throughout the process and were subject to continued renaming, reordering, and other revisions. Such an approach allowed for continuous growth in understanding of the topic being studied, and the potential reframing of research questions in order to develop an increasingly useful knowledge of the topic being studied.[12] It allowed for the

---

10. Ibid., xi.
11. Cresswell, *Qualitative Inquiry*.
12. Ibid.

centrality of thinking and intuition that Corbin and Strauss stress as central to good qualitative research.[13]

Cresswell[14] and others, including Strauss and Corbin,[15] draw a strong line between open coding and a second step, axial coding. While open coding focuses on relatively low-level concepts, axial coding attempts to draw out connections between these concepts to form higher-level categories. Cresswell suggests that while open coding begins at the initiation of data collection, axial coding begins only after the completion of all field work.[16] Corbin does not deal with open and axial coding separately, but rather argues that the division is an artificial one, as the human brain automatically begins to make such higher-order connections as it works with the data.[17] The key to this approach, Corbin argues, is the ability to keep categories fluid and flexible and to continue to reflect on them, especially as the researcher begins to contemplate interrelations among various data sets, in this case, the experience of the four individual schools.

The final step in the analysis process arises in the formation of theory. Corbin stresses that the researcher must continue to evaluate data until such a point when "theoretical saturation" is reached, or a point where all categories are well developed in terms of properties, dimensions, and variations.[18] At this point, the researcher must begin the work of integration, or identifying a *core* category and developing and refining a theoretical construction that draws explanatory value from the entire set of data.[19] The researcher then moves beyond description to conceptualization, building a broad, meaningful explanatory theory that contributes to the initial research questions and to the broader phenomenon being studied. The outcomes of this process form the heart of chapter 3.

---

13. Corbin and Strauss, *Basics of Qualitative Research*.
14. Cresswell, *Qualitative Inquiry*.
15. Strauss and Corbin, *Basics of Qualitative Research*, 1st ed. (1990).
16. Cresswell, *Qualitative Inquiry*.
17. Corbin and Strauss, *Basics of Qualitative Research*.
18. Ibid.
19. Ibid., 263.

Appendix B

Protocol for Examination of Historical Documents

- Are these historical narratives composed in a professional, interpretive manner, or in a celebratory, institutional framework?
- What is the background of the author? Why did he/she compose this historical narrative? What biases might he/she bring to the task?
- When was the historical narrative(s) written? Why was the historical narrative composed at this particular time? What is missing from the narratives in terms of chronology? How recent are the narratives?
- What are the key turning points as portrayed in the historical narrative(s)? If multiple narratives, do they agree? Are these turning points tied to the legitimacy of the institution?
- What is the role of the governing board in these turning points? Who else has proven influential during these critical times?
- If the historical narrative(s) reveal conflict, how is it treated? Is there another side to the story? How was the conflict handled? Who was involved?
- What does the history reveal about the institution's mission's evolution over time? Has discernment regarding mission contributed to either turning points or conflict?
- What does the history reveal about the institution's constituency? Has the understanding of constituency shifted through the years?
- What does the history reveal about the institution's place in the broader ecclesial context? In the broader society?

- If the narrative is composed in a celebratory, institutional framework, what would be the key historical questions not addressed?

Appendix C

Protocol for Analysis of Board Meeting Minutes and Board Policy Manual

Type of Minutes

- Does the board utilize a board policy manual or something of the sort?
- What is the general character of the minutes? Do they capture only action items or do they give some character to the discussion?
- Who keeps minutes, and how are they filed?
- How soon after the meeting are minutes available?

Content of Policy Manual

- If a board policy manual exists, when was it instituted?
- What types of issues does the policy manual address?
- How often is it updated? Does it seem to be a document that informs action of the board, or is it merely an antiquated document?

Content of Minutes

- What are the most important issues addressed/recorded in the minutes? Over how many meetings of the board do such issues flow?
- To what degree does the board deal with issues of legitimacy of the institution? How is this expressed?

- Is conflict visible in the minutes? If so, how is it dealt with? Does it linger over multiple meetings? Does it appear to be resolved through formal or informal structures?
- What do the minutes say about power in the board? Were decisions unanimous? Were discussions referred to the chairperson or smaller groups?
- Do the minutes reveal a strong sense of community among the board? Are there clear divisions among members? If so, are they along ethnic or other lines?
- To what degree do the minutes and record or board activity represent engagement with fiduciary, strategic, and generative governance?
- If engagement in generative governance is noted, how? What issues? How did these issues arise? What nurtured or hindered these discussions? What environment nurtured the conversations?

Appendix D

Protocol for Observation of Board Meeting

Description of Environment and Meeting

- Detail the environment being observed, including:
    - Number of people present
    - Names and roles of people present
    - Backgrounds of board members (tenure, education, church experience, professional responsibilities) – drawn from preliminary data from CEO
    - Diagram of seating arrangement
    - Description of environment, including aesthetics, weather, lighting
    - Copy of agenda and pre-board meeting correspondence
- How does the meeting commence?
- To what degree were processes or procedures clear? Did the meeting follow a clear agenda?
- What is the overall tone of the conversation? Does it change throughout the meeting?
- What is the role of the chairperson? Is it uniform throughout the meeting?
- What is the role of the CEO? Is it uniform throughout the meeting?
- How does the meeting end?

Power Dynamics

- What are the power dynamics visible among the various members? How does the chairperson or others present wield authority?
- Do dynamics such as age, gender, or ethnicity contribute to power dynamics?
- What was the character of any informal times, such as coffee breaks, meals, etc? Did work continue during these times, and if so, in what forms?
- Is there evidence of informal networks within the board?

Conflict

- If conflict is evident among any parties, how is it evidenced?
- What subjects seem to lead to conflict?
- How is conflict handled when it arises?

Use of Time

- What are key elements of the meeting that fit the fiduciary mode of governance? Approximately what percentage of the whole in terms of time?
- What are key elements of the meeting that fit the strategic mode of governance? Approximately what percentage of the whole in terms of time?
- What activities or discussions seem unusual or significant? What makes these stand out?
- What are the turning points in the meeting? Do they happen formally or informally?
- What issues consumed the most time? What issues consumed the most energy?

Generative Governance/Boundary Spanning

Boundary Spanning

- To what degree does the board engage in Middleton's conceptions of boundary spanning, such as
  - Developing of exchange relationships with external parties to ensure the flow of resources into and out of organization.
  - Interpreting information gained from exchange relationships to make the internal organizational adjustments necessary to meet environmental demands.
  - Buffering the organization from the environment and thus protect it from external interference.
  - Reducing environmental constraints by influencing external conditions to the organization's advantage.
- What are key elements of the meeting that fit the generative mode of governance? Approximately what percentage of the whole in terms of time?
- Do board members draw on their experiences in external environments? If so, how? With what issues?
- How do the board members' backgrounds (such as pastors, businesspeople, educators) contribute to the discussions?
- When generative governance takes place, what conditions seem to stimulate it? What sustains such discussions? What impedes or hinders? To what degree do board members show comfort with such discussions?

Appendix E

Protocol for Structured Interviews

Board Chairperson

- Tell me about yourself, your background, profession, family? (dialogue)
- What are some of the major challenges you see for the church in your society?
- What are some the major challenges you see more generally in society?
- In what ways is x institution addressing these issues?
- In what ways is the board discussing x institution's role in these church and societal issues?
- What has been your favorite or most rewarding moment while serving on the board of x institution?
- Describe the relationship among the board members of institution x.
- What has been the most challenging moment for you while serving on the board of the x institution? (Draw especially to see if there are legitimacy issues involved).
- What do you see as your primary roles as chairperson of the board of x institution?
- What insights are you able to bring to the board from your own professional life?

Other Board Member

- Tell me about yourself, your background, profession, family? (dialogue)
- What has been your favorite or most rewarding moment while serving on the board of x institution?
- What has been the most challenging moment for you while serving on the board of the x institution? (Draw especially to see if there are legitimacy issues involved).
- What do you see as your primary roles as a member of the board of x institution?
- What are some of the major challenges you see for the church in your society?
- What are some the major challenges you see more generally in society?
- In what ways is x institution addressing these issues?
- In what ways is the board discussing x institution's role in these church and societal issues?
- What is the most valuable and productive aspect of board meetings? (Attempt to draw on presence of informal power structures).
- What insights are you able to bring to the board from your own professional life?
- What would you like to see the board of x institution do better?

CEO

- Tell me about yourself, your background, profession, family? (dialogue)
- What has been your favorite or most rewarding moment while serving x institution?
- What has been the most challenging moment for you while serving x institution?
- Describe your relationship with the board chairperson and with the board in general?

- What do you do in order to prepare for board meetings? When is the board the most productive? What makes for the most successful meetings?
- What do you see as the major function(s) of the board of your school?
- What are some of the major challenges you see for the church in your society?
- What are some the major challenges you see more generally in society?
- In what ways is x institution addressing these issues?
- In what ways is the board discussing x institution's role in these church and societal issues?
- What insights do board members bring from their outside, professional life?
- What would you like to see the board of x institution do better?

Chief Academic Officer or Other Senior Staff Member

- Tell me about yourself, your background, profession, family? (dialogue)
- What has been your favorite or most rewarding moment while serving x institution?
- What has been the most challenging moment for you while serving x institution?
- Describe your interaction with the board.
- What do you see as the major function(s) of the board of your school?
- What are some of the major challenges you see for the church in your society?
- What are some the major challenges you see more generally in society?
- In what ways is x institution addressing these issues?
- In what ways is the board discussing x institution's role in these church and societal issues?
- What would you like to see the board of x institution do better?

Bibliography

Abraham, A. "Contextualized Theological Education for Oral Learners with Particular Reference to the Unreached, Unengaged People Groups in North India: Lessons Learnt and the Challenges." In *Beyond Literate Western Practices: Continuing Conversations in Orality and Theological Education,* edited by S. Chiang and G. Lovejoy, 37–44. Hong Kong: Condeo Press/International Orality Network, 2014.

Abzug, R., and J. Galaskiewicz. "Nonprofit Boards: Crucibles of Expertise or Symbols of Local Identities." *Nonprofit and Voluntary Sector Quarterly* 30 (2001): 51–73.

Abzug, R., and J. S. Simonoff. *Nonprofit Trustees in Different Contexts.* Aldershot, England: Ashgate, 2004.

Adjei, M. B. "Is The Seminary Relevant? A Critical Examination of the Relevance of Leadership Preparation at Ghana Christian University for Training Transformational Leaders." Unpublished doctoral dissertation. Seattle, WA: Bakke Graduate School, 2009.

Agar, M. H. *The Professional Stranger: An Informal Introduction to Ethnography.* San Diego, CA: Academic Press, 1980.

Ahoga, A. "Christianisme et context de vie." In *Christianisme authentique en Afrique contemporaine,* edited by R. Pohor and I. Coulibaly, 21–44. Abidjan, Côte d'Ivoire: Les Presses FATEAC, 2014.

Akrong, A. "The Challenges of Theological Education in Ghana." *Journal of African Christian Thought* 10, no. 2 (2007): 24–31.

Aleshire, D. *Earthen Vessels: Hopeful Reflections on the Work and Future of Theological Schools.* Grand Rapids, MI: Eerdmans, 2008.

———. "Governance and the Future of Theological Education." *Theological Education* 44, no. 2 (2009): 11–20.

———. "The Future Has Arrived: Changing Theological Education in a Changed World." Presented at Institute for Excellence in Global Theological Education (4 May 2011) Addis Ababa, Ethiopia.

———. "Response to 'Stewards of the Gospel.'" In *Stewards of the Gospel,* edited by R. Vallett. Grand Rapids: Eerdmans, 2011.

Allen, Y. *A Seminary Survey: A Listing and Review of the Activities of Theological Schools in Africa, Asia, and Latin America.* New York: Harper, 1960.

Amanze, J. N. "Contextuality: African Spirituality as a Catalyst for Spiritual Formation in Theological Education in Africa." *Ogbomosho Journal of Theology* XVI, no. 2 (2011): 1–23.

Andringa, R. C., and T. W. Engstrom. *Nonprofit Board Answer Book: Practical Guide for Board Members and Chief Executives.* (Expanded ed.). Washington, DC: Board Source, 2002.

Anheier, H. K., and L. M. Salamon. "The Nonprofit Sector in Comparative Perspective." In *The Nonprofit Sector, a Research Handbook,* edited by W.W. Powell and R. Steinberg (2nd ed.), 89–114. New Haven, CT: Yale University Press, 2006.

Antone, H., W. Longchar, H. Bae, H. P. Ho, and D. Werner, eds. *Asian Handbook for Theological Education and Ecumenism.* Oxford: Regnum, 2013.

Asamoah-Gyadu, J. K. "Called to Make a Difference: Theological Education and Mission in Twenty-First Century Africa." *Ogbomosho Journal of Theology* XV, no. 2 (2010): 1–16.

Banks, R. *Reenvisioning Theological Education: Exploring a Missional Alternative to Current Models.* Grand Rapids, MI: Eerdmans, 1999.

Barro, A. C. "A educação teológica e os seus desafíos para uma sociedade em transformação." In *Educação teológica transformadora,* edited by A. C. Barro and M. W. Kohl, 171–192. Londrina, Brazil: Descoberta, 2006.

———. "Holistic Mission as a Vision for the Seminary." Presented at Asia Theological Association (ATA) Consultation on Models of Theological Education: Manila, Philippines, 11 May 2011.

Baumgaertner, W. L. "Accountability to Church and State." In *The Good Steward: A Guide to Theological School Trusteeship,* 111–120. Washington, DC: AGB, 1983.

———. "The Theological Trustee's Testament." *AGB Reports,* 31, no. 2 (1989): 23–25.

Bediako, K. *Theology and Identity: The Impact of Culture upon Christian Thought in the Second Century and in Modern Africa.* Carlisle, UK: Regnum Books International, 1999.

Benefiel, R. "The Ecology of Evangelical Seminaries." *Theological Education* 44, no. 1 (2008): 21–27.

Bergquist, W. H., and K. Pawlak. *Engaging the Six Cultures of the Academy.* San Francisco, CA: Jossey-Bass, 2008.

Bermeo, N., and P. Nord, eds. *Civil Society before Democracy: Lessons from Nineteenth-Century Europe.* Lanham, Md: Rowman & Littlefield, 2000.

Billman, K. D., and B. C. Birch, eds. *C(H)AOS Theory: Reflections of Chief Academic Officers in Theological Educations.* Grand Rapids: Eerdmans, 2011.

Blackman, R. *Organisational Governance*. London, UK: Tearfund, 2006.

Blier, H. M., and B. G. Wheeler. *Report on a Study of Doctoral Programs That Prepare Faculty for Teaching in Theological Schools*. New York: Auburn Center for Theological Education, 2010.

Bolman, L. G., and T. E. Deal. *Reframing Organizations: Artistry, Choice, and Leadership*. (4th ed.). San Francisco, CA: Jossey-Bass, 2003.

Boorstin, D. *The Americans: The National Experience*. New York: Random House, 1965.

Borneman, J. and A. Hammoudi, eds. *Being There: The Fieldwork Encounter and the Making of Truth*. Berkeley, CA: University of California Press, 2009.

Borthwick, P. *Western Christians in Global Mission: What's the Role of the North American Church*. Downers Grove, IL: Intervarsity Press, 2012.

Bosch, D. J. *Transforming Mission: Paradigm Shifts in the Theology of Mission*. 20th Anniversary Edition. Maryknoll, NY: Orbis, 2011.

Bounds, E. M. "Theological Reflection in Contextual Education." In *Contextualizing Theological Education*, edited by T. Brelsford and P. A. Rogers, 17–28. Cleveland, OH: Pilgrim Press, 2008.

Bradley, J. *Voluntary Associations in Tsarist Russia: Science, Patriotism, and Civil Society*. Cambridge, MA: Harvard University Press, 2009.

Bradshaw, P., B. Hayday, R. Armstrong, J. Levesque, and L. Rykert. "Nonprofit Governance Models: Problems and Perspectives." Paper presented at the ARNOVA Conference, Seattle, WA, 1998.

Brelsford, T., and P. A. Rogers, eds. *Contextualizing Theological Education*. Cleveland, OH: Pilgrim Press, 2008.

Brelsford, T., and J. Senior. "Theological Thinking as Contextual Practice." In *Contextualizing Theological Education*, edited by T. Brelsford and P. A. Rogers, 42–55. Cleveland, OH: Pilgrim Press, 2008.

Brereton, V. L. *Training God's Army: The American Bible School, 1880-1940*. Bloomington and Indianapolis, IN: Indiana University Press, 1990.

Brooks, D. "Goodbye, Organization Man." *The New York Times* (2014, September 15): p. A27.

Brown, J. *The Imperfect Board Member: Discovering the Seven Disciplines of Governance Excellence*. New York: Wiley, 2006.

Brudney, J. L., and V. Murray. "Do Intentional Efforts to Improve Boards Really Work?" *Nonprofit Management and Leadership* 8, no. 4 (1998): 333–348.

Burch Basinger, R. "Where policy is good governance." *InTrust Magazine* (Summer 2008). Retrieved 7 Dec 2011. http://www.intrust.org/magazine/pastarticle.cfm?column=33&id=567.

Caldwell, L. W. "How Asian is Asian Theological Education?" In *Tending the Seedbeds: Educational Perspectives on Theological Education in Asia*, edited by A. Harkness, 23–46. Manila: Asia Theological Association, 2010.

Cannell, L. M. *Theological Education Matters: Forming Leaders for the Church*. Newburgh, IN: EDCOT Press, 2006.

———, ed. "Theme: The Social Philosophy of the Christian Educator, Gathering the Work of Ted Ward." *Common Ground Journal* 10, no. 2 (2013).

———. "Nonformal Education: A Retrospective." *Common Ground Journal* 11, no. 2 (2014): 144–153.

The Cape Town Commitment. (2011). The Lausanne Movement. Retrieved November 29, 2011. www.lausanne.org/en/documents/ctcommitment.html.

Carpenter, J., P. Glanzer, and N. Lantinga. *Christian Higher Education: A Global Reconnaissance*. Grand Rapids: Eerdmans, 2014.

Carver, J. *Boards That Make a Difference: A New Design for Leadership in Nonprofit and Public Organizations* (3rd ed.). San Francisco, CA: Jossey-Bass, 2006.

Chait, R. P., W. P. Ryan, and B. E. Taylor. *Governance as Leadership: Reframing the Work of Nonprofit Boards*. Hoboken, NJ: John Wiley, 2005.

Chait, R. P. "'GAL' turns five!" *Board Member* 8–11 (2010, March/April).

Charmaz, K. "Grounded Theory in the 21st Century: Applications for Advancing Social Justice." In *Strategies of Qualitative Inquiry*, edited by N. K. Denzin and Y. S. Lincoln. Thousand Oaks, CA: SAGE, 2008.

Charter, M. L. "Theological Education for New Protestant Churches of Russia: Indigenous Judgments on the Appropriateness of Educational Methods and Styles." Unpublished doctoral dissertation, Trinity Evangelical Divinity School. Deerfield, Illinois, 1997.

Cheesman, G. *The Bible College Movement in the UK*. Frankfurt, Germany: Vdm Verlag, 2009.

Cherenkov, M. "Toward Appropriate Missiology for Post-Soviet Evangelicals: Global Missiological Trends and Local Realities." Unpublished Manuscript, 2009.

Chiang, S., and G. Lovejoy, eds. *Beyond Literate Western Practices: Orality and Theological Education*. Hong Kong: Condeo Press/International Orality Network, 2013.

———, eds. *Beyond Literate Western Practices: Continuing Conversations in Orality and Theological Education*. Hong Kong: Condeo Press/International Orality Network, 2014.

Chong, C. "The Rise of the Net-Generation: Implications for Educational Renewal in the Seminary Classroom." In *Building Lives for Ministry: Collected Essays of Alliance Bible Seminary 110th Anniversary Consultation on Theological Education*, edited by Wai-Luen Kwok, 88–120. Hong Kong: Alliance Bible Seminary, 2009.

———. "Christian Education Encounters 21st Century Globalization: The Singapore Experience." *Christian Education Journal* 3, no.10, Supplement, (2013): S205–S219.

Chow, W. "An Integrated Approach to Theological Education." *Evangelical Review of Theology* 19, no. 2 (1995): 220–228.

Christensen, C. M., and H. J. Eyring. *The Innovative University: Changing the DNA of Higher Education from the Inside out*. San Francisco, CA: Jossey-Bass, 2011.

Cohen, M. D., and J. G. March. *Leadership and Ambiguity: The American College Presidency* (2nd ed.). Boston, MA: Harvard Business School Press, 1986.

Cole, V. B. "Toward Integration in the Theological School Curriculum." *Evangelical Review of Theology* 23, no. 2 (1999): 141–162.

Colwill, D. "The Use of Metaphor in Consulting for Educational Change." In *Consulting for Organizational Change*, edited by A. F. Buono and D. W. Jamieson, 113–135. Charlotte, NC: Information Age Publishing, 2010.

Cooley, R., and D. Tiede. "What Is the Character of Administration and Governance in the Good Theological School?" *Theological Education* 30, no. 2 (1994): 61–70.

Coppedge, W. "Training in the Ugandan Context." In *Beyond Literate Western Practices: Continuing Conversations in Orality and Theological Education*, edited by S. E. Chiang and G. Lovejoy, 31–36. Hong Kong: Condeo Press/International Orality Network, 2014.

Corbin, J. and A. Strauss. *Basics of Qualitative Research*. (3rd ed.). Los Angeles, CA: SAGE, 2008.

Cornelius, P. P. "Bridging the Expectation-Reality Gap: Exploring a Transformational Model for Theological Education in India." Unpublished Doctoral Dissertation. Fuller Theological Seminary, School of Intercultural Studies. Pasadena, California, 2014.

Costa, N. and R. Kassis. *Fann al-Hawkamah al-Rashedah: Daleel li-Najah al-Mu'assasat)The Art of Good Governance: A Guide for Successful Nonprofit Organizations)*. Beirut, Lebanon: Dar Manhal al-Hayat, 2012.

Costas, O. "Educación teológica y misión." In *Nuevas alternativas de educación teológica*, edited by C. R. Padilla. Buenos Aires: Nueva Creación, 1986.

Cowley, W. H. *Presidents, Professors, and Trustees: The Evolution of American Academic Government*. San Francisco, CA: Jossey-Bass, 1980.

Cranton, P. *Understanding and Promoting Transformative Learning: A Guide for Educators of Adults* (2nd ed.). San Francisco, CA: John Wiley, 2006.

Cresswell, J. W. *Qualitative Inquiry and Research Design: Choosing Among the Five Traditions.* (2nd ed.). Thousand Oaks, CA: SAGE Publications, 2007.

Crisp, O., and L. Edmondson, eds. *Civil Rights in Imperial Russia.* Oxford: Clarendon Press, 1989.

Crompton, L. C. "The New Future of Governance." *Board Member* 18, no. 6 (2009).

Delaney, K. J. "Methodological Dilemmas and Opportunities in Interviewing Organizational Elites." *Sociology Compass* 1, no. 1 (2007): 208–221.

Deininger, F., and O. Eguizabal. *Foundations for Academic Leadership.* Nürnberg, Germany: VTR Publications, 2013.

Dharamraj, H. "We Reap What We Sow: Engaging Curriculum and Context in Theological Education." *Evangelical Review of Theology* 38, no. 3 (2014).

DiMaggio, P. J., and W. W. Powell. "The Iron Cage Revisited: Institutional Isomorphism and Collective Rationality in Organizational Fields." *American Sociological Review* 48, no. 2 (1983): 147–160.

Diniz, L. "The Changing Face of Non-Traditional NGO Governance: The Case of the Chinmaya Rural Primary Health Care and Training Centre (CRTC), India." *FES Outstanding Graduate Student Paper Series* 10, no. 1 (2005). Retrieved April 17, 2009, from http://www.yorku.ca/fes/research/docs/2004/Diniz_2004_OGSPS.pdf.

Doornenbal, R. J. A. *Crossroads: An Exploration of the Emerging-Missional Conversation with a Special Focus on 'Missional Leadership' and Its Challenges for Theological Education.* Delft, the Netherlands: Eburon Delft, 2012.

Duryea, E. D. "Evolution of University Organization." In *The University as an Organization*, edited by J. A. Perkins, 15–38. New York: McGraw-Hill, 1973.

Dyatlik, T. "Chto ozhidaiut pastory i pomestnye tserkvi byvshego Sovetskogo Soiuza ot bogoslovskogo obrazovaniya v nachale XXI veka?" (What Do Pastors and Local Churches of the Former Soviet Union Expect from Theological Education at the beginning of the 21st century?). *Bogoslovskie Razmyshleniya* (Theological Reflections), 10 (2009): 72–96.

Dyrness, B. *Let the Earth Rejoice!: A Biblical Theology of Holistic Mission.* Grand Rapids, MI: WIPF, 1998.

Edgar, B. "The Theology of Theological Education." *Evangelical Review of Theology* 29, no. 3 (2005): 208–217.

Eadie, D. "Meeting the Governing Challenge: Applying the High-Impact Governing Model in your Organization." Oldsmar, FL: Governing Edge Publications, 2007.

Eichenwald, K. "In String of Corporate Troubles, Critics Focus on Boards." *New York Times* (2003, September 21). Retrieved April 8, 2009, from http://www.nytimes.com.

Elmer, D. H. "Theology Informs Mission and Education." In *Theological Education as Mission*, edited by P. Penner, 111–136. Schwarzenfeld, Germany: Neufeld Verlag, 2005.

Elmer, D. H., and L. McKinney, eds. *With an Eye to the Future: Development and Mission in the 21st Century: Essays in Honor of Ted Ward*. Monrovia, CA: MARC Publications, 1996.

Enns, M. "Theological Education in Light of Cultural Variations of Reasoning: Some Educational Issues." In *Theological Education as Mission*, edited by P. Penner, 137–152. Schwarzenfeld, Germany: Neufeld Verlag, 2005.

Escobar, S. *The New Global Mission: The Gospel from Everywhere to Everyone*. Downers Grove, IL: IVP Academic, 2003.

Estafanos, S. "Defying the Pharaohs: Contemporary Educational Challenges for the Evangelical Church in Egypt." *Christian Education Journal* 3, no. 10, Supplement, (2013): S-162–173.

Esterline, D. V. "Multicultural Theological Education and Leadership for a Church without Walls." In *Shaping Beloved Community*, edited by D. V. Esterline and O. U. Kalu, 15–25. Louisville, KY: Westminster John Knox Press, 2006.

Esterline, D. V., and O. U. Kalu, eds. *Shaping Beloved Community*. Louisville, KY: Westminster John Knox Press, 2006.

Esterline, D. V., D. Werner, and T. Johnson. *Global Survey on Theological Education: 2011-2013*. Presented at WCC Consultation in Busan, Korea, November 2013.

Evans, A. F., R. A. Evans, and D. A. Roozen. *The Globalization of Theological Education*. Maryknoll, NY: Orbis, 1993.

Farley, E. *Theologia: The Fragmentation of Unity of Theological Education*. Philadelphia, PA: Fortress, 1983.

———. "Why Seminaries Don't Change: A Reflection on Faculty Specialization." *Christian Century* 114, no. 5 (1997).

Feliciano-Soberano, J. "Patterns of Epistemological Beliefs among Filipino Students at a Graduate Seminary in Manila: Cultural Perspectives and Pedagogical Implications." Unpublished doctoral dissertation. Trinity Evangelical Divinity School. Deerfield, Illinois, 2011.

Ferenczi, J. *International Directory of Theological Education*. Chicago, IL: American Theological Library Association, 2001.

Ferris, R. W. *Renewal in Theological Education: Strategies for Change*. Wheaton, IL: Billy Graham Center, Wheaton College, 1990.

Freire, P. *Pedagogy of the Oppressed*. (30th anniversary ed.). New York: Continuum, 2000.

Freiwirth, J. and M. E. Letona. "System-wide Governance for Community Empowerment." *The Nonprofit Quarterly* 13, no. 4 (2006): 24–27.

Friedman, T. *The World is Flat, 3.0: A Short History of the 21st Century* (3rd ed.). New York: Picador, 2007.

Gener, T. "Every Filipino Christian a Theologian: A Way of Advancing Local Theology in the 21st Century." In *Doing Theology in the Philippines*, edited by E. Acoba, John D. Suk, and Asian Theological Seminary, 3–23. Manila: OMF Publications, 2005.

Gies, J. C. *The Good Steward: A Guide to Theological School Trusteeship*. Washington, DC: Association of Governing Boards, 1983.

Glaser, B. G. *Basics of Grounded Theory Analysis*. Mill Valley, CA: Sociology Press, 1992.

Glaser, B., and A. Strauss. *The Discovery of Grounded Theory*. Chicago, IL: Aldine, 1967.

González, J. *The History of Theological Education*. Nashville, TN: Abingdon Press, 2015.

Greenleaf, R. K. *Servant Leadership*. New York: Paulist Press, 1977.

———. *Seminary as Servant: Essays on Trusteeship*. Peterborough, NH: Windy Row Press, 1983.

Groome, T. "Wisdom for Life: The Horizon of Theological Literacy." In *Theological Literacy for the Twenty-First Century*, edited by R. L. Petersen and N. M. Rourke, 352–370. Grand Rapids, MI: Eerdmans, 2002.

Hagle, J., J. S. Brown, and L. Davison. *The Power of Pull: How Small Moves, Smartly Made, Can Set Big Things in Motion*. New York: Basic Books, 2010.

Hall, E. *Beyond Culture*. New York: Anchor, 1976.

Hall, P. D. "Cultures of Trusteeship." In *Inventing the Nonprofit Sector and Other Essays on Philanthropy, Voluntarism, and Nonprofit Organizations*, edited by P. D. Hall, 135–206. Baltimore, MD: Johns Hopkins University Press, 1992.

Hardy, S. *Excellence in Theological Education*. Green Point, South Africa: Modern Printers, 2006.

Harkness, A. "De-schooling the Theological Seminary: An Appropriate Paradigm for Effective Pastoral Formation." In *Tending the Seedbeds: Educational Perspectives on Theological Education in Asia*, edited by A. Harkness, 103–128. Quezon City, Philippines: Asia Theological Association, 2010.

Harvey, W. S. "Methodological Approaches for Interviewing Elites." *Geology Compass* 4, no. 3 (2010): 193–205.

Heclo, H. *On Thinking Institutionally.* Oxford: Oxford University Press, 2008.
Heifetz, R., A. Grashow, and M. Linsky. *The Practice of Adaptive Leadership: Tools and Tactics for Changing Your Organization and the World.* Cambridge, MA: Harvard Business Press, 2009.
Heim, S. M. "Renewing Ways of Life: The Shape of Theological Education." In *Theological Literacy for the Twenty-First Century,* edited by R. L. Petersen and N. M. Rourke, 55–67. Grand Rapids, MI: Eerdmans, 2002.
Herzog, F. "Athens, Berlin, and Lima." *Theology Today* 51, no. 2 (1994): 270–277.
Hester, D. C. "Practicing Governance in the Light of Faith." In *Building Effective Boards for Religious Organizations,* edited by T. P. Holland and D. C. Hester, 58–82. San Francisco, CA: Jossey-Bass, 2000.
Hiebert, P. G. *Transforming Worldviews: An Anthropological Understanding of How People Change.* Grand Rapids, MI: Baker, 2008.
Highsmith, D. T. "The Board of Trustees as Institutional Change Agent." Unpublished doctoral dissertation. University of South Carolina, Columbia, SC, 1999.
Hofestadt, G. *Culture's Consequences: Comparing Values, Behaviors, Institutions, and Organizations across Cultures.* (2nd ed.). Thousand Oaks, CA: SAGE, 2001.
Holland, T. P. and D. C. Hester, eds. *Building effective boards for religious organizations: A handbook for trustees, presidents, and church leaders.* San Francisco, CA: Jossey-Bass, 2000.
Hopewell, J. "A Congregational Paradigm for Theological Education." *Theological Education* 21 (1984): 60–70.
Hopkins, B. R. *Legal Responsibilities of Nonprofit Boards. BoardSource Governance Series:* Vol 2. (2nd ed.). Washington, DC: BoardSource, 2009.
Houle, C. O. *Governing Boards.* San Francisco, CA: Jossey-Bass, 1989.
Houston, W. H. "Theological Models of Biblical Holism with Reference to Theological Colleges in Africa." Unpublished D.Min. dissertation. Gordon-Conwell Theological Seminary, South Hamilton, MA, 2008.
Howell, A. M. "Beyond Translating Western Commentaries: Bible Commentary Writing in African Languages." *Journal of African Christian Thought* 13, no. 2 (2010): 21–33.
Hunter, E. R. "Stakeholder Perspectives of Contextual Engagement of PhD Programs at Select Evangelical Seminary in the Majority World." Unpublished doctoral dissertation. Trinity Evangelical Divinity School. Deerfield, IL, 2014.
Ingram, R. T. *Ten Basic Responsibilities of Nonprofit Boards.* Washington, DC: BoardSource, 2003.

James, E. *The Nonprofit Sector in International Perspective: Studies in Comparative Culture and Policy.* New York: Oxford University Press, 1989.

Jenkins, P. *The New Faces of Christianity: Bible Believers in the Global South.* New York: Oxford University Press, 2006.

Jones, L. G. "Something Old, Something New." *Christian Century* 131, no. 4 (2014).

Jones, D., J. Greenman, and C. Pohl. "The Public Character of Theological Seminaries: An Evangelical Perspective." *Theological Education* 37, no. 1 (2000): 1–16.

Kafang, Z. B. *Higher Theological Education: An Overview of Six Protestant Theological Institutions in Nigeria.* Jos, Nigeria: Pyla-Mak Services Ltd, 2009.

Kalu, O. "Elijah's Mantle: Ministerial Formation in Contemporary African Christianity." *International Review of Mission* 94, no. 37 (2005): 263–277.

———. "Multicultural Theological Education in a Non-Western Context." In *Shaping Beloved Community*, edited by D. Esterline and O. Kalu, 225–241. Louisville: Westminster John Knox Press, 2006.

Katongole, E., and C. Rice. *Reconciling All Things: A Christian Vision for Justice, Peace, and Healing.* Downers Grove, IL: Intervarsity Press, 2008.

Kaufman, R. A. *Needs Assessment: Concepts and Applications.* Miami, FL: Education Technology Publications, 1979.

Kellerman, B. *The End of Leadership.* New York: Harper Collins, 2012.

Kelsey, D. *Between Athens and Berlin: The Theological Education debate.* Grand Rapids, MI: Eerdmans, 1993.

Kerr, C., and M. L. Gade. *The Guardians: Boards of Trustees of American Colleges and Universities.* Washington, DC: Association of Governing Boards, 1989.

Kinsler, R. *Diversified Theological Education: Equipping all God's people.* Pasadena, CA: William Carey International University Press, 2011.

Kirk, A. "Re-envisioning the Theological Curriculum as if the *Missio Dei* Mattered." In *Theological Education as Mission*, edited by P. Penner, 15–38. Schwarzenfeld, Germany: Neufeld Verlag, 2005.

Klein, C. R. "Boundary Spanning: Building Bridges between and Organization and Its Environment." In *Building Effective Boards for Religious Organizations*, edited by T. P. Holland and D. C. Hester, 122–138. San Francisco, CA: Jossey-Bass, 2000.

———. *Perspectives on the Current Status of an Emerging Policy Issues for Theological Schools and Seminaries.* AGB White Paper No. 1. Washington: AGB, 1991.

Knight, G. R. *Philosophy and Education: An Introduction in Christian Perspective.* (4th ed.). Berrien Springs, MI: Andrews University Press, 2006.

Kohl, M. W. "Theological Education: What Needs to Be Changed?" In *Educating for Tomorrow: Theological Leadership for the Asian Context*, edited by M. W. Kohl and A. N. L. Senanayake, 29–58. Bangalore, India; SAIACS Press, 2007.

Knowles, M. S., F. H. Elwood, and R. A. Swanson. *The Adult Learner: The Definitive Classic in Adult Education and Human Resources*. (6th ed.). New York: Butterworth-Heinemann, 2005.

Landy, H. "Executives Took, but Directors Gave." *New York Times* (2009, April 4). Retrieved 8 April 2009, from http://www.nytimes.com.

Lang, A. S. *Financial Responsibilities of Nonprofit Boards. BoardSource Governance Series:* Vol 2. (2nd ed.). Washington, DC: BoardSource, 2009.

Lara Proença, W. "De 'casa de profetas' a seminaries teológicos: A preparação vocacional em perspectiva histórica." In *Educação teológica transformadora*, edited by A. C. Barro and M. W. Kohl, 11–48. Londrina, Brazil: Descoberta, 2006.

Lee, M. "The Asianization of Theological Education." *Journal of African Christian Thought* 9, no. 2 (2006): 38–42.

Lewis, G. D. "Governance: What Is It?" *Theological Education* 44, no. 2 (2009): 21–28.

Lewis, G. D., and L. H. Weems. *A Handbook for Seminary Presidents*. Grand Rapids, MI: Eerdmans, 2006.

Lincoln, T. D. "How Master of Divinity Changes Students: A Research-Based Model." *Teaching Theology and Religion* 13, no. 3 (2010): 208–222.

Luiskutty, C. T. and J. Jaison. "Towards Greater Effectiveness in Training." *Journal of Theological Education & Mission* 1, no. 1 (2010): 26–38.

Lynn, E., and B. L. Wheeler. *Missing Connections: Public Perceptions of Theological Education and Religious Leadership*. (Auburn Studies No. 6). New York: Auburn Theological Seminary, 1999.

Lynn, R. L. "Coming over the Horizon." In *Good Stewardship: A Handbook for Seminary Trustees*, edited by B. E. Taylor and M. L. Warford, 51–66. Washington, DC: Association of Governing Boards, 1991.

McKenna, D. L. "Mission and Ministry." In *Good Stewardship: A Handbook for Seminary Trustees*, edited by B. E. Taylor and M. L. Warford, 9–22. Washington, DC: Association of Governing Boards, 1991.

McKenna, D. L. *Stewards of a Sacred Trust*. Winchester, VA: ECFA Press, 2010.

MacLeod, M. "Unconventional Educational Practices in Majority World Theological Education: A Qualitative Research Study." Unpublished manuscript. Indianapolis, IN: Overseas Council, 2013.

Maggay, M. "Towards Contextualization from Within: Some Tools and Culture Themes." In *Doing Theology in the Philippines*, edited by E. Acoba, John D. Suk, and the Asian Theological Seminary, 37–50. Manila: OMF Publications, 2005.

Mapile, L. "Social Concern and Theological Education: A Philippines' Perspective." In *Tending the Seedbeds: Educational Perspectives on Theological Education in Asia*, edited by A. Harkness, 213–236. Quezon City, Philippines: Asia Theological Association, 2010.

Marsden, G. *Reforming Fundamentalism: Fuller Seminary and the New Evangelicalism*. Grand Rapids, MI: Eerdmans, 1987.

———. *The Soul of the American University*. New York: Oxford University Press, 1994.

Marshall, C., and G. B. Rossman. *Designing Qualitative Research*. (4th ed.). Thousand Oaks, CA: SAGE Publications, 2006.

Mathews, A. "The Theological is Also Personal: The 'Place' of Evangelical Protestant Women in the Church." In *Theological Literacy for the Twenty-First Century*, edited by R. L. Petersen and N. M. Rourke, 134–149. Grand Rapids, MI: Eerdmans, 2002.

McLarin, B., and T. Campolo. "Adventures in Missing the Point: How the Culture-Controlled Church Neutered the Gospel." Grand Rapids: Zondervan, 2003.

Mezirow, J. *Transformative Dimensions of Adult Learning*. San Francisco, CA: Jossey-Bass, 1991.

Middleton, M. "Nonprofit Boards of Directors: Beyond the Governance Function." In *The Nonprofit Sector*, edited by W.W. Powell. New Haven, CT: Yale University Press, 1987.

Miller, G. T. *Piety and Profession: American Protestant Theological Education, 1870-1970*. Grand Rapids, MI: Eerdmans, 2007.

———. *Piety and Plurality: Theological Education since 1960*. Eugene, OR: Cascade Publications, 2014.

Miller, S. L., A. T. Ruger, and B. G. Wheeler. *Great Expectations: Fundraising Prospects for Theological Schools*. New York: Auburn Center for the Study of Theological Education, 2009.

Miller, W. C. "The Governance of Theological Education: A Case Study of Nazarene Theological Seminary, 1945-1976." Unpublished doctoral dissertation. Kent State University, Kent, OH, 1983.

Moore, M. "Nonprofits to Face Sarbanes-Like Scrutiny from IRS." *Boston Business Journal*. (2009, January 9). Retrieved 26 January 2009, from http://boston.bizjournals.com

Morck, R. K., and L. Steier. *The Global History of Corporate Governance*. Chicago, IL: University of Chicago Press, 2005.

Motty, B. "Forward." In *Beyond Literate Western Practices: Continuing Conversations in Orality and Theological Education*, edited by S. E. Chiang and G. Lovejoy, 13–14. Hong Kong: Condeo Press/International Orality Network, 2014.

Nason, J. W. *The Nature of Trusteeship: The Role and Responsibilities of College and University Boards*. Washington, DC: Association of Governing Boards of Universities and Colleges, 1982.

Neto, J. A. M. "Un análisis bíblico-histórico de la formación con base en la iglesia local y sus implicaciones para las iglesias evangélicas tradicionales del nordeste brasileño." Unpublished Doctoral Dissertation. Seminario Teológico Centroamericano, Guatemala City, Guatemala, 2012.

Niebuhr, H. R., D. D. Williams, and J. M. Gustafson. *The Advancement of Theological Education*. New York: Harper Brothers, 1957.

Nobbie, P. D., and J. L. Brudney. "Testing the Implementation, Board Performance, and Organizational Effectiveness of the Policy Governance Model in Nonprofit Boards of Directors." *Nonprofit and Voluntary Sector Quarterly* 32, no. 4 (2003): 571–595.

Noelliste, D. "Theological Education in the Context of Socio-Economic Deprivation." *Evangelical Review of Theology* 3 (2005): 270–283.

Noll, M. *The New Shape of World Christianity*. Downers Grove, IL: IVP Academic, 2009.

Ochola, J. M. "A comparison of values and aspirations of the members of the board of trustees and of the faculty at two theological schools in Kenya." Unpublished doctoral dissertation. University of Southern Mississippi, Hattiesburg, MS, 2001.

Odendahl, T. and A. M. Shaw. "Interviewing Elites." In *Handbook of Interview Research*, edited by J. F. Gubrium and J. A. Holstein. San Francisco, CA: SAGE, 2001.

Oliver, C. "Policy Governance and Other Governance Models Compared." *Board Leadership* 64 (2002): 2–6.

Ostrower, F., and M. Stone. "Governance: Research Trends, Gaps, and Future Prospects." In *The Nonprofit Sector: A Research Handbook* (2nd ed.), edited by W. W. Powell and R. Steinberg, 612–627. New Haven, CT: Yale University Press, 2006.

Ott, B. *Beyond Fragmentation: Integrating Mission and Theological Education*. Oxford, UK: Regnum Books, 2001.

———. *Understanding and Developing Theological Education*. Translated by Tom Keefer. Carlisle: Langham Global Library, 2015.

Ott, C., and H. A. Netland. *Globalizing Theology: Belief and Practice in an Era of World Christianity*. Ada, MI: Baker Academic, 2006.

Padilla, A. "Living in the Hyphen: Theological Literacy from an Hispanic American Perspective." In *Theological Literacy for the Twenty-First Century*, edited by R. L. Petersen and N. M. Rourke, 229–241. Grand Rapids, MI: Eerdmans, 2002.

Padilla, C. R. *New alternatives in Theological Education*. Oxford, UK: Regnum, 1985.

———. "Integral Mission and its Historical Development." In *Justice, Mercy and Humility*, edited by T. Chester. Carlisle: Paternoster, 2003.

———. *Mission between the Times*. Carlisle, UK: Langham, 2010.

Palmer, P. J. *The Courage to Teach: Exploring the Inner Landscape of a Teacher's Life*. San Francisco, CA: John Wiley, 2007.

Paligorova, T. *Industry 2020*. Prague: Penta Investments, 2001. Retrieved January 26, 2009 from http://www.pentainvestments.com/files/vizia2020/3-001-PaligorovaTeodora-ENG.doc.

Patterson, E. L. "Theological Boardsmanship: A Descriptive and Comparative Study of Some Identified Elements of Board Effectiveness." Unpublished doctoral dissertation. Claremont Graduate School, Claremont, CA, 1992.

Patty, S. "A View of Theological Education in Central and Eastern Europe: A Joint Project of Mission Eurasia and Josiah Venture in Partnership with Dialogues in Action." Unpublished manuscript, 2015.

Pearson, S. C., ed. *Supporting Asian Christianity's Transition from Mission to Church: A History of the Foundation for Theological Education in South East Asia*. The Historical Series of the Reformed Church in America, No. 68. Grand Rapids: Eerdmans, 2010.

Penner, P. "Introduction." In *Theological Education as Mission*, edited by P. Penner, 7–14. Schwarzenfeld, Germany: Neufeld Verlag, 2005.

Petersen, R. L., and N. M. Rourke. *Theological Literacy for the Twenty-First Century*. Grand Rapids, MI: Eerdmans, 2002.

Pfeffer, J. "Size, Composition, and Functions of Hospital Boards of Directors: A Study of Organization-Environment Linkage." *Administrative Science Quarterly* 18 (1973): 349–363.

Phiri, I. and D. Werner. *Handbook of Theological Education in Africa*. Oxford: Regnum, 2013.

Pilli, T. "Toward a Holistic View of Theological Education." In *Theological Education as Mission*, edited by P. F. Penner, 171–184. Schwarzenfeld, Germany: Neufeld Verlag, 2005.

Pohor, R., and I. Coulibaly. *Christianisme authentique en Afrique contemporaine*. Abidjan, Côte d'Ivoire: Les Presses FATEAC, 2014.

Pohor, R., and M. Kenmogne. *Théologie et vie chrétienne en Afrique*. Yaoundé, Cameroon: ADG Editions, 2012.

Reed, J. *The Paradigm Papers: New Paradigms for the Post-Modern Church*. Ames, IA: BILD International, 1997.

Renz, D. O. "Reframing Governance." *The Nonprofit Quarterly* 13, no. 4 (Winter 2006): 6–13.

Ringenberg, W. C. *The Christian College: A History of Protestant Higher Education in America*. (2nd ed.). Grand Rapids, MI: Baker, 2006.

Robert, D. "Shifting Southward: Global Christianity since 1945." *International Bulletin of Missionary Research* 24, no. 2 (2000): 50–58.

Rowe, W. T. "Symposium: 'Public Sphere'/'Civil Society' in China? Paradigmatic Issues in Chinese Studies, III." *Modern China* 19, no. 2 (1993): 139–157.

Ruger, A., and C. A. Meinzer. *Through Toil and Tribulation: Financing Theological Education*. New York: Auburn Center for the Study of Theological Education, 2014.

Sachs, W. L. "The Religious Mission of the Board. In *Building Effective Boards for Religious Organizations*, edited by T. P. Holland and D. C. Hester, 44–57. San Francisco, CA: Jossey-Bass, 2000.

Said, E. *Orientalism*. New York: Vintage, 1978.

Salamon, L. M., H. K. Anheier, R. List, S. Toepler, S. W. Sokolowski, and Associates, eds. *Global civil society: Dimensions of the nonprofit sector*. Baltimore, MD: Johns Hopkins Comparative Nonprofit Sector Project, 1999.

Sanneh, L., and J. Carpenter, eds. *The Changing Face of Christianity: Africa, the West, and the World*. New York: Oxford University Press, 2005.

Saracco, N. "La búsqueda de nuevos modelos de educación teológica." *Encuentro y diálogo* 4 (1988).

Savage, T. J. "Beyond Hierarchies: Transforming Power and Leadership." In *Building Effective Boards for Religious Organizations*, edited by T. P. Holland and D. C. Hester, 109–121. San Francisco, CA: Jossey-Bass, 2000.

Schein, E. H. *Organizational Culture and Leadership*. (3rd ed.). San Francisco, CA: Jossey-Bass, 2004.

Schwartz, M. P. *Results of a National Survey of Theological School Board Characteristics, Policies, and Practices* (AGB Occasional Papers). Washington, DC: AGB, 1994.

Scott, K. T. *Creating Caring and Capable Boards: Reclaiming the Passion for Active Trusteeship*. San Francisco, CA: Jossey-Bass, 2000.

Searle, J., and M. Cherenkov. *A Future and a Hope: Mission, Theological Education, and the Transformation of Post-Soviet Society*. Eugene, OR: Wipf & Stock, 2014.

Senanayake, A. N. L. "Developing Culturally Relevant curriculum for Theological Education in Asia." In *Educating for Tomorrow: Theological Leadership for the Asian Context*, edited by M. W. Kohl and A. N. L. Senanayake, 77–88. Bangalore, India: SAIACS Press, 2007.

Senge, P. M. *The Fifth Discipline: The Art and Practice of the Learning Organization.* (Rev. ed.). New York: Doubleday, 2006.

Sessoms, R. "On Tablets of Human Hearts." (forthcoming, 2015).

Shamgunov, I. "Listening to the Voice of the Graduate: An Analysis of Professional Practice and Training for Ministry in Central Asia." Unpublished doctoral dissertation. University of Oxford, UK, 2009.

Shaw, P. W. H. "New Treasures with the Old: Addressing Culture and Gender Imperialism in High Level Theological Education." In *Tending the Seedbeds: Educational Perspectives on Theological Education in Asia*, edited by A. Harkness, 47–74. Quezon City, Philippines: Asia Theological Association, 2010.

Shaw, P. W. H. *Transforming Theological Education: A Handbook for Integrative Learning*. Carlisle, UK: Langham Global Library, 2014.

Smith, D. H. *Entrusted: The Moral Responsibilities of Trusteeship*. Bloomington, IN: Indiana University Press, 1995.

Smith, G. T. "Theological Education as Formation in Wisdom." Presented at ATA Consultation on Models of Theological Education: Manila, Philippines, 2011.

Smith, L. "A Strategic Framework for Faculty Development." Unpublished manuscript, 24 April 2013.

Snook, S. G. *Developing Leaders Through Theological Education by Extension: Case Studies from Africa*. Wheaton, IL: Billy Graham Center, 1992.

Soloviy, R. *Vynykaiucha tserkva*. Cherkassy, Ukraine: Colloquium, 2014.

Sorensen, C. A. "Formation, Transformative Learning, and Theological Education." Unpublished doctoral dissertation. University of Auckland, New Zealand, 2007.

Spradley, J. P. *The Ethnographic Interview*. New York: Holt, Rinehart, and Winston, 1979.

Stackhouse, M. *Apologia: Contextualization, Globalization, and Mission in Theological Education*. Grand Rapids, MI: Eerdmans, 1988.

Stahlke, L. *Governance Matters: Relationship Model of Governance, Leadership, and Management*. Toronto, ON: GovernanceMatters, 2003.

Stelio Rega, L. "Revendo paradigmas para a formaçao teológica e ministerial." In *Educação teológica transformadora*, edited by A. C. Barro and M. W. Kohl, 171–192. Londrina, Brazil: Descoberta, 2006.

Steuernagel, V. "The Relevance and Effects of European Academic Theology on Theological Education in the Third World." *Evangelical Review of Theology* 27, no. 3 (2003): 203–212.

Strauss, A., and J. Corbin. *Basics of Qualitative Research: Grounded Theory Procedures and Techniques*. Newbury Park, CA: SAGE, 1990.

Suazo Jiménez, D. *La función profética de la educación teológica evangélica en América Latina*. Barcelona, Spain: Editorial Clie, 2012.

Sule-Saa, S. S. "Owning the Christian Faith Through Mother-Tongue Scriptures: A Case Study of the Dagomba and Konkomba of Northern Ghana." *Journal of African Christian Thought* 13, no. 2 (2010): 47–53.

Sunquist, S. "Asian Theological Education: The Long View." In *A Cultured Faith: Essays in Honour of Prof. G.P.V. Somaratna on His Seventieth Birthday*, edited by P. Mihindiskulasariya, I. Poobalan, and R. Caldera. Colombo, Sri Lanka: CTS Publishing, 2011.

Tankler, M. "Harmonizing Individual and Ecclesiastical Expectations with the Institution of Theological Education." Unpublished Doctoral Dissertation. Asbury Theological Seminary. Wilmore, KY, 2013.

Taylor, B. E., R. P. Chait, and T. P. Holland. "The New Work of the Nonprofit Board." *Harvard Business Review* (Sep-Oct 1996): 4–11.

Taylor, B. E., and M. L. Warford. *Good Stewardship: A Handbook for Seminary Trustees*. Washington, DC: Association of Governing Boards of Universities and Colleges, 1991.

Tennent, T. C. *Theology in the Context of the World Christianity: How the Global Church is the Way We Think about and Discuss Theology*. Grand Rapids, MI: Zondervan, 2007.

Theocharous, M. "Not Living on Bread Alone: Theological Education as Prophetism." *Evangelical Review of Theology* 38, no. 3 (2014).

Thoman, R. "Leadership Development, Part 1: Churches Don't Have to Go It Alone." *Christian Education Journal* 6, no. 2 (2009): 282–299.

Thomas, J. "Practical Theology: A Transformative Praxis in Theological Education toward Holistic Formation." *Journal of Theological Education and Mission* 1, no. 1 (2010): 76–86.

Thornton, W. P. "Orality and Theological Education in Latin American Culture." In *Beyond Literate Western Practices: Continuing Conversations in Orality and Theological Education*, edited by S. Chiang and G. Lovejoy, 55–62. Hong Kong: Condeo Press/International Orality Network, 2014.

Thrall, B., B. McNicol, and K. McElrath. *The Ascent of a Leader: How Ordinary Relationships Develop Extraordinary Character and Influence.* San Francisco, CA: Jossey-Bass, 1999.

Throup, M. "Towards Integration: Reenvisioning Theological Education as Worship." *The Theological Educator* 1 (2011). Retrieved 14 Aug 2011. www.eeaa.org/TTE.htm.

Tiénou, T. "Epanouissement du christianisme en Afrique." In *Christianisme authentique en Afrique contemporaine*, edited by R. Pohor and I. Coulibaly, 13–20. Abidjan, Côte d'Ivoire: Les Presses FATEAC, 2014.

Tracy, D. "On Theological Education: A Reflection." In *Theological Literacy for the Twenty-First Century*, edited by R. L. Petersen and N. M. Rourke, 13–22. Grand Rapids, MI: Eerdmans, 2002.

Vidich, A. J. and S. M. Lyman. "Qualitative Methods: Their History in Sociology and Anthropology." In *The Discipline and Practice of Qualitative Research*, edited by N. K. Denzin, and Y. S. Lincoln, 1–28. Thousand Oaks, CA: SAGE, 2000.

Walls, A. "Christian Scholarship and the Demographic Transformation of the Church." In *Theological Literacy for the Twenty-First Century*, edited by R. L. Petersen and N. M. Rourke, 166–183. Grand Rapids, MI: Eerdmans, 2002.

———. *The Cross-Cultural Process in Christian History.* Maryknoll, NY: Orbis, 2002.

———. *The Missionary Movement in Christian History: Studies in Transmission of Faith.* Maryknoll, NY: Orbis, 2004.

Warford, M. "The Calling of Stewards." In *Good Stewardship: A Handbook for Seminary Trustees*, edited by B. E. Taylor and M. L. Warford, 9–22. Washington, DC: Association of Governing Boards, 1991.

Warford, M. "Stewards of Hope: The Work of Trustees." In *Building Effective Boards for Religious Organizations*, edited by T. P. Holland and D. C. Hester, 3–23. San Francisco, CA: Jossey-Bass, 2000.

Ward, T. "Preparing and Equipping the Leaders of Leaders." *Common Ground* 10, no. 2 (2013): 11–12.

Watson, H. M. "The Theological Educator: An Indian Perspective." *Currents in Theology and Mission* 40, no. 2 (2013): 120–125.

Weber, T. P. "The Seminaries and the Churches: Looking for New Relationships." *Theological Education* 44, no. 1 (2008): 65–91.

Werner, D., D. Esterline, N. Kang, and J. Raja, eds. *Handbook of Theological Education in World Christianity: Theological Perspectives, Ecumenical Trends, Regional Surveys.* Oxford, UK: Regnum, 2010.

Wheeler, B. G. *In Whose Hands: A Study of Theological School Trustees.* (Auburn Studies No. 9). New York: Auburn Theological Seminary, 2002.

Wheeler, B. G., G. D. Lewis, S. L. Miller, A. T. Ruger, and D. L. Tiede. *Leadership That Works: A Study of Theological School Presidents.* New York: Auburn Center for the Study of Theological Education, 2010.

Wheeler, B. G., S. L. Miller, and K. Schuth. *Signs of the Times: Present and Future Theological Faculty.* (Auburn Studies No. 10). New York: Auburn Theological Seminary, 2005.

Winter, R. *Theological Education by Extension.* Pasadena, CA: William Carey Library, 1969.

Woodyard, J. *The M. J. Murdock Trust Review of Graduate Theological Education Programs in the Pacific Northwest.* Vancouver, WA: M. J. Murdock Trust, 1994.

Wright, C. J. H. *The Mission of God: Unlocking the Bible's Grand Narrative.* Downers Grove, IL: Intervarsity Press, 2006.

———. "The Challenge of the Brain Drain within Theological Education." 2012 Global Consultation on Theological Education. South Hamilton, MA, 2012.

Yamamori, T., and C. R. Padilla, eds. *The Local Church: Agent of Transformation.* Buenos Aires, Argentina: Ediciones Kairos, 2004.

Yung, H. *Mangoes or Bananas? The Quest for Authentic Asian Christian Theology.* Eugene, OR: Wipf and Stock, 1997.

Zokoué, I. "Educating for Servant Leadership in Africa." *Evangelical Review of Theology* 9, no. 1 (1990): 3–13.

Global Hub for Evangelical Theological Education

ICETE is a global community, sponsored by nine regional networks of theological schools, to enable international interaction and collaboration among all those engaged in strengthening and developing evangelical theological education and Christian leadership development worldwide.

The purpose of ICETE is:
1. To promote the enhancement of evangelical theological education worldwide.
2. To serve as a forum for interaction, partnership and collaboration among those involved in evangelical theological education and leadership development, for mutual assistance, stimulation and enrichment.
3. To provide networking and support services for regional associations of evangelical theological schools worldwide.
4. To facilitate among these bodies the advancement of their services to evangelical theological education within their regions.

Sponsoring associations include:
Africa: Association for Christian Theological Education in Africa (ACTEA)

Asia: Asia Theological Association (ATA)

Caribbean: Caribbean Evangelical Theological Association (CETA)

Europe: European Evangelical Accrediting Association (EEAA)

Euro-Asia: Euro-Asian Accrediting Association (E-AAA)

Latin America: Association for Evangelical Theological Education in Latin America (AETAL)

Middle East and North Africa: Middle East Association for Theological Education (MEATE)

North America: Association for Biblical Higher Education (ABHE)

South Pacific: South Pacific Association of Evangelical Colleges (SPAEC)

www.icete-edu.org

Langham Literature and its imprints are a ministry of Langham Partnership.

Langham Partnership is a global fellowship working in pursuit of the vision God entrusted to its founder John Stott –

to facilitate the growth of the church in maturity and Christ-likeness through raising the standards of biblical preaching and teaching.

Our vision is to see churches in the majority world equipped for mission and growing to maturity in Christ through the ministry of pastors and leaders who believe, teach and live by the Word of God.

Our mission is to strengthen the ministry of the Word of God through:
- nurturing national movements for biblical preaching
- fostering the creation and distribution of evangelical literature
- enhancing evangelical theological education

especially in countries where churches are under-resourced.

Our ministry

Langham Preaching partners with national leaders to nurture indigenous biblical preaching movements for pastors and lay preachers all around the world. With the support of a team of trainers from many countries, a multi-level programme of seminars provides practical training, and is followed by a programme for training local facilitators. Local preachers' groups and national and regional networks ensure continuity and ongoing development, seeking to build vigorous movements committed to Bible exposition.

Langham Literature provides majority world preachers, scholars and seminary libraries with evangelical books and electronic resources through publishing and distribution, grants and discounts. The programme also fosters the creation of indigenous evangelical books in many languages, through writer's grants, strengthening local evangelical publishing houses, and investment in major regional literature projects, such as one volume Bible commentaries like *The Africa Bible Commentary* and *The South Asia Bible Commentary*.

Langham Scholars provides financial support for evangelical doctoral students from the majority world so that, when they return home, they may train pastors and other Christian leaders with sound, biblical and theological teaching. This programme equips those who equip others. Langham Scholars also works in partnership with majority world seminaries in strengthening evangelical theological education. A growing number of Langham Scholars study in high quality doctoral programmes in the majority world itself. As well as teaching the next generation of pastors, graduated Langham Scholars exercise significant influence through their writing and leadership.

To learn more about Langham Partnership and the work we do visit **langham.org**

www.ingramcontent.com/pod-product-compliance
Lightning Source LLC
Chambersburg PA
CBHW071737150426
43191CB00010B/1614